# WITNESS TO

# MORMONS

## IN LOVE

## *The Mormon Scrapbook*
## *Revised Edition*

*A Christian's Guide for Reaching Latter-day Saints*

Unless otherwise indicated, Bible Quotes are from the Authorized King James Version of the Bible
Cover design by Britney Thompson; B. Renae Design Concepts
Book design by Britney Thompson; B. Renae Design Concepts

**WITNESS TO MORMONS IN LOVE: The Mormon Scrapbook/Revised Edition**
©2014 by Daniel G. Thompson
Printed by CreateSpace, An Amazon.com Company
ISBN: ISBN-13: 978-1500601799
ISBN-10: 1500601799

**FOR INFORMATION:**
Gospel Truth 4 U Publications
P. O. Box 305
Ephraim, Utah 84627
Phone: (435) 283-0178
E-mail: gospeltruth4U@hotmail.com
Online orders: TriGrace.org

# WITNESS TO

# MORMONS

## IN LOVE

## *The Mormon Scrapbook*
## *Revised Edition*

*A Christian's Guide for Reaching Latter-day Saints*

## Daniel G. Thompson

Gospel Truth 4 U
P u b l i c a t i o n s

# Contents

# Acknowledgments

No one in ministry is an island unto himself. Throughout my years in Utah, I have been surrounded by godly men and women who have a passion for the LDS people. The contents of *Witness to Mormons in Love* are my gleanings from these men and women of God. Thanks to all who contributed—knowingly or unknowingly—to the ideas and methods contained in this witnessing manual.

I want to thank my wife and family for their patience with me. Countless hours were spent in the production of this book that might otherwise have been spent with them. *Witness to Mormons in Love* would not be in print today if it were not for their support and encouragement.

I want to also thank the Tri-Grace Ministries Staff for giving me the time and space necessary to work on the contents of this book. Everyone stepped up and filled in to compensate for my absence from the normal daily activities of Tri-Grace Ministries. Their selfless service and devotion to the work of the Lord in Utah blesses me greatly.

I want to thank my editor, my mother, who spent many long nights agonizing over and correcting grammar and punctuation. She is one of the truest servants of God that I have ever known. Thanks, Mom. You're the greatest.

Finally, I want to thank my Aunt Becki and my daughter Britney for assisting with the typing, graphic designs, editing and publishing of *Witness to Mormons in Love, The Mormon Scrapbook, Revised Edition*.

The completion of this witnessing manual was certainly a team effort that is devoted to the building up of the Kingdom of God here on earth and to the praise of our glorious God and Savior Jesus Christ.

# Foreword

Over the years, I have heard many disconcerting comments about Mormonism such as:

- *Why pick on the Mormons? They're Christians, too!*

- *My Mormon neighbors are the nicest people I have ever met, they must be Christians.*

- *Mormonism can't be all bad—they believe in Jesus.*

- *I don't see why Christians are so down on the LDS Church—they give away free Bibles.*

- *We went to Salt Lake City and heard the Mormon Tabernacle Choir. What a blessing!*

Why produce a manual geared entirely toward witnessing to Mormons? God has given me a great love for the Mormon people, and I fear that Christians around the globe are overlooking the lost condition of their Mormon friends. I want the Christian community to realize that Mormonism is counterfeit Christianity. As Satan appears to be an angel of light, and as his ministers appear to be ministers of righteousness, even so the false religion of Mormonism has transformed itself to appear as another Christian religion. However, Mormonism is not Christian in any way, shape, or form. This book is first and foremost written to prepare Christians to witness to their Mormon friends before it is eternally to late.

Another deep concern that prompted me to produce this book is the welfare of the Body of Christ. The Apostle Paul voiced the following warning to the early church:

*"But I fear, lest somehow, as the serpent deceived Eve by his craftiness, so your minds may be corrupted from the simplicity that is in Christ."* (**2 Corinthians 11:3—NKJV.**)

In many ways, the true Church of Jesus Christ is being deceived by the Church of Jesus Christ of Latter Day Saints *(the LDS or Mormon Church.)* Subtle deceptions within Mormonism, like a tasteless poison, are claiming victim after victim, many from the ranks of Christian churches. Paul goes on to say,

*"For if he who comes preaches another Jesus whom we have not preached, or if you receive a different spirit which you have not received, or a different gospel which you have not accepted—you may well put up with it!"* (**2Corinthians 11:4—NKJV.**)

Each warning voiced by Paul in these verses applies to Mormonism. The LDS Church preaches a different Jesus, promotes another spirit, and teaches a different gospel. Unfortunately, many in the Christian church today are accepting Mormons as fellow believers. We want to expose Mormonism for what it really is: a false religion that will ultimately lead people to hell.

My family and I have lived in the heart of rural Utah since 1991, so we understand the frustration and discouragement associated with witnessing to Mormons. We have experienced the heartache of watching LDS friends withdraw and refuse to talk with us any more about religious matters. Because our community is predominantly LDS and we have had conversations with hundreds of LDS people, we understand Mormon thinking, LDS doctrine, and the grip the Mormon Church has on its members. We have learned from experience that our approach must be compassionate and knowledgeable or we will alienate them, building walls of distrust and anger instead of bridges toward spiritual understanding. It is my sincere prayer that the enclosed information will help you lead your Mormon friends and family into a saving relationship with the true Jesus of the Bible.

—Daniel G. Thompson

# C H A P T E R 1
# GETTING STARTED

# S E C T I O N 1
# How to Use This Book

This book presents a unique witnessing method that has proven to be effective in challenging Mormons to question their faith in the LDS Church. It has opened doors to allow honest discussion with LDS people and to build relationships rather than destroy them. Ultimately, these methods have proven effective in turning LDS people from the false religion of Mormonism to a personal relationship with Jesus Christ.

## Before You Begin

This book is only one of many methods on the market today that can be used effectively to witness to Mormons. There is no such thing as the perfect witnessing technique. Don't fool yourself into thinking that this or any other method is like Aladdin's magic lamp—just rub it and 'poof' Mormons become Christians. What you will learn in this book are effective ways to enter into meaningful dialogue with LDS people. Your effectiveness will depend upon three things: (1) your attitude, (2) your relationship with God, and (3) your ability to rightly divide the Word of Truth, the Bible (**2 Timothy 2:15**.)

While the information in this book may look like an overwhelming amount of material, be assured it is not. *Witness to Mormons in Love* has as its primary focus three truths of Christianity—

(1) the Doctrine of God; (2) Biblical Salvation *(the Gospel)*; and (3) the Teachings of Jesus. Almost every issue you will study is related in some way to these three topics. Knowing the God of the Bible, understanding the gospel of Jesus Christ and following His teachings are the crucial ingredients to true conversion.

## Glossary of Mormon Terms

You must understand Mormon terminology before you can effectively witness to your Mormon friends. The 'Glossary of Mormon Terms', located in the back of this book, can be described as a crash course on LDS doctrine. Many Christians wrongly assume that common Biblical terms used by both Mormons and Christians have the same meanings. Nothing could be further from the truth. Mormonism has taken virtually all of the Biblical words and redefined them, completely altering the true message of God's Word.

Many well-meaning Christians have tried to witness to their Mormon friends but have been ineffective because they did not understand LDS terminology. The importance of this study cannot be overemphasized. Look for the 🛑 Icon as you study this book. It will direct you to the Glossary of Mormon Terms to find and read pertinent LDS definitions as they relate to each topic—as an example:

🛑 **Turn to the Glossary of Mormon Terms and read the LDS definitions of 'Adam' and 'Ancient of Days'.**

It is vital that you take the time to study each LDS term. The discussions in this book will make more sense when the background information for each LDS topic is fully understood.

You should also understand that most, if not all, Mormons wrongly assume that LDS and Christian terms mean the same things. We have, therefore, created a handout for Mormons titled, *'The Articles of Faith of Christianity',* which can be given to your LDS friends. This handout was carefully worded so active Latter-day Saints will understand the differences between LDS and Christian doctrines.

Also watch for the Visual Aid Icon 👁 as you study this book. It will direct you to the TriGrace.org website where you will find free witnessing visuals and video tutorials explaining the TGM witnessing visuals.

👁 **Go now to: TriGrace.org**
**Under 'Resources' find and print the free PDF download of *The Articles of Faith of Christianity*. Then watch the corresponding TGM Tutorial explaining how to use this visual aid when witnessing to LDS people.**

## Witness to Mormons Reference Guides

The *Reference Guides* contain the scripture references you will want to remember as you witness to Mormons. The vital topics and proof texts found in this book are included in the reference guides which should fit inside the covers of your Bible. It is important that you familiarize yourself with these guides as you study this book. If while you are witnessing you get a 'brain freeze', don't panic! Just grab the appropriate reference guide. It will be your crutch until you become familiar with the various topics and pertinent scripture passages.

👁 **Go to: Trigrace.org**
**Under 'Resources' find and print the free PDF download of the *Witness to Mormons Reference Guides*.**

## Why We Care

LDS people do not understand why Christians care enough to share Biblical truth with them. Mormons will often say, "We are happy in our religion! We believe in Jesus! We are okay, so why don't you just leave us alone!"

When they say this, Figure 1.1 will help to explain why we care and why we do not believe they are 'okay' or 'happy' in their religion.

Throughout the late 20th and early 21st centuries, suicide has occurred in epidemic proportions in the State of Utah. And, we believe this problem may be worse than this *Deseret*

*News* graphic shows. Because these tragic deaths have been such a stigma within Utah culture, many are glossed over as hunting accidents, unsolved homicides, or accidental deaths. We live in the heart of Utah and can tell you suicide is abnormally commonplace. There are very few extended LDS families in Utah that have not suffered the loss of at least one loved one to suicide.

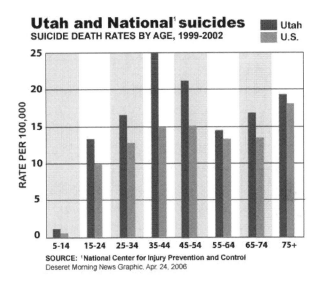

**Figure 1.1**

So, when a Mormon says, "Why don't you leave us alone—we are okay!" We simply show them the *Suicide Visual* and say, "We don't think this is okay. Do you?"

The back side of the *Suicide Visual* exposes another Utah stigma—Depression. Also in the late 20th and early 21st centuries, the use of anti-depressant drugs in Utah was twice the national average. Provo Valley has often been termed 'Happy Valley' due to the unprecedented numbers of women on anti-depressants. Again, this is strong evidence that Mormons are not okay or happy.

It should also be noted that both the suicide and depression problems are largely associated with the middle to upper class segments of Utah society which are predominantly the Latter-day Saints. We, therefore, believe these problems are directly connected to pressures associated with the LDS religion. To understand why, see Sections

41 and 42 of this book which explain 'The Impossible Gospel' of Mormonism.

👁 **Go to: TriGrace.org**
**Under 'Resources' find and print the free PDF download of *The Suicide—Depression Visual*. Then watch the corresponding TGM Tutorial explaining how to use this visual aid when witnessing to LDS people.**

## Growing in Your Understanding

As you begin your study, it is crucial for you to understand the complexity of converting a Mormon to Biblical Christianity. Don't be fooled into thinking that Mormonism is Christian in any way. A person who puts their faith in the doctrines of the LDS Church cannot be a true Christian. As you study these materials, you will begin to understand why.

Also realize that Mormonism is much more than just a false religious system. It is an all-encompassing culture. Everything in life, religiously and socially, is tied to 'The Church'. For many LDS people, generations of relatives have lived and died in this culture. To abandon their religion is viewed as a betrayal of their entire heritage. When Mormons decide to leave the LDS Church, they are thought to be totally deceived and are labeled 'apostates' or 'sons of perdition'.

🛑 **Turn to the Glossary of Mormon Terms and read the LDS definitions of 'Apostate', 'Outer Darkness', and 'Sons of Perdition'.**

The Mormon community as a whole treats apostate Mormons with the utmost contempt. It is not uncommon to see their marriages dissolve and friends and family turn their backs. They may eventually be ostracized by the entire LDS community, sometimes causing the loss of employment or the demise of a family business.

It is difficult to imagine the conflicting emotions experienced by an LDS person when confronted with Biblical truth. Considering what it may cost them, even when they are convinced what you are saying is true, it is not surprising that it often takes years for a Mormon to reach the place where they are willing to turn from their religion to Biblical Christianity.

Jesus emphasized how important it was for people to 'count the cost' before making the decision to follow Him (see **Luke 14:26-30**.) We cannot rush this process in our desire to see Mormons come to salvation. Our attitude is as important as our approach as we reach out to these lost people. Be patient with them, treat them with love and respect, be understanding, and most of all PRAY for them!

> **1 Corinthians 13:1,** *"Though I speak with the tongues of men and of angels, and have not charity [love], I am become as sounding brass, or a tinkling cymbal."*

**QUESTIONS** are included at the end of each section. Correctly answered, these questions will provide a summary of each section's content. Here are the review questions for Section 1.

## QUESTIONS FOR REVIEW
**Your effectiveness in witnessing to LDS people depends upon what three things?**
1.

2.

3.

**What are the three primary truths of Christianity discussed in this book?**
1.

2.

3.

**What helpful Witnessing tool will assist in your witnessing efforts when you get a 'brain freeze'?**

**What should you do each time you encounter a** 🛑 **Icon?**

**When you see the** 👁 **icon where should you go to download the free Tri-Grace witnessing visuals?**

# SECTION 2
# History of Mormonism

🛑 **Turn to the Glossary of Mormon Terms and read the LDS definition of 'Joseph Smith'.**

## Joseph Smith and Early Mormonism

To understand Mormonism, it is necessary to look at the life of its founder, Joseph Smith, Jr. He is considered by Latter-day Saints to be a prophet of God and the founder of the only true religion on the face of the earth today. The theology of the LDS Church is based upon the writings and revelations of this man who claimed to 'restore the everlasting gospel' of Jesus Christ to those living at this time in history.

Joseph Smith was born on December 23, 1805, in the town of Sharon, Vermont. The Smith family was poor, and Joseph's father was a farmer. It was reported that Joseph Smith, Sr. was also a 'gold digger' and 'treasure hunter' who searched for hidden treasure by means of seer stones and other types of divination. Due to his father's influence, two of young Joseph's earliest hobbies were money digging and stone peeping.

In 1817, the Smith family moved to Palmyra, New York. At this time, Palmyra was experiencing an unusual religious fervor. A revival swept through the community and many members of the Smith family joined the Presbyterian Church. According to Joseph, arguments broke out in the ensuing months between the different religious groups as to which denomination was the most correct. Joseph, a teenager at this time, claimed to be concerned about which sect was right and which he should join.

In Joseph Smith's historical account, his concerns led him to **James 1:5**,

> *"If any of you lack wisdom, let him ask of God, that giveth to all men liberally, and upbraideth not; and it shall be given him."*

After reflecting on this verse, Joseph went to the solitude of the woods to pray. According to LDS History, while young Joseph was in the act of praying, two personages appeared to him—one of them pointing to the other, said, *"This is My Beloved Son. Hear Him!"* These personages, whom Joseph claimed were God the Father and Jesus Christ, then proceeded to tell him all the Christian churches were wrong, all of their creeds were an abomination in God's sight, and that all their professors *(pastors)* were corrupt. He was told he should not join any of them.

Approximately three years later, on the evening of September 21, 1823, an 'angel' named Moroni supposedly appeared three times to Joseph Smith. Upon each appearance, Moroni stated that he was sent from God to reveal ancient gold plates inscribed with the history of the early inhabitants of the Americas. These plates were also said to contain 'the fullness of the everlasting gospel'. Joseph was to look for the plates buried in a hill called Cumorah near his home, but the plates were not to be removed until further notice.

Four years later, Joseph was instructed by the angel Moroni to dig up and to translate the plates. The gold plates were supposedly written in 'reformed Egyptian hieroglyphics', and this translation is now called the Book of Mormon.

The LDS Church would like the world to believe Joseph Smith translated the Book of Mormon directly from the gold plates. However, the eyewitness accounts as to how the translation took place is strange to say the least. It is reported that Joseph placed a seer stone in a hat, placed his face in the hat, and then folded the brim around his cheeks. In the darkness of the hat, the words would supernaturally appear on the seer stone one phrase at a time. He then conveyed these words to his scribes who recorded them for him.

👁 **Go to: TriGrace.org**
**Under 'Resources' find and print the free PDF download of *Book of Mormon Translation from a Hat*. Then watch the corresponding TGM Tutorial explaining how this visual aid can be used when witnessing to LDS people.**

With the publication of the Book of Mormon in 1830, Mormonism was soon founded. Following the translation, Joseph Smith claimed the gold plates had been taken to Heaven by the angel Moroni which eliminated any possibility of examining the only ancient manuscript of the Book of Mormon.

Joseph was, however, a charismatic and persuasive leader who convinced many people to believe his writings in spite of the lack of evidence. In the ensuing years, Mormonism grew rapidly.

Due to the controversial Mormon practice of polygamy and other peculiar doctrines, the new LDS church was forced to move frequently—traveling from Palmyra, New York, to Kirtland, Ohio, to Far West, Missouri. The Mormons finally landed in Nauvoo, Illinois, where the church flourished for several years.

In 1844, the *Nauvoo Expositor*, a newspaper published by men who had been excommunicated from the LDS Church, publicly exposed Joseph Smith's practice of polygamy and criticized his leadership. A group of Joseph's followers broke into the newspaper office, destroyed the printing press, and burned the copies of the newspaper. Consequently, Joseph was accused of inciting a riot and was jailed in Carthage, Illinois.

Before he could come to trial, armed militia stormed the jail and on June 27, 1844, killed both Joseph and his brother, Hyrum, in a hail of bullets. The Mormon Church portrays Joseph as a martyr—'a lamb led to the slaughter'. The truth, however, is that Joseph killed two men and wounded another with smuggled pistols before he died.

After the death of Joseph Smith, the Mormons split into two main factions. In 1847, Brigham Young led the largest group westward to the valley of the Great Salt Lake in Utah. Today this Utah faction is known as The Church of Jesus Christ of Latter-day Saints (the LDS Church or the Mormon Church.)

The smaller group, led by Emma Smith and Joseph's son, settled in Independence, Missouri, and continues to this day as the Reorganized Church of Jesus Christ of Latter Day Saints (the RLDS Church or the Community of Christ.)

## The Book of Mormon in a Nutshell

In about 600 B.C., before the Babylonian captivity of ancient Israel, a Hebrew prophet named Lehi left Jerusalem with his family to escape the impending destruction of the Jewish nation. The Book of Mormon is the story of Lehi and the generations of ancestors that followed as their travels led them to the Americas. Two of Lehi's sons, Nephi and Laman, became the patriarchal leaders of the new world. Nephi was godly and followed the ways of his Hebrew heritage. His followers were called Nephites. In contrast, Laman was evil and became the leader of his descendants, the Lamanites.

**STOP Turn to the Glossary of Mormon Terms and read the LDS definition of 'Lamanites'.**

The Book of Mormon story evolved over many years and told of struggles that ensued through internal fighting, lack of faith, and evil practices. Eventually, in a great battle on a hill called Cumorah, the Lamanites annihilated the Nephites. According to Mormon teachings, the Lamanites lived on, inhabiting the entire land and were the principle ancestors of Native American Indians.

Spiritual teachings, many taken directly from the Bible, are woven throughout the Book of Mormon. The climax of the story occurred when Jesus Christ, immediately following His resurrection, visited the inhabitants of the New World to teach them his doctrine and establish the Christian church in the Americas.

The gold plates containing this incredible story had been hidden by the last Nephite, a man named Moroni, in the hill called Cumorah. This same Moroni later appeared as an 'angel of light' to Joseph Smith in the early 1800s and revealed to him the location of the plates.

## Mormonism in a Nutshell

The ultimate goal of every devout LDS couple is to become a God and a Goddess exactly like their Heavenly Father and Mother. The LDS

Church calls this doctrine 'exaltation'. The first and most important step toward eventual godhood *(exaltation)* is to be married and then sealed for time and all eternity in an LDS temple. Thus begins a tedious climb toward exaltation. Achieving godhood involves obeying not only all the laws of the LDS Church while on this earth, but also continuous work in the afterlife until, at some unknown point in eternity, the LDS couple will finally have earned the right to rule their own world.

Every LDS man who has been deemed worthy will then become a God, and his wife will become a Goddess. The people of his world will one day worship and pray to him just as the people of this world worship and pray to our Heavenly Father. The purpose of the LDS Heavenly Mother is to help her God husband populate his world. Therefore, the fate of every LDS woman who earns the right to be called a Goddess is to be eternally pregnant, producing multitudes of spirit babies for her husband God.

🛑 **Turn to the Glossary of Mormon Terms and read the LDS definition of 'Exaltation'.**

## QUESTIONS FOR REVIEW

**What happened to the gold plates, the only ancient manuscript of the Book of Mormon?**

**According to the Book of Mormon, where did the Native American Indians originate?**

**How did Joseph Smith 'translate' the Book of Mormon?**

**What is the Mormon doctrine of 'exaltation?'**

# S E C T I O N 3
# Attitude and Approach

When witnessing to LDS people, a godly attitude and approach is more important than the witnessing method you plan to use. In the following passage, Paul gives us the perfect pattern to follow, **2 Timothy 2:23-26** says,

*"But foolish and unlearned questions avoid, knowing that they do gender strifes. And the servant of the Lord must not strive; but be gentle unto all men, apt to teach, patient, in meekness instructing those that oppose themselves; if God peradventure will give them repentance to the acknowledging of the truth; And that they may recover themselves out of the snare of the devil, who are taken captive by him at his will."*

With a godly attitude, a godly approach logically follows. The servant of the Lord should avoid issues that cause pointless strife and debate and patiently teach Biblical truth with an attitude of meekness and humility.

Remember, only God's Spirit will eventually convince people of their religious errors and bring them to the truth. And, turning from Mormonism to true Biblical Christianity is ultimately a Mormon's decision, not yours.

## What to Avoid

Following are some topics we would advise you to avoid in your initial discussions:

- The Adam-God doctrine
- The Mountain Meadow Massacre
- Sacred (secret) temple rituals
- Holy underwear and/or temple garments
- The no-coffee rule
- Mocking the Mormon prophets or the Mormon Church

As you witness to LDS people, they will feel offended by many of the truths you present. The goal is not to totally avoid offense but rather to avoid needlessly offending them with non-crucial side issues. Later, after they have come to know the Lord as their personal Savior, you *(in conjunction with the Holy Spirit)* can show them why the entire LDS religious system is false.

Finally, be wise and avoid personal attacks. You will be more successful as you witness to Mormons if you avoid personal pronouns.

- Don't say, 'You are not a Christian'. Instead say, 'Mormonism is not Christian'.

- Don't say, 'You believe this or that'. Instead ask, 'Doesn't the LDS Church teach this or that?'

Generalize the way you say things so your hearers will not feel as though you are attacking them personally. Jesus instructed his disciples to be *"wise as serpents and harmless as doves"* (**Matthew 10:16**.) Learn to be wise as you share the good news of the gospel with LDS people.

## QUESTIONS FOR REVIEW
**When witnessing to LDS people, what is more important than the method you plan to use?**



**Circle the Correct Statement:**
   One should avoid all issues that are offensive to Mormons.
or
   One should avoid issues that cause pointless strife and debate.

**Outline 2 Timothy 2:23-26—What are the three main points of this passage?**

1.

2.

3.

# SECTION 4
# Contention and Mockery

The Mormon culture does not tolerate contention or mockery when discussing spiritual matters. As you are witnessing, if LDS people sense a tone of contention or mockery in your voice, they will quickly end the conversation. Why? Following is what the Book of Mormon says about these two terms.

## Contention
**Book of Mormon**—Jesus is supposedly speaking and in **3 Nephi 11:29** says,
   *"Verily, verily I say unto you, he that hath the spirit of contention is not of me, but is of the devil, who is the father of contention, and he stirreth up the hearts of men to contend with anger, one with another."*

## Mockery
**Book of Mormon**
   **Alma 5:30-31,** *"I say unto you, is there one among you that doth make a mock of his brother, or that heapeth upon him persecutions? Wo unto such an one, for he is not prepared, and the time is at hand that he must repent or he cannot be saved!"*

These concepts are compatible with Biblical principles:
   **2 Timothy 2:24,** *."..And the servant of the Lord must not strive ..."*

   **Galatians 5:22-23,** *"But the fruit of the Spirit is love, joy, peace, longsuffering, gentleness, goodness, faith, meekness, temperance (or self-control) ..."*

As a child of God, you should always demonstrate a Spirit-controlled temperament. It is common sense to realize that you will not lead LDS people to the Lord by being rude or condescending.

Contention and mockery are LDS buzz words that can also be a great defense for us as we witness. The Christian gospel is exclusive—there is only one true way of salvation. When LDS people understand that we are challenging the false doctrines of their church with Biblical truth, they may get confrontational or contentious with us.

If you are the one who keeps things under control, Mormons will respect you. When a conversation begins to heat up, you should be the one to calm it down by saying something like this:

> "I am not interested in continuing this discussion if it is going to become contentious. I think we can each share our beliefs without contention, don't you?"

When LDS people realize they are the ones being 'contentious', they will usually calm down and sometimes even apologize.

Some Mormons, especially in public settings, may try to belittle your message by mocking what you are saying. At the first hint of mockery, you might say something like this:

> "Are you mocking what I am saying? I would never mock my brother the way you are mocking me."

After hearing this, Mormon people who know their scriptures will usually back off. If they continue to mock, you might turn to **Alma 5:30-31** in the Book of Mormon and read it aloud to them.

## Proverbs on Strife and Contention

The Bible has much to say about senseless strife and contention. Read the following verses from **Proverbs** to gain a Biblical perspective on this issue:

- **10:12**, *"Hatred stirreth up strifes: but love covereth all sins."*

- **15:18**, *"A wrathful man stirreth up strife: but he that is slow to anger appeaseth strife."*

- **18:6**, *"A fool's lips enter into contention, and his mouth calleth for strokes" [in other words, he deserves a beating].*

- **18:19**, *"A brother offended is harder to be won than a strong city: and their contentions are like the bars of a castle."*

- **22:10**, *"Cast out the scorner, and contention shall go out; yea, strife and reproach shall cease."*

- **26:21**, *"As coals are to burning coals, and wood to fire; so is a contentious man to kindle strife."*

- **28:25**, *"He that is of a proud heart stirreth up strife…"*

- **13:10**, *"Only by pride cometh contention: but with the well advised is wisdom."*

Be well advised! If you don't consider these warnings, your witnessing efforts may be in vain.

## Compassionate Boldness

Before we conclude this chapter, we must consider another Biblical truth—the true gospel of Jesus Christ is by nature offensive. Mormons will often feel offended by the truths you are sharing in spite of how kindly or compassionately you may be talking with them.

We are commanded to *"earnestly contend for the faith"* (**Jude 1:3**), but this kind of contention is not senseless contention, it is necessary for the ones with whom we are talking.

You must understand that the Book of Mormon passages **3 Nephi 11:29** and **Alma 5:30-31** dealing with contention and mockery are NOT teaching Biblical truth! Contention and mockery are not always of the devil, nor are they always wrong.

There are many Biblical examples where men of God were very contentious, and they were in the right. For example, read the story of Elijah and the prophets of Baal found in **1 Kings 18:20-40**. In this story, Elijah mocks the prophets of Baal.

Also consider the fact that Jesus was very contentious at times with the religious rulers of his day (read **Matthew chapter 23.**) In this story, Jesus goes to the religious center of Israel, the Jewish temple, and he uses the strongest language possible to condemn the Jewish religious rulers.

The Apostle Paul started riots when he preached the gospel in Ephesus (**Act 19:21-41**.) Yes, we are commanded to 'contend earnestly' for the true gospel of Jesus Christ.

> **Jude 1:3**, *"Beloved, when I gave all diligence to write unto you of the common salvation, it was needful for me to write unto you, and exhort you that ye should earnestly contend for the faith which was once delivered unto the saints."*

Maybe the best way to describe our witnessing efforts would be COMPASSIONATE BOLDNESS. Yes, we are to be compassionate, kind, merciful, and humble as we share the gospel, but we also are to boldly proclaim the truth even if it is not received well by those who need to hear our message. I think the key thought is that we are to avoid senseless contention.

> **Romans 12:18**, *"If it be possible, as much as lieth in you, live peaceably with all men."*

## QUESTIONS FOR REVIEW

**What two LDS buzz words will be helpful to remember as you witness to Mormons?**

**1.**

**2.**

**Explain why 3 Nephi 11:29 and Alma 5:30-31 are NOT Biblical truths?**

**Should we always feel as though we did something wrong if an LDS person is offended by our message?**

# CHAPTER 2
# THE LDS SCRIPTURES

## SECTION 5
# Using the Bible and The LDS Scriptures

**NOTE**: The Bible is the inspired, authoritative, complete, and ONLY written Word of God. Christianity does not believe in modern-day inspired scriptures, so we do not believe the additional scriptures of the LDS Church are in any way inspired (nor are they historically true.) In your witnessing efforts, you should use Biblical proof texts as often as possible to support every doctrinal point.

🛑 **Turn to the Glossary of Mormon Terms and read the LDS definition of 'Scriptures, LDS'.**

### The scriptures

The LDS Church has four written volumes that are believed by Mormons to be inspired scriptures. These are the Bible, the Book of Mormon, the Doctrine and Covenants, and The Pearl of Great Price. When you use the term 'Scriptures' as you witness to LDS people, they will automatically assume you are referring to all four books recognized as scripture by the LDS Church.

**The Holy Bible** used by the Mormon Church is the Authorized King James Version of the Bible. It is safe to use the Bible published by the LDS Church when witnessing to Mormons because the text has not been altered—only the footnotes and cross-references reflect LDS doctrine.

**The Book of Mormon** is the most important volume of scripture to Mormons. It claims to be another testament of Jesus Christ and is believed to be the only ancient historical record of the early Americas. The Book of Mormon contains an account of a small band of Hebrew Israelites who supposedly migrated to the Americas in about 600 B.C. and eventually became the people group known as the Native American Indians. The Book of Mormon also claims Jesus visited the Americas shortly after his resurrection and established the Christian church in the New World in exactly the same manner as he had done in Israel.

**Doctrine and Covenants** is a volume of modern-day revelations of the Mormon Church written mostly by Joseph Smith—with a few additional revelations by other LDS prophets.

🛑 **Turn to the Glossary of Mormon Terms and read the LDS definition of 'Doctrine and Covenants'.**

**The Pearl of Great Price** is a selection of LDS scriptures that support the 'restored gospel' of The Church of Jesus Christ of Latter-day Saints. These revelations were supposedly 'translated' and/or produced by the Prophet Joseph Smith.

**NOTE**: Virtually all of the foundational and unique doctrines of the LDS Church come from the last two volumes of scriptures, the Doctrine and Covenants *(D&C)* and the Pearl of Great Price. Very few of the unique doctrines of Mormonism can be found in either the Bible or the Book of Mormon.

### LDS View of the Bible

🛑 **Turn to the Glossary of Mormon Terms and read the LDS definition of 'Bible'.**

It is critical for you to understand the LDS view of the Bible. Although the Bible is officially recognized as scripture by the LDS Church, it is considered to be the least authoritative of their four volumes of scripture. A phrase you will hear often is, "We believe the Bible to be the Word of

God as far as it is translated correctly" *(LDS Article of Faith #8.)*

LDS leaders have consistently instructed their people not to trust the Bible because they claim it was not 'translated correctly'. In addition, they teach many 'plain and precious truths' have been changed or entirely removed from the Bible. Because of this, Mormon people cling devotedly to the doctrines of their church even though LDS teachings often contradict the Bible. They use the Bible as proof that they are a Christian religion while at the same time denying the fundamental doctrines contained within it.

Tri-Grace Ministries has created two visual aids dealing with the trustworthiness of the Bible. These handouts will help LDS people to understand the true history of the Bible and will show why it could not have been changed the way the Book of Mormon describes.

- *The Truth About the Plain and Precious Truths of the Bible Visual* proves the Bible could not have been altered at the time in history when the Book of Mormon claims it was altered—after 100 A.D.

- *The Reliability of the New Testament Text Visual* is an outline taken from James White's explanations of the textual variants contained within the ancient handwritten Greek N.T. documents *(James White is the Director of Alpha and Omega Ministries.)* This handout explains why the vast majority of the textual variants do not affect the text in any way and then shows that even the most significant variants do not alter any of the doctrines taught by our Lord and His Apostles.

These two handouts demonstrate beyond a shadow of a doubt that (1) NO Commandments, (2) NO Doctrines, and (3) NO Principles taught in the Bible have been altered in any significant way. We can confidently state that our Bible contains the exact same message as it did in ancient times when it was inspired by the Holy Spirit and written by His prophets and apostles.

👁 **Go to: TriGrace.org**
**Under 'Resources' find and print the free PDF downloads of *The Plain and Precious Truths Visual* and *Reliability of the New Testament Text*. Then watch the corresponding TGM Tutorials explaining how to use these visual aids when witnessing to LDS people.**

## Who Really Changed Their Scriptures?

The LDS Church has done exactly what they accuse Christianity of doing—the LDS Church has made significant changes to ALL of the LDS scriptures.

- The *1830 Book of Mormon* was described by Joseph Smith as 'the most correct of any book on earth'. It, however, contained many mistakes. These errors were later corrected by the LDS Church—some of these corrections were doctrinally and/or historically significant.

- The *1835 Doctrine and Covenants* is perhaps the most glaring example of the LDS Church making significant changes to their scriptures. In 1835, the D&C contained two sections: the Doctrine of the Church and the Covenants and Commandments. In 1921 the LDS Church removed the first section. The entire section describing the Doctrine of the Church (70 pages long) was totally eliminated from the Doctrine and Covenants.

- *Joseph Smith's 'New Translation' of the Bible* shows the corrections and additions Joseph Smith made to the Bible. This work by Joseph is known to Latter-day Saints as the 'Inspired Version' or 'JST' *(Joseph Smith Translation.)* Today these 'corrections' can be found in the footnotes in LDS Bibles. The most glaring of these changes are found in Genesis chapter 50 and Isaiah chapter 29 where Joseph inserted prophecies from the Book of Mormon into the Bible. And, these passages contain prophecies about himself! Yes, Joseph Smith inserted himself into the Bible twice!

**STOP** Turn to the glossary of Mormon Terms and read the LDS definition of 'Inspired Version of the Bible or the Joseph Smith Translation (JST)'.

## 'Turn the Tables' On Mormonism

We would suggest after using the TGM visual, *The Truth About the Plain and Precious Truths of the Bible,* (that proves Christianity NEVER changed the message of the Bible)—you then 'turn the tables' on Mormonism by exposing your LDS friends to the fact that the LDS Church DID make significant changes to their scriptures. Mormons will be shocked when they realize their church is guilty of doing the very thing they criticize Christianity of doing.

**👁** Go to: TriGrace.org
**Under 'Resources' find and print the free PDF downloads of: *'4 Reasons Why the Book of Mormon Should Be Correct', 'Who took the 'D' out of the D&C?'* and the *'Bible is the Word of God as Far as It is Translated Correctly'.* Then watch the corresponding TGM Tutorials explaining how to use each of these visual aids.**

Showing LDS people the changes that were made to the LDS scriptures in a printed handout will make your point. But, for those who want to take the conversation to the next level, showing your LDS friends the actual source materials will be even more effective. The following LDS books can be purchased at reasonable prices on Amazon.com – The *1830 Book of Mormon* and the *1835 Doctrine and Covenant* reproductions can be purchased for about $25 each. A book titled, *Joseph Smith's 'New Translation' of the Bible*, can be purchased for about $15.

**STOP** Turn to the Glossary of Mormon Terms and read the LDS definition of 'Book of Abraham'.

## The Lost Book of Abraham Video/DVD

Another great resource that challenges the trustworthiness of the Pearl of Great Price is a video titled, *The Lost Book of Abraham.* It can be purchased from the Institute for Religious Research by going to their website: www.irr.org

## The Book of Mormon vs. Mormonism

Mormonism is a false religion, governed over the years by unregenerate men. Each new LDS 'prophet' has, therefore, introduced his own preferences into the teachings of the LDS Church. Consequently, LDS doctrine has changed dramatically over the years. There are many inconsistencies found when comparing official LDS Church doctrine with the LDS scriptures.

When witnessing, your main focus should be to direct LDS people to the Bible, God's Word. Your secondary focus, at times, will be to show them that not only the Bible but also the LDS scriptures don't always agree with Mormonism *(especially the Book of Mormon.)*

For Christians, the Book of Mormon carries no weight of authority because it is not historically accurate nor is it inspired by God. For Mormons, however, the Book of Mormon is their primary focus. We know from experience that they become very troubled when presented with teachings from the Book of Mormon that directly contradict the current doctrines of their church.

Because the LDS Church forbids the reading of 'Anti-Mormon' literature, some Mormons will not read anything that is not sanctioned by their church. However, if you ask them questions about their scriptures, they often will talk freely. The doctrines of the Bible and the Book of Mormon are not in total harmony, but the Book of Mormon does contain some traditional Christian theology. We encourage you to use the LDS scriptures to challenge Mormon people.

We believe the Holy Spirit uses truth to convict men in spite of the source. Consider this Biblical example—in the book of Numbers, God used a donkey to proclaim truth to a false prophet named Balaam. Then God used this pagan prophet to bless the children of Israel and proclaim a wonderful messianic prophecy. If God can use a donkey and a pagan prophet to fulfill His purposes, why not the Book of Mormon?

Be honest with your Mormon friends and tell them up front that you do not believe the Book of Mormon is historically true or inspired by God. But, explain that when a topic is in agreement with the Bible, you can agree with that principle. They will usually find this acceptable because they are told the Book of Mormon and the Bible agree. If they want to know why you do not believe the Book of Mormon is historically true, take them directly to the Book of Mormon and show them the various historical problems as outlined in Section 6, 'Book of Mormon Anachronisms'.

**IMPORTANT POINT**: The Book of Mormon contains very few of the prominent doctrines of the LDS Church. In fact, many of the key LDS doctrines are contradicted in the Book of Mormon.

## Reasoning With Mormons

When you choose to focus your discussions on the Bible and Book of Mormon, LDS people may try to introduce the Doctrine and Covenants or Pearl of Great Price into the conversation. The following dialogue illustrates one good way to steer the conversation back to the Bible and the Book of Mormon.

**Christian:** Can you show me one place in the Bible or Book of Mormon that says there is more than one true and living God?

**Mormon:** I don't know if I can, but **Doctrine and Covenants, section 132:37**, tells us Abraham, Isaac, and Jacob have already been exalted and have become gods.

**Christian:** The Doctrine and Covenants are Latter-day scriptures aren't they?

**Mormon:** Yes, the LDS Church believes in modern-day revelation. Joseph Smith was a living prophet used by God to give us our latter-day scriptures.

**Christian:** I know the LDS Church believes in a plurality of Gods, and I would expect the more recent revelations of your church, like the Doctrine and Covenants, would support this doctrine. What I want to know is, where in your ancient scriptures, the Bible or the Book of Mormon, does it say there is more than one true God? I want to know if your Latter-day prophets agree with the ancient prophets.

## Using the King James Bible

The Mormon Church recognizes only the Authorized King James Version (KJV) of the Bible. To a Mormon, all other translations are perversions—this is especially true with older LDS people. Therefore, we recommend you use the KJV when talking with your Mormon friends. And, it is best if you use a Bible printed by the LDS Church. All of the Biblical proof texts used in this booklet are quoted from the authorized KJV.

## QUESTIONS FOR REVIEW

**What are the four volumes of scriptures recognized by the LDS Church?**

   1.

   2.

   3.

   4.

**Which of the LDS scriptures is the most important to Mormons?**


**LDS people believe the Bible to be the Word of God as far as it is _____  _____ .**
   **What does this mean to a Mormon?**


*The Truth About the Plain and Precious Truths of the Bible* **visual will prove that:**

**No** _____ ,

**No**_____ **and**

**No**_____ **have been changed.**

**Which of the LDS scriptures has the Mormon Church changed in some significant way?**


**The Book of Mormon is not historically true nor is it inspired by God. What is the purpose behind using it to witness to LDS people?**

# Book of Mormon Anachronisms

In literary works, it is not uncommon to encounter details that are out of place in reference to time. These are called anachronisms. Writers mistakenly place objects in a timeframe before they existed or were invented. An example of this is the mention of a chiming clock in Shakespeare's play, *Julius Caesar.* Since chiming clocks did not exist in ancient Rome, this detail did not fit within the historical setting of the play.

But because the Book of Mormon is not simply a play, anachronisms found in it are more serious. Joseph Smith claimed these writings, published in 1830, had been translated from gold plates supposedly containing the actual history of the ancient Americas from about 2,500 B.C. to A.D. 400. This claim has been frequently challenged over the years for a variety of reasons, among them the many anachronisms.

## General Anachronisms—Book of Mormon

**"windows" that will "be dashed in pieces" (Ether2:23—about 2,500 B.C.)** This was supposedly written at the time of the Tower of Babel. The earliest glass windows—stained glass windows—were invented in the first century B.C. by the Romans. Transparent glass window panes were invented much later. **Ether 3:1** also mentions **"transparent glass."**

**"horses and chariots" (Alma 18:9-12 and 3 Nephi 3:22—600 B.C. to about A.D. 400.)** Horses and wheel technology did not exist in the ancient Americas. The Spaniards introduced horses when they arrived in the 1500's. There are no archeological proofs for either horses or chariots in the New World during Book of Mormon times.

**"steel swords" (Ether 7:9, 2 Nephi 5:14-15, Jarom 1:8—about 2500 B.C. to A.D. 400.)** Steel technology did not exist in the ancient Americas.

Not one steel sword nor any evidence of swords has been discovered in the archeology of the New World. Native Americans in Book of Mormon times never reached the 'Iron Age', therefore steel would have been an impossibility.

**"wild elephants" (Ether 9:19—about 2500 B.C.)** This passage says the people found the wild elephants of the Americas to be especially useful. The only animal that could possibly fit the description of an elephant was the woolly mammoth which became extinct in prehistoric times, long before the Book of Mormon history.

**"Nephite coinage set forth… Now these are the names of the different pieces of their gold, and of their silver, according to their value" (Alma 11:3-19—82 B.C.)** No gold or silver coins mentioned in the Book of Mormon have ever been found in the archeology of the Americas.

**"adieu" (Jacob 7:27—about 421 B.C.)** 'Adieu' is a French term. The French language did not even exist until A.D. 700.

***The King James Bible*—(600 B.C. to A.D. 400.)** Long passages that were copied directly from the *King James Bible* are another huge problem for the Book of Mormon. The first edition of the KJV was published in A.D. 1611. Compare **I Nephi 20 & 21 with Isaiah 48 & 49; 2 Nephi 7 & 8 with Isaiah 50 & 51; 2 Nephi 12 with Isaiah 2; and 2 Nephi 24 with Isaiah 14.**

## Greek anachronisms—Book of Mormon

Finding Greek words in the Book of Mormon is another major flaw because the original characters in the story were supposedly Hebrew speaking Israelites who left Jerusalem at about 600 B.C., before the Babylonian captivity. It is not possible that these Hebrews would have had a working knowledge of the Greek language because 250 years and two Aramaic speaking world empires would come and go before the Greek conqueror, Alexander the Great, would emerge on the world scene. Through Alexander's influence, the Greek language eventually became the common trade language after 350 B.C. It is, therefore, highly problematic to say these Hebrew people would use words from an unfamiliar and foreign language in their common vocabulary.

Since the people described in the Book of Mormon story had no contact with the Old World after 600 B.C., Greek words found throughout the Book of Mormon are linguistic anachronisms.

**"Alpha and Omega" (3 Nephi 9:18—34 A.D.)** Since the people would not have known Greek, Jesus' statement that He was the 'Alpha and Omega' (the first and last letters of the Greek alphabet) would have been meaningless.

**"Christ" (2 Nephi 25:14-29—about 550 B.C.)** 'Christ' is the Greek equivalent of the Hebrew word, 'Messiah'. Both words mean the exact same thing—the 'anointed one'. Christ and Messiah are used interchangeably throughout the Book of Mormon!

**"Christians" (Alma 46:13-16—73 B.C.)** This is a Greek word, and the Bible says believers were first called Christians in Antioch (**Acts 11:26**) in about A.D. 63.

**"Timothy & Jonas" (3 Nephi 19:4—about 34 A.D.)** These are Greek names. Why would Hebrew families give their children Greek names?

**"alms" (3 Nephi 13:1-4—34 A.D.)** 'Alms' is a Greek word that has no Hebrew counterpart.

## Attempts to Justify the Anachronisms

Although these General and Greek Anachronisms strike at the very heart of the integrity of the Book of Mormon, there are Mormon responses to dodge them. Following is a plausible dialog between a Christian and a Mormon.

**Christian:** How do you account for the anachronisms I've just shown you?

**Mormon:** Well, I'm not sure, but there seems to be a lot of archeological evidence to prove the Book of Mormon is true. Central America is full of ancient ruins. You can actually take 'Book of Mormon Tours' to Central America.

**Christian:** I have done some research on the ancient Mayan, Aztec and Inca civilizations; and

from everything I have discovered they don't fit the culture found in the Book of Mormon. The plant life, animals, technology and the religious cultures are all different. Besides, if they were the Nephites and Lamanites of the Book of Mormon, why do we call them Mayans, Aztecs, and Incas? (See Section 7, 'More Historical Problems', for an in-depth answer to this response.)

*[Another typical LDS response]* **Mormon:** We don't need archeological proof. We believe by faith that the Book of Mormon is true and we have received a spiritual witness of its truthfulness from God. I know the Book of Mormon is true, that Joseph Smith was a true prophet of God, and that the Mormon Church is true.

**Christian:** *(See Chapter 4, 'Dealing with Feelings', Sections 13-16.)*

## QUESTIONS FOR REVIEW:
**What is an anachronism?**

**Which General Anachronism do you think best disproves the Book of Mormon?**

**Why?**

**Which Greek Anachronism do you think best disproves the Book of Mormon?**

**Why?**

# Other Historical Problems

This section follows the discussion on the anachronisms in the Book of Mormon because there are more than just time-related problems to consider. The 'historical' entries below appear in the Book of Mormon but are either not credible, are highly improbable, or are impossible to prove.

## Vanishing Native American Christianity

The book of **4 Nephi** says for almost 200 years (A.D. 36-201) all Native Americans were practicing Christians. To this day, there is no evidence that Christianity flourished in the ancient Americas. How could 200 years of Christianity totally vanish from the archeological record of the New World?

## Hill Cumorah Battles

Recorded in **Mormon 6:11-16** (A.D. 385) and **Ether 15:1-11** (prior to 600 B.C.)—these two battles claimed millions of lives! These battles supposedly took place at the Hill Cumorah, a small hill, located near Joseph Smith's home in Palmyra, New York. There is, however, no evidence that these great battles took place at all—no steel swords, no brass breastplates, no chariots, no brass/iron/steel arrow tips, etc. *(See also **Jarom 1:8**—399 B.C.)*

## A temple like that of King Solomon

In **2 Nephi 5:15-16** (about 570 B.C.) there is the record of a handful of people (by all estimates less than 100 men, women, and children) supposedly building a temple similar to Solomon's temple. If it took Solomon seven years—using more than 100,000 laborers—to build his magnificent temple (**2 Chronicles 2:1-2**), how long would it have taken Nephi and his small band of followers?

## Source Fix/Living Hope Video Resources

*DNA vs the Book of Mormon*—For more than 170 years, the Church of Jesus Christ of Latter-day Saints has declared the Book of Mormon to be a literal history of the ancient Americas. It recounts the story of an Israelite family who migrated to and populated the American continents.

The Book of Mormon teaches that these Israelites are the principal ancestors of modern-day Native Americans. New discoveries in DNA research currently allow scientists to test this historical claim. Thousands of Native Americans from more than 150 tribes have been tested to determine their ancestry.

Now the same DNA evidence used in courts of law can credibly speak to the validity of The Book of Mormon. The evidence answers one basic question: Are Israelites the principal ancestors of Native Americans?

*DNA vs. The Book of Mormon* presents the evidence from DNA researchers, including Mormon scientists, who are wrestling with the DNA dilemma that now faces Mormonism.

*The Bible vs the Book of Mormon*—The Book of Mormon claims to be 'a volume of holy scripture comparable to the Bible'. Both the Bible and the Book of Mormon declare themselves to be ancient and historical—the very word of God.

These claims have historically been taken on faith. But is there any evidence to support them one way or the other? More to the point, is there any basis for placing one's faith in the Bible or the Book of Mormon? It's an important question. This presentation puts the Bible and the Book of Mormon to the same tests. History, archaeology, textual criticism, and other disciplines combine to shed light on what is true and what is false.

Truth never fears investigation. Faith need not—and should not—be blind. Discover for yourself which of these books is worthy of being called 'scripture' and which is worthy of your trust.

To purchase these and other resources, visit the SourceFlix website at: **SourceFlix.com**

## Circumstantial Evidences vs. Archeological Proof

LDS people may try to use circumstantial evidence to prove the historical accuracy of the Book of Mormon. Don't be fooled by this ploy that might or might not support Book of Mormon history. Circumstantial evidences such as ancient stone boxes, or the discovery of concrete in ancient America, or pools with stairs that may have been used as baptismal fonts are not proofs for the Book of Mormon.

Archeological proof is very different from circumstantial evidence.

### Archeological proof would:

- Confirm the names of the ancient people groups and/or important persons who are mentioned in the Book of Mormon

- Identify the prominent cities which the Book of Mormon describes in detail

- Reveal historical evidences for the major events in the Book of Mormon—such as the Hill Cumorah Battles

- Locate even part of an ancient manuscript of the Book of Mormon—there are NO manuscripts or fragments of manuscripts of the Book of Mormon that pre-date Joseph Smith. All existing Book of Mormon manuscripts are English manuscripts which is a huge problem for Mormonism.

- Uncover specific items the Book of Mormon mentions like chariots, steel swords, brass breastplates, Mormon coins, iron/steel arrow tips etc. in the New World

NOTE: I have searched both secular and Mormon sources for archeological proof that positively identifies any Book of Mormon person, place, or event. I have yet to find even one proof that the Book of Mormon is historically true. Challenge your Mormon friend to show you any LDS Church resource that would answer these questions.

To better understand the dilemma Mormonism faces when it comes to Book of Mormon evidences:

👁 **Go to: TriGrace.org**
**Under 'Resources', go to the Tutorials and listen to *Book of Mormon Archaeology?***

## Biblical Proof

Archeological proof for the Bible exists in abundance! You can go to Christian bookstores and find an assortment of books containing thousands of archeological finds which prove the persons, places and events recorded in the Bible.

One example is *The Popular Handbook of Archaeology and the Bible* by Joseph M. Holden and Norman Geisler, Harvest House Publishing, 2013, which contains hundreds of such proofs.

## QUESTIONS FOR REVIEW
**What is the difference between circumstantial evidence and archeological proof?**

**What archeological proof exists to support the historical truthfulness of the Book of Mormon?**

**What archeological proof exists to support the historical truthfulness of the Bible?**

*(see TGM Tutorial, Book of Mormon Archaeology?)*
**What dilemma does Dr. Kerry Muhlestein face in regard to Book of Mormon Archaeology?**

**What dilemma does Rod Meldrom face in regard to Book of Mormon Archaeology?**

# SECTION 8

# Using the Book of Mormon 'INTRODUCTION'

As you discuss the topics outlined in this book, you should be familiar with the following two quotations. These quotes are important because neither the Bible nor the Book of Mormon support the most important doctrines of the LDS Church. The following quotes are from the *1981 edition of the Book of Mormon, 'INTRODUCTION'*.

## 1st Paragraph Quotation,

*"The Book of Mormon is a volume of holy scripture comparable to the Bible. It is a record of God's dealings with the ancient inhabitants of the Americas and contains, as does the Bible, the fullness of the everlasting gospel."*

**NOTE:** This statement is based on a passage found in **Doctrine and Covenants 42:12**.

After reading this in the Book of Mormon, ask your Mormon friend the following questions:

- Do both the Bible and Book of Mormon contain the fullness of the everlasting gospel?

- What does the word 'fullness' mean?

- What does the word 'everlasting' mean?

- If 'the fullness of the everlasting gospel' means the complete gospel, then everything Mormonism teaches about the gospel should be contained in both books, correct?

The following quotation clarifies this issue,

*"FULLNESS OF THE GOSPEL. 'By fullness of the gospel is meant all the ordinances and principles that pertain to the exaltation in the celestial kingdom.'"* (*Doctrines of Salvation*, Joseph Fielding Smith, Vol. 1, p. 160.)

## 6th Paragraph Quotation,

*"Joseph Smith said: 'I told the brethren that the Book of Mormon was the most correct of any book on earth, and the keystone of our religion, and a man would get nearer to God by abiding by its precepts, than by any other book.'"*

After reading this quotation, ask your Mormon friend the following questions:

- Do you believe the Book of Mormon is the most correct book on earth?

- What does it mean when it says that the Book of Mormon is the keystone of your religion?

- Do you believe you will get nearer to God by abiding by the precepts contained in the Book of Mormon than by any other book?

After examining both quotes, ask this:

If the Bible and the Book of Mormon are in agreement on any given topic, would it be correct to conclude that the truth being taught must be a correct doctrine or principle?

The answer for a Mormon has to be, 'Yes!'

## QUESTIONS FOR REVIEW

**If the fundamental doctrines of Mormonism are not found in either the Bible or Book of Mormon, why would it be to your advantage to point out the quotations highlighted in this section?**

**In Paragraph 1 of the 'INTRODUCTION' what is meant by the 'fullness of the everlasting gospel?'**

**What does Paragraph 6 imply in regard to the Bible?**

# CHAPTER 3
# PREPARING TO WITNESS

## SECTION 9
# Two Witnessing Techniques

In any witnessing situation, and especially with Mormons, two essential techniques must be a part of your witnessing effort. They are *Truth vs. Error* and the *Hungering and Thirsting Principle*.

### 'Truth vs. Error'

Much of the information in this book is Biblical truth that is designed to confront the doctrinal errors of Mormonism. As you present these truths, it is important for you to use the Bible as the basis for your discussions.

If you do not use the Bible as your foundation, it will just be your opinion vs their opinion—and I guarantee the Mormon will like their opinion better than yours. When you use the Bible, it will be their opinion vs God's word. The Holy Spirit uses the word of God to convict people of their sin, so use the word of God!

The *Truth vs. Error* witnessing technique will be most effective if you have the person you are talking with read the scriptural proof texts related to each topic. When they finish reading a passage, ask, "What do you think this is this saying?"

When they see that what they have just read contradicts what their church has taught them, *Truth vs. Error* comes into play. What you are doing is allowing the Holy Spirit to take Biblical truth and use it to convict them of error.

*Isaiah 55:11* tells us God's word will not return void but will accomplish that which He pleases.

### The 'Hungering and Thirsting Principle'

The *Hungering and Thirsting Principle* is as important as *Truth vs. Error*. While *Truth vs. Error* is designed to cause Mormons to question their religion, the *Hungering and Thirsting Principle* is designed to cause them to desire what true Christians have found in Jesus Christ. After exposing the fallacies of their false religious system, it is absolutely essential that you replace what has been destroyed with the real thing.

The gospel is good news! Through your own salvation testimony you will be able to show how a personal relationship with Jesus Christ is infinitely more satisfying than the hopeless works of any religious system.

LDS people do not understand what it means to have peace with God, complete forgiveness of sins, eternal life, and a relationship with Jesus through the indwelling presence of the Holy Spirit. You can help them to see that Christ is the only One who will bring lasting peace to a hungering soul. This is the *Hungering and Thirsting Principle*.

### QUESTIONS FOR REVIEW
**Explain *Truth vs. Error* in your own words.**

**Explain the *Hungering and Thirsting Principle* in your own words.**

**Why are both witnessing techniques important?**

# SECTION 10
# Conversation Starters

Most Mormons are very open to talk about their religion. If you are wondering how you can get into religious discussions with LDS people, here are two ideas to help you.

## Use the Book of Mormon

**STOP Turn to the Glossary of Mormon Terms and read the LDS definition of 'Book of Mormon'.**

To a Mormon, the Book of Mormon is the most important document ever written. Mormons will first challenge you to read it then ask you to pray for God to reveal its truthfulness to you.

Study from the Book of Mormon the passages relating to the topics found in this book. This will take time and effort but will pay huge dividends when witnessing to LDS people. You will then be able to tell them you have been studying the Book of Mormon and have some questions—would they be willing to answer your questions?

It would be anti-Mormon for them to refuse, so begin by taking them through one of the topical studies you will learn in this book. Chapter 5, 'The Doctrine of God', is a perfect place to start.

## Are Families Forever?

**STOP Turn to the Glossary of Mormon Terms and read the LDS definition of 'Eternal Families'.**

The familiar quote, 'Families are Forever', is straight from the heart of Mormonism. This warm, fuzzy doctrine is one of the greatest drawing cards of the Mormon Church but is also one of its deepest deceptions. As you discuss Mormonism with your Mormon friends, you will likely hear at some point, "Don't you want to live as a family with your wife and children forever?"

This false doctrine was introduced to Mormonism by Joseph Smith in the Doctrine and Covenants, sections 131 and 132.

In 1995, LDS President Gordon B. Hinckley made a proclamation, titled, *The Family: A Proclamation to the World.* In it he said:

> "The divine plan of happiness enables family relationships to be perpetuated beyond the grave. Sacred ordinances and covenants available in holy temples make it possible for individuals to return to the presence of God and for families to be united eternally." *(True to the Faith, The LDS Church, 2004, p. 60.)*

Mormonism is a patriarchal society that believes all worthy Mormon men will be allowed to take their posterity *(their wife/wives and children)* with them to the Celestial Kingdom—IF they have been sealed in an LDS Temple, by one holding the proper priesthood authority. This gives Mormons a false sense of security concerning their eternal future, and even non-practicing Mormons cling to the hope that they will 'make it' because they were sealed to good Mormon parents. But this doctrine is illogical and cannot work, even within Mormonism.

## Consider the 'Families are Forever' scenario:

As a child you are sealed to your LDS family in a Mormon temple for time and all eternity. As you grow to adulthood, you then marry a Mormon and are sealed to that person for time and all eternity. Unfortunately, the person you married was also sealed as a child to their family for all eternity. Now you have a serious problem! Which sealing takes priority?

Then, as you and your spouse have children, you will seal them to your new family; but when your children grow up and get married, they will marry Mormons who have been sealed to their families. So, again, which sealing takes priority? This becomes an eternally complicated problem.

There is one final glitch to this fantasy—the ultimate goal of every devout Mormon couple is to be exalted to godhood. When exaltation is achieved, each worthy couple will become a god and goddess of their own world. If this is true, how can families be together for all eternity? Instead of being together, the best Mormon families will literally be scattered across the universe on different planets!

When confronted with these incongruities, a Mormon may respond, 'We don't understand everything now, but God will work out all the details in the end'.

Mormons have no reasonable explanation for the 'eternal families' dilemma; and though they may appear to dismiss the problem, we know from experience that this topic haunts them.

### Christian Families—Together Forever

The idea that 'families can be together forever' is more true in Christianity than in Mormonism. While we do not envision living in our earthly family units in Heaven, every family member who accepts Jesus as Savior is adopted into God's eternal family. All believers will live together as members of God's forever family.

But, unlike Mormonism, the focus of our eternal existence will not be on the relationships we enjoyed while here on earth—our eternal focus will be on GOD.

### QUESTIONS FOR REVIEW
**How can you use the Book of Mormon to start a conversation with a Mormon?**

**If you follow LDS doctrine to its final conclusion, can families be together forever?**

**Why not?**

**Why is the idea that 'Families can be Together Forever' more true for Christians than Mormons?**

# SECTION 11
# Is Mormonism Christian?

**STOP Turn to the Glossary of Mormon Terms and read the LDS definitions of 'Christianity', 'Cross', and 'Fall, The'.**

In recent years, the LDS Church has gone to great lengths to be accepted as another 'Christian Denomination'. Nothing bothers LDS people more than the fact that the Christian community will not accept Mormonism as Christian.

**Go to: TriGrace.org
Under 'Resources' find and print the free PDF download of *Heavenly Father's Plan of Salvation*. Then watch the corresponding TGM Tutorial explaining *Heavenly Father's Plan of Salvation*.**

**NOTE:** Heavenly Father's Plan of Salvation is a great conversation starter with Mormons. Just hand them this visual aid and ask them to explain the LDS plan of salvation to you.

When they finish, point out the fact that you think they missed something that is very important—***JESUS!*** Neither Jesus nor the atonement of Jesus is mentioned anywhere in *Heavenly Father's Plan of Salvation*! How can a Christian religion forget to mention Jesus when explaining Heavenly Father's Plan of Salvation?

If you are going to use this visual with LDS people it is best if you purchase the 'official' LDS laminated full-color Heavenly Father's Plan of Salvation from an LDS bookstore. It can be purchased on-line *(in 2014 when this book was published)* from the LDS Deseret Bookstores at the following URL: http://deseretbook.com/At-a-Glance-Plan-Salvation-Richard-Maher/i/4098480

Is Mormonism Christian? To a Christian who understands Mormonism, the answer is simple, NO WAY! You could just tell your Mormon friends they are NOT Christian, but this will cause a fight and hurt feelings. There is a better way! This topic can be an excellent opportunity to witness.

**A Suggested Dialogue:**
**Christian:** Hello, I think I overheard you talking about your religion, I am a Christian and I was just wondering what Church you attend?
**Mormon:** I attend the Church of Jesus Christ of Latter-day Saints... and, we are Christians too!

**Christian:** So you are a Mormon?
**Mormon:** Well, yes, but we prefer to be called Latter-day Saints.

**Christian:** Can I ask you a question—why do you think Mormonism is a Christian religion?
**Mormon:** Because we believe in Jesus. His name is in the title of our church, The Church of Jesus Christ of Latter-day Saints. Don't you think we are Christians?

**Christian:** Can I ask another question before I give you an answer? I have studied the Book of Mormon and I honestly don't believe it was inspired by God, I also do not believe Joseph Smith was a true prophet, Would it be honest for me to tell people I am a Mormon?
**Mormon:** Of course not!

**Christian:** Why not?
**Mormon:** Because if you don't believe what we believe you shouldn't say you are LDS.

**Christian:** That's why I would say you shouldn't call Mormonism a Christian religion. You can correct me if I am wrong, but from what I have studied, the LDS Church doesn't agree with any of the fundamental doctrines of Christianity.
**Mormon:** What do you mean by that? I don't think we're so far apart!

This type of conversation will often open the door to a great witnessing opportunity.

Many religions of the world believe in the historical man called Jesus: Muslims, Jehovah's Witnesses, Mormons, etc. But, none of these religions are Christian. The Bible says *"the devils also believe, and tremble"* (**James 2:19**.)

The topics in this book will teach you how to effectively challenge the fact that Mormonism is NOT Christian and will help you introduce your LDS friends to the true gospel of Jesus Christ.

## QUESTIONS FOR REVIEW
**Why do LDS people think Mormonism is another Christian denomination?**

**When an LDS person says, 'We are Christians too!'—Explain how you should respond?**

**Why isn't Mormonism a Christian denomination?**

# S E C T I O N 12
# Moroni 10:3-5

LDS people are taught to use Moroni 10:3-5 as a means of challenging non-Mormons to read the Book of Mormon. They will read the following verses found in **Moroni 10:3-5,**

*"Behold, I would exhort you that when you shall **read these things**, if it be wisdom in God that ye should **read them**, that ye would remember how merciful the Lord hath been unto the children of men, from the creation of Adam even down until the time that ye shall **receive these things**, and **ponder it in your hearts**. And when ye shall **receive these things**, I would exhort you that ye would ask God, the Eternal Father, in the name of Christ, if these things are not true; and if ye shall ask with a sincere heart, with real intent, having faith in Christ, he will manifest the truth of it unto you, by the power of the Holy Ghost. And by the power of the Holy Ghost ye may know the truth of all things."*

They will then ask, 'Would you be willing to read the Book of Mormon, and ask God to reveal the truthfulness of it to you?'

This question presents a perfect witnessing opportunity.

## How to Use Moroni 10:3-5

You can use this passage to your advantage by immediately REVERSING the question.

The admonition from Moroni, the last Nephite prophet, is not just about praying and asking God if the book is true. In five places *(bold type above)* it mentions how important it is to read, receive, and ponder what is written in the book. So, ask your Mormon friend,

- Have you read the Book of Mormon?

- Did you pray and ask God to show you the truthfulness of the Book of Mormon?

- What did God tell you?

Follow-up with,

- Then I assume you totally believe what the Book of Mormon teaches?

They will almost certainly answer positively to all of those questions, so explain that you have been studying the Book of Mormon and have some questions you would like to have answered.

Use the discussions pertaining to:

### 'The Doctrine of God'
### Sections 17-24

or

### 'The Impossible Gospel'
### Sections 41-42

Find out if they actually believe what the Book of Mormon teaches.

## QUESTIONS FOR REVIEW
**Moroni 10:3-5 not only instructs you to pray, it also tells you to do what three things?**

1.

2.

3.

**Explain how you can reverse the question and use Moroni 10:3-5 to get into a meaningful discussion with a Mormon?**

# CHAPTER 4
# DEALING WITH FEELINGS

## SECTION 13
## The LDS Testimony

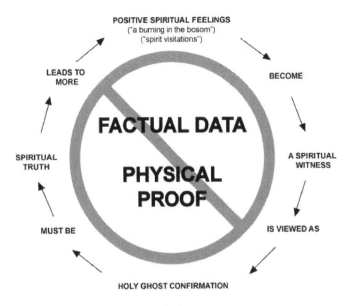

POSITIVE SPIRITUAL FEELINGS
("a burning in the bosom")
("spirit visitations")

LEADS TO MORE

BECOME

SPIRITUAL TRUTH

FACTUAL DATA PHYSICAL PROOF

A SPIRITUAL WITNESS

MUST BE

IS VIEWED AS

HOLY GHOST CONFIRMATION

FIGURE 4.1

**STOP** Turn to the Glossary of Mormon Terms and read the LDS definition of 'Feelings'.

The Mormon Church supports much of its belief system with positive spiritual feelings which are commonly referred to as 'a testimony', 'a burning in the bosom', or 'a spiritual witness'.

These spiritual feelings may be the result of actual encounters with false spirits. Spirit visitations are encouraged by the LDS religion and are believed to be personal revelations of truth. Therefore, in the Mormon mind, factual data such as archaeology or ancient manuscripts are not considered necessary when spiritual issues have been validated by a 'spiritual witness'.

The LDS Testimony is based upon a passage of Mormon scripture found in the Doctrine and Covenants which says,

*"You must study it out in your mind; then you must ask me if it be right, and if it is right I will cause that your bosom shall burn within you; therefore, you shall feel that it is right. But if it be not right you shall have no such feelings, but you shall have a stupor of thought that shall cause you to forget the thing which is wrong."* (**Doctrine and Covenants 9:8-9.**)

FIGURE 4.1 illustrates the circular reasoning behind this phenomenon. Study it to gain a clearer understanding of how a Mormon justifies his/her beliefs.

As you can see, the basis for truth and/or error centers entirely upon feelings. This kind of irrational thinking is the most difficult issue to deal with when witnessing to Mormons. For many Mormons, the facts you present will pale in comparison to their 'positive spiritual feelings'. We, however, believe God's written word, the Bible, is more powerful than their feelings.

If you hope to accomplish anything of eternal value, you must establish a solid foundation upon which to base your discussions, and that foundation is the Bible. When you use the Bible, you won't be the one convincing them of their error—the Holy Spirit will do that. The work of God's Spirit, through the written Word, will convince them of truth and win them to Christ.

**INTERESTING NOTE**: When Mormon people get backed into a theological corner, they will often 'bear their testimony'. They will say something like this, "No matter what you say, I know Joseph Smith was a true prophet, I know the Book of Mormon is true, I know the LDS Church is true, and I know we have a living prophet to guide us."

When your Mormon friends say this, don't get discouraged. They are only parroting what they have been instructed to do when they cannot defend their faith. They try to appear unshaken by resorting to their 'testimony', but in reality, this is proof that the Holy Spirit is convicting them.

**In your own words, explain the LDS 'Testimony'.**

**Why do you think this is such a difficult issue to deal with when witnessing to Mormons?**

S E C T I O N **14**

# Responses to the LDS Testimony

Following are two ways you can respond to the 'LDS testimony'.

## 1. Share Your Own Testimony

After a Mormon shares their testimony, this is a great opportunity for you to share your testimony. You can sincerely thank them for sharing something so personal and important with you—then ask, 'Would you like to hear my testimony?' They will usually say yes.

Your testimony will be very different from the LDS testimony. The LDS testimony is about their religion—it will almost always be composed of 4 or 5 simple statements,

1. *I know the LDS Church is true.*
2. *I know Joseph Smith was a true prophet of God.*
3. *I know the Book of Mormon is true.*
4. *I know Thomas S. Monson is the living prophet in the Church today. (This will change when Thomas Monson dies and a new prophet takes his place.)*

[And about half the time they will say...]

5. *I know Jesus Christ is the Savior.*

The Christian testimony, on the other hand, is not about a religion, it is about a personal relationship with Jesus. Many Mormons hunger for a relationship with Jesus, so a heartfelt testimony telling of your personal walk with Jesus will be something they will never forget. When you do this, be sure to include Biblical passages as the basis for your salvation experience

## ALWAYS—when you finish a conversation with a Mormon—PRAY with them.

Mormons do not pray like Christians. Mormon prayers are very proper and sterile, like leaving a message on an answering machine. When a Christian prays, because we have a personal relationship, we are talking directly with God. After hearing a Christian pray, Mormons will sometimes comment, "Wow, that was really beautiful. You sounded like you were actually talking to God." Your testimony and your heartfelt prayers will impact Mormons more than you will ever know.

## 2. Challenge the source of their testimony using 'The Canadian Copyright Episode'

The Canadian Copyright Episode is a story from the early days of Mormonism which is recorded in *A Comprehensive History of the Church of Jesus Christ of Latter-day Saints*, published by the LDS Church.

The story involves several prominent early Mormon leaders, David Whitmer and Oliver Cowdery wrote and signed 'The Testimony of the Three Witnesses' and Hyrum Smith and Hirum Page signed 'The Testimony of the Eight Witnesses' in the the Book of Mormon intro.

These early Mormon leaders were trying to find a way to raise the necessary funds to publish the Book of Mormon. In this historical narrative,

"Hyrum Smith is represented by David Whitmer as saying that it had been suggested to him that some of the brethren might go to Toronto, Canada, and sell the copyright of the book *[of Mormon]* for considerable money, that is, sell the right to publish the book in the Canadian provinces, not dispose of the copyright absolutely.

He persuaded Joseph to inquire of the Lord, with the result… that he 'received a revelation that some of the brethren should go to Toronto, Canada, and they would sell the copyright'.

Accordingly, Oliver Cowdery and Hirum Page, the latter being one of the eight witnesses, went to Canada to sell the copyright, but failed. David Whitmer represents that this failure threw the little group of believers into great trouble, and they went to the Prophet and asked him to account for the failure.

The Prophet frankly acknowledged his inability to understand the cause of the failure, and inquired of the Lord. He received for answer… this: 'Some revelations are of God: some revelations are of man: and some revelations are of the devil.'" (*A Comprehensive History of The Church of Jesus Christ of Latter-day Saints*, Vol. 1, by the LDS Church, p. 162-163.)

In this story, Joseph Smith received a 'revelation' that he thought came from God, but when it failed he had to admit it did not come from God. He then offered two alternative sources for this revelation—one was that it might have come from his own mind, the other that it could have come from the devil.

This creates a serious problem for the LDS testimony which is based entirely upon feelings. If Joseph Smith could not tell if his revelations came from—God, his own mind, or the Devil, how can any LDS person be certain their 'testimony' came from God?

The LDS testimony is further complicated by the many Mormon splinter groups, all of which believe Joseph Smith was a true prophet of God and the Book of Mormon is true. These groups also follow the 'feelings test' found in **D&C 9:8-9** which tells them to pray and seek for a 'burning in their bosom'. Yet, each of these groups receive different answers when they pray to the LDS Heavenly Father.

- The FLDS (in Colorado City, Arizona) believe the prophet of their group is the only true prophet on earth.

- The True and Living Church of Jesus Christ (the TLC in Manti, Utah) believe their prophet is the only true prophet.

- The United Apostolic Brethren (also known as the 'UAB' or Allred group) believe their prophet is the only true prophet.

Which Mormon group is right, The LDS, The TLC, The FLDS, or the UAB? They all use the same test—so why do they all get different answers to their heartfelt prayers? The reason is simple—the LDS 'feelings test' found in **D&C 9:8-9** DOESN'T WORK!

👁 **Go to: TriGrace.org**
**Under 'Resources' find and print the free PDF download of the *2 Step LDS Testimony Visual*. Then watch the TGM Tutorial explaining how this visual is used with LDS people.**

## QUESTIONS FOR REVIEW
**What Bible verses will you use if you have the opportunity to share your own personal testimony with a Mormon?**

**What should you ALWAYS attempt to do as you conclude a conversation with a Mormon?**

**Put yourself in an LDS person's place and explain why 'The Canadian Copyright Episode' would be so devastating to their feelings based testimony.**

# SECTION 15

# "Believe Not Every Spirit."—1 John 4:1

## A Spiritual Witness

A Mormon may say, "I know what I believe is true because the spirit told me it was true!"

When a person says this, you should ask, 'What spirit told you it was true? How do you know the spirit was a spirit sent from God?' The following Biblical passages will help.

> **1 John 4:1**, *"Beloved, believe not every spirit, but try the spirits whether they are of God: because many false prophets are gone out into the world."*

## Try the Spirits

How Can a Person *'try the spirits'*? All spiritual messages must agree with the Lord's apostles.

> **1 John 4:1, 6,** *"Beloved, believe not every spirit, but try the spirits whether they are of God: because many false prophets are gone out into the world...We are of God: he that knoweth God heareth us; he that is not of God heareth not us. Hereby know we the spirit of truth, and the spirit of error."*

## Satanic Spirits Are Deceptive

False spirits don't always appear to be evil, and false prophets don't always look fake.

> **2 Corinthians 11:13-15,** *"For such are false apostles, deceitful workers, transforming themselves into the apostles of Christ. And no marvel; for Satan himself is transformed into an angel of light. Therefore it is no great thing if his ministers also be transformed as the ministers of righteousness; whose end shall be according to their works."*

## Not All 'Prophets' Are True

Jesus warned us to beware of false prophets because many will be deceived and follow them.

> **Matthew 24:4-5, 11, & 24,** *"Jesus answered and said unto them, Take heed that no man deceive you. For many shall come in my name, saying, I am Christ; and shall deceive many... And many false prophets shall rise, and shall deceive many... For there shall arise false Christs, and false prophets, and shall shew great signs and wonders; insomuch that, if it were possible, they shall deceive the very elect."*

## God Is Not the Author of Confusion

Contradictory revelation is confusion, and God is not the author of confusion. True revelation that comes from God cannot contradict previously given revelation. If a person receives a 'spiritual witness' that is contrary to what inspired prophets have already proclaimed in the Bible—it did not come from God.

> **1 Corinthians 14:32-33,** *"And the spirits of the prophets are subject to the prophets. For God is not the author of confusion, but of peace, as in all churches of the saints."*

## QUESTIONS FOR REVIEW

**Do both good and evil spirits exist in our world today?**

**Why might it be dangerous to trust a person who claims to be a prophet of God?**

**How can you discern between the spirit of truth and the spirit of error?**

# Trusting Your Heart

The LDS Church encourages its members to trust their hearts and to doubt the Bible. In this way they have been deceived into trusting what they should not trust and doubting what they should not doubt.

As you systematically prove Mormon doctrine to be untrue or when you factually dismantle the historical accuracy of the Book of Mormon, your LDS friend may respond with heartfelt emotion, "But I believe with all my heart the LDS Church is true. I have to trust my heart!"

Foundational to Mormonism is belief in Joseph Smith and his revelations from God. As you prove Joseph Smith to be a false prophet, you may hear, "I don't care what you say. In my heart I know Joseph Smith was a true prophet of God!"

## Bible Warning—Do Not Trust Your Heart!

It is an eye-opener for Mormon people to see what the Bible says about trusting their hearts.

> **Jeremiah 17:9**, *"The heart is deceitful above all things and desperately wicked: who can know it?"*

> **Proverbs 28:26**, *"He that trusteth in his own heart is a fool: but whoso walketh wisely he shall be delivered."*

> **Mark 7:20-23**, *"And he [Jesus] said, 'That which cometh out of the man that defileth the man. For from within out of the heart of men proceed evil thoughts, adulteries, fornications, murders, thefts, covetousness, wickedness, deceit, lasciviousness, an evil eye, blasphemy, pride, foolishness: All these evil things come from within and defile the man.'"*

## Do Trust the Bible!

Mormon people need to learn to trust the Bible. This is one of the most important lessons to share with LDS people. If they don't believe the Bible, where will they ever find truth?

> **John 17:17** Jesus prayed, *"Sanctify them through thy truth: thy word is truth."*

> **2 Timothy 3:16-17**, *"All scripture is given by inspiration of God, and is profitable for doctrine, for reproof, for correction, for instruction in righteousness. That the man of God may be perfect, throughly furnished unto all good works."*

## Study and Pray to Find Truth

It is interesting that both the Bible and the Book of Mormon (Remember **Moroni 10:3-5**?) admonish readers to base truth upon the written scriptures and prayer, not on personal feelings that contradict recorded revelation. This is what the Bible says about studying and praying to find truth:

> **2 Timothy 2:15**, *"Study to shew thyself approved unto God, a workman that needeth not to be ashamed, rightly dividing the word of truth."*

> **James 1:5**, *"If any of you lack wisdom, let him ask of God, that giveth to all men liberally, and upbraideth not; and it shall be given him."*

## QUESTIONS FOR REVIEW

**Why can't we trust our hearts?**

**What should we trust?**

**Does this mean we should not pray?**

**Do Christians also have emotional feelings about the truths we believe?**

**What is the ultimate basis for truth—our heartfelt feelings or God's written word?**

# CHAPTER 5
# THE DOCTRINE OF GOD

## SECTION 17
# There is Only One God—Period!

Mormonism is a 'polytheistic' religion that holds to a belief in many Gods.

**STOP** Turn to the Glossary of Mormon Terms and read the LDS definitions of 'Godhead', 'God', and 'Eternal Progression'.

Christianity is a 'monotheistic' religion that holds to a belief in only one true God.

## There is only one true God

Ironically, both the Bible and the Book of Mormon agree with Christianity on this point! We can use this to our advantage with LDS people.

**NOTE:** Remember, we do not use the Book of Mormon because we believe it is true. It is not true history nor is it inspired by God. We use the Book of Mormon because Mormons believe it is true, and the fact that it contradicts the LDS doctrine of God is a big problem for Mormons.

**The Bible** is totally consistent—there is only one true God.

> **Isaiah 43:10,** *"Ye are my witnesses, saith the LORD, and my servant whom I have chosen: that ye may know and believe me, and understand that I am he; before me there was no God formed, neither shall there be after me."*

> **Isaiah 44:6, 8,** *"Thus saith the LORD the King of Israel, and his redeemer the LORD of hosts; I am the first, and I am the last; and beside me there is no God... Fear ye not, neither be afraid have not I told thee from that time, and have declared it? Ye are even my witness: Is there a God beside me? Yea, there is no God; I know not any."* (See also **Isaiah 45:5, 18**.)

> **Deuteronomy 4:35, 39,** *"Unto thee it was shewed, that thou mightiest know that the LORD he is God; there is none else beside him... Know therefore this day, and consider it in thine heart, that the LORD he is God in heaven above, and upon the earth beneath: there is none else."*

## The Book of Mormon

> **Alma 11:26-29,** *"And Zeezrom said unto him: Thou sayest there is a true and living God? And Amulek said: Yea, there is a true and living God. Now Zeezrom said: Is there more than one God? And he answered, no."*

**NOTE:** The Book of Mormons is also totally consistent on this point—there is only one true God. Never does the Book of Mormon support the LDS belief that more than one true God exists.

## Typical Mormon Interpretation

Mormons will try to convince you that these verses really mean there is only one God of this earth or only one God that they worship.

## Two Christian Responses

**First,** ask your Mormon friend to show you one place in the Bible or the Book of Mormon where it says there is more than one true God.

**NOTE:** A few Mormons pride themselves on being 'scriptorians' and may try to use some Bible passages, taken out of context, to challenge this idea. These passages are discussed in detail in Chapter 8, *LDS 'Proof Texts' for Plural Gods?*

**Second,** you can ask them which LDS God is the God of this earth? Don't they believe Heavenly Father, Jesus Christ, and the Holy Ghost are three separate individuals and all three are Gods of this earth?

You will get a variety of responses from Mormons on this question. LDS doctrine is very confusing when it comes to the roles of Heavenly Father, Jesus Christ, and the Holy Ghost. As a result LDS people have differing opinions as to which God is the God of this earth and which God they should worship. Most will say Heavenly Father is the God of this earth and the only God we should worship.

**STOP** Turn to the Glossary of Mormon Terms, and under 'Godhead' read the statement made by LDS Apostle Bruce R. McConkie—he tells us what 'Gods' the LDS people worship.

## QUESTIONS FOR REVIEW
**According to Mormonism, How many Gods exist and, how many Gods do Mormons worship?**

**Who is speaking in Isaiah chapters 43, 44, and 45?**

**Why is this significant?**

**What statements in these Biblical passages eliminate any possibility of there being other true Gods?**

# SECTION 18
# The Godhead— The Trinity

**STOP** Turn to the Glossary of Mormon Terms and read the LDS definitions of 'Trinity', 'Heavenly Father', and 'Heavenly Parents'.

The LDS Church prefers to use the term 'Godhead' rather than 'Trinity'. The LDS Godhead is three separate beings, three separate Gods. God the Father or Heavenly Father is one God, Jesus Christ is a separate and distinct God and the Holy Ghost is the third distinct God.

It is interesting to note that, according to LDS theology, the Holy Ghost and the Holy Spirit are two very different things.

**STOP** Turn to the Glossary and read the LDS definitions of 'Holy Ghost' and 'Holy Spirit'.

## The Trinity—God is a three-in-one Being.
Again, both the Bible and the Book of Mormon agree on this point.

### The Bible
**Matthew 28:19,** *"Go ye therefore, and teach all nations, baptizing them in the name of the Father, and of the Son, and of the Holy Ghost."*
['In the name of' is singular—Father, Son, and Spirit share the same name.]

**John 10:30,** *"I and my Father are one."*

**Deuteronomy 6:4,** *"Hear, Oh Israel, the LORD our God, is one LORD."* (see **Mark 12:29-30**.)

### The Book of Mormon
**Alma 11:44,** *"...every thing shall be restored to its perfect frame, as it is now, or in the body, and shall be brought and be arraigned before the bar of Christ the Son, and God the Father, and the Holy Spirit, which is one Eternal God."*

**2 Nephi 31:21,** *"And now, behold, this is the doctrine of Christ, and the only and true doctrine of the Father, and of the Son, and of the Holy Ghost, which is one God, without end. Amen."*

*(See also 'The Testimony of the Three Witnesses'.)*

The Bible and the Book of Mormon both state the Father, the Son, and the Holy Ghost are One God, not three Gods.

## Typical Mormon Interpretation

Mormons will say these verses mean the Father, Son, and Holy Ghost are one God in purpose; therefore, they are called one God.

## Christian Response

Can you show me one passage in the Bible or the Book of Mormon where it says the Father, the Son, and the Holy Ghost are three separate Gods that are only united in purpose?

**NOTE:** In several passages *(especially **John 17**)* the Father and the Son are perfectly united in purpose, but never does it say they are separate Gods. The Bible and the Book of Mormon consistently say there is only one God *(see Section 30, 'One God In Purpose—**John 17:11**'.)*

## <u>QUESTIONS FOR REVIEW</u>
**When the Bible says, Jesus and the Father are 'One', why can't this mean two separate Gods that are one in purpose?**

The following statements are found in the Book of Mormon: *"...which is one Eternal God"* and *"...which is one God."* Are these statements singular or plural?

**Why is this important?**

# S E C T I O N **19**
# The Trinity— One Substance

The members of the Christian Trinity are three 'Persons' or 'Persona' or 'Personalities' which denotes the fact that they are three independent 'consciousnesses'. The different Persons of the Christian Trinity are eternally unique and distinct, yet they are one Nature, one Being, one Substance, one God—again, both the Bible and the Book of Mormon agree on this point!

## The Bible

**John 1:1-3, 14,** *"In the beginning was the Word, and the Word was with God, and the Word was God. The same was in the beginning with God. All things were made by him; and without him was not any thing made that was made... And the Word was made flesh, and dwelt among us, (and we beheld his glory; the glory as of the only begotten of the Father,) full of grace and truth."*

**John 14:7-11,** *"If ye had known me, ye should have known my Father also: and from henceforth ye know him, and have seen him. Philip saith unto him, Lord, shew us the Father, and it sufficeth us. Jesus saith unto him, Have I been so long time with you, and yet hast thou not known me, Philip? He that hath seen me hath seen the Father; and how sayest thou then, Shew us the Father? Believest thou not that I am in the Father, and the Father in me? The words that I speak unto you I speak not of myself: but the Father that dwelleth in me, he doeth the works. Believe me that I am in the Father, and the Father in me: or else believe me for the very works' sake."*

**John 10:30,** *"I and my Father are one."*

## The Book of Mormon

**NOTE:** Remember, we do not believe the Book of Mormon is true, so Christians would never use the following Book of Mormon passages to prove the Godhead is one substance—except when witnessing to Mormons. With Mormonism in mind, these verses make a strong case against the Father, the Son, and the Holy Ghost being three different Beings, three different Gods. These Book of Mormon passages, however, present a modalistic view of God—it should not be assumed that the author or anyone using these verses holds to a 'modalistic' view of the Trinity!

> **Mosiah 15:1-4,** *"And now Abinadi said unto them: I would that ye should understand that God himself shall come down among the children of men, and shall redeem his people. And because he dwelleth in flesh he shall be called the Son of God, and having subjected the flesh to the will of the Father, being the Father and the Son; the Father, because he was conceived by the power of God; and the Son, because of the flesh; thus becoming the Father and Son; And they are one God, yea, the very Eternal Father of heaven and earth."*

> **Alma 11:38-39,** *"Zeezrom saith again unto him: Is the Son of God the very Eternal Father? And Amulek said unto him: Yea he is the very Eternal Father of heaven and of earth."*

## Typical Mormon Response

Mormons will say, 'The Trinity makes no sense at all! I don't understand how anyone can believe in the Trinity! How can Heavenly Father and his Son be the same God? When Jesus was in the garden, praying to his Father, they are two separate persons! Do you think Jesus was praying to himself?'

## Christian Answer

Use the *Trinity Diagram* and explain to them the Biblical concept of the Trinity *[see Chapter 6, Section 21, 'Explaining the Trinity']*.

## QUESTIONS FOR REVIEW

In your own words, what does John 14:7-11 teach about Jesus and the Father?

In your own words, what does Mosiah 15:1-4 teach about Jesus and the Father?

What phrases in Mosiah 15:1-4 and Alma 11:38-40 are 'modalistic' in nature?

Why don't these phrases agree with the Biblical view of the Trinity?

# S E C T I O N  20
# The Virgin Birth

🛑 Turn to the Glossary of Mormon Terms and read the LDS definition of 'Virgin Birth'.

The Mormon doctrine of a Godhead composed of three separate Gods forces Mormonism to reject the Holy Ghost as the agent through which Christ's miraculous conception occurred. If this were true, Christ would then have to be called the 'Son of the Holy Ghost'. Instead, they teach that God the Father (who has a physical body of flesh and bones) had a physical relationship with Mary, and she conceived Jesus in the same natural way that all children are conceived on this earth. This heretical doctrine destroys the Biblical truth that Christ was virgin born.

## Conceived by the Holy Ghost
### The Bible

> **Matthew 1:18-20,** *"Now the birth of Jesus Christ was on this wise: When as his mother Mary was espoused to Joseph, before they came together, she was found with child of the Holy Ghost. Then Joseph her husband, being a just man, and not willing to make her a publick example, was minded to put her away privily. But while he thought on these things, behold, the angel of the LORD appeared unto him in a dream, saying, 'Joseph, thou son of David, fear not to take unto thee Mary thy wife: for that which is conceived in her is of the Holy Ghost.'"*

### The Book of Mormon

> **Alma 7:10,** *"And behold, he shall be born of Mary, at Jerusalem which is the land of our forefathers, she being a virgin, a precious and chosen vessel, who shall be overshadowed and conceive by the power of the Holy Ghost, and bring forth a son, yea, even the Son of God."*

It is clear in both the Bible and the Book of Mormon that Jesus was conceived or begotten miraculously by the Spirit of the Triune God, the Holy Ghost.

### Typical Mormon Response

Mormons usually don't know how to respond to these scripture passages. In an effort to defend his position, one devout Mormon man said, "I believe God the Father conceived Jesus by artificial insemination." He kept a serious face in spite of the fact that his wife laughed out loud.

They also might respond that the Holy Ghost only 'assisted' in the process. It was by the 'power of the Holy Ghost' that the conception happened, but it was actually God the Father who literally impregnated Mary. *[How exactly that would work I have no idea.]*

### Christian Answer

LDS prophets state emphatically that Jesus was not begotten by the Holy Ghost, he was conceived by God the Father, an exalted man of flesh and bones.

*"Christ was begotten by an Immortal Father in the same way that mortal are begotten by mortal fathers"* (see Glossary of Mormon Terms, 'Virgin Birth'.)

If God the Father is an exalted man who has a body of flesh and bones, as LDS doctrine proclaims, and if the LDS Heavenly Father conceived Jesus in the same natural way that mortal men are conceived—Mary would not have been a virgin when Jesus Christ was born. Mormonism cannot honestly claim they believe in the virgin birth of Christ.

## QUESTIONS FOR REVIEW

**How can Christians claim Jesus was conceived by the Holy Ghost and still believe He is the Son of God?**

**Why do LDS people have such a problem accepting that Jesus was conceived by the Holy Ghost?**

**Why is a literal 'virgin birth' problematic when the LDS theology of the Godhead is taken into consideration?**

## CONCLUSION:

To Summarize Chapter 5, TGM has created a Visual Aid which condenses the contrasts between the Bible & Book of Mormon doctrines of God and the LDS theology of God. *[We offer two options—formatted different but containing the same info.]*

👁 **Go to: TriGrace.org**
**Under 'Resources' find and print the free PDF download of the *Truth About God Visual*. Then watch the corresponding TGM Tutorial explaining how to use this Visual Aid with LDS people.**

# CHAPTER 6
# THINKING ABOUT GOD

## SECTION 21
# Explaining The Trinity

🛑 **Turn to the Glossary of Mormon Terms and read the LDS definition of 'Trinity'.**

LDS people struggle more with the doctrine of the Trinity than with any other Christian doctrine. They don't understand how Christians can honestly believe the Father, Son, and Holy Ghost are one Being, one God. This subject will come up time and again, so it is crucial to have Biblical answers for your Mormon friends.

**NOTE:** To be honest, this is a complex discussion. As human beings we cannot comprehend a God who is incomprehensible. How can we wrap our finite minds around an infinite God? We can, by faith, UNDERSTAND what the Bible teaches about God, but no one will ever COMPREHEND God. This chapter will help Mormons UNDERSTAND the truths about the LORD God of the Bible.

## Explaining the Trinity—Part 1

**LDS ARGUMENT #1**—If Jesus and the Father are the same God, how do you explain this passage?

> **Matthew 26:39,** *"He went a little farther, and fell on his face, and prayed, saying, 'O my Father, if it be possible, let this cup pass from me: nevertheless not as I will, but as thou wilt.'"*

Mormons will ask, "Who do you think Jesus was praying to, Himself? When Jesus was in the garden, he was praying to his Father in heaven. They are obviously two separate individuals! I don't understand how you can believe they are just one God."

### Christian Response

Tell your LDS friend, "If you think Christianity hasn't considered this question, you are mistaken. This is not a problem for people who, by faith, believe what the Bible reveals about God. If you have a few minutes, I would love to answer your question and explain the Christian doctrine of the Trinity to you."

👁 **Go to: TriGrace.org**
**Under 'Resources' find and print the free PDF download of *The Trinity Diagram.* Then watch the TGM Tutorial explaining how to use this Visual Aid with Mormon people.**

### Using the Trinity Diagram

The *Trinity Diagram* is a visual aid that presents a Biblical explanation of the Trinity.

HONESTLY, the very BEST way for you to learn this witnessing method is to watch the TGM Tutorial explaining how we use the *Trinity Diagram* with LDS people. I could explain it all in writing but that would be redundant and would not be as effective as the Tutorial. So, if you have not yet watched it…

**PLEASE** 🛑 **Go to TriGrace.org and** 👁 **watch the *Trinity Diagram Tutorial*.**

### A Brief Synopsis of the *Trinity Diagram*

There is nothing on earth or in the universe that compares to God. He is the self-existent Creator of all that exists—He is holy, a one-of-a-kind Being, so trying to explain Him is a complex undertaking. Many have tried to find simple explanations for the Trinity but all simple illustrations fall short.

There is, however, one thing that God tells us was created 'in His image'. **Genesis 1:26-27** tells us 'man' was created in God's image!

Therefore, logic would tell us that our best shot at understanding the Triune God is to study what this means, *"So God created man in his own image, in the image of God created he him; male and female created he them."* And, that is what the *Trinity Diagram* does.

## Trinity Diagram Side 1
## The Image of God and Man

The beginning of the *Trinity Diagram* uses **Matthew 28:19** to explain that God has a Name, and all three members of the Godhead share the same Name. God's name is 'Jehovah', so the Father is 'Jehovah', the Son is 'Jehovah', and the Holy Ghost/Spirit is 'Jehovah'. These three co-equal and co-eternal Persons are Jehovah God. He has eternally been a three-in-one being.

**NOTE:** *'Jehovah'* is an old English term for God's Hebrew name that has been adopted by Mormonism. *'Yahweh'* is probably a better translation of the Hebrew name for God. We, however, use the word *'Jehovah'* because this is the term with which Mormons are familiar.

Next we use **Genesis 1:26-27** to explain that God made man in His own Image. So, if we want to understand the image of God, we need to look at the only creature that was created 'in His image'—man.

We then use **1 Thessalonians 5:23** to show that, similar to the Triune God, man is also a three-in-one being. Man is a trichotomy. Mankind is composed of a spirit and a soul and a body. The combination of these three things makes a complete human being. Therefore, when considering my own makeup, it would be proper for me to say that my spirit is Daniel Thompson, my soul is Daniel Thompson and my body is Daniel Thompson. I am a three-in-one being—similar to the idea that the Father is Jehovah, the Son is Jehovah and the Holy Ghost is Jehovah.

**IMPORTANT NOTE:** Before continuing, it is important to point out the immense differences between the infinite God and finite man. Though man is created in God's image, God and man are very different.

- God is the Self-Existent Creator of all
  - Man is a mere creature
- God is Eternal *(exists eternally as God)*
  - Man is created and is not eternal.
- God is Omniscient *(has all knowledge)*
  - Man is constantly learning
- God is Omnipotent *(possesses all power)*
  - Man has no power of his own
- God is Omnipresent *(everywhere present)*
  - Man is limited to time and space

## Who was Jesus praying to, Himself?

Since man was created with an image similar to that of his Creator, we can understand some simple truths about God. One of those simple truths is the fact that both God and Man commune within themselves.

- All humans 'THINK' to themselves—from the time we wake in the morning till we go to bed at night, we are thinking about what we will wear, what we will eat, how we will plan our day, etc. Why do we think/reason within ourselves if we are just one being?

- All human beings, at times, 'DEBATE' with themselves—for instance, if you are on a diet and you are offered a piece of cake, do you have a debate within yourself? I think the cartoonist got it right when he portrayed a little devil on one shoulder saying "Yea, yea, yea!" and a little angel on the other shoulder saying "No, no, no!" Why do we debate with ourselves?

- We also 'FIGHT' within our being—when we are tempted with a desirable sin, we experience a fight inside of us. Both Paul and James speak of a war going on within our 'members' **(Romans 7:23** *and* **James 4:1**.) The 'war' is a fight inside of us between good and evil. Don't we all experience this 'war' within?

- And finally, do we not, at times, even 'TALK OUT LOUD' to ourselves? Yes, at times, all of us talk out loud to ourselves! Why do we talk to ourselves? Are we all crazy? Of course not! We commune with ourselves because we were created in God's image.

## Trinity Diagram Side 2—Understanding the Trinity according to the Bible

Next we turn to the back side of the *Trinity Diagram* and discuss the Biblical passages that prove the Tri-Unity of God. These verses will visually demonstrate the fact that the Father is Jehovah God, Jesus Christ is Jehovah God, and the Holy Ghost/Spirit is Jehovah God.

🛑 Carefully study the back side of the *Trinity Diagram* and consider each Bible passage.

## Conclusion

We then conclude with a discussion about how these truths help us understand the Trinity.

According to the Bible, the LORD God (Jehovah God) is a Triune Being: He is 1) the Father, 2) the Son, and 3) the Holy Ghost/Spirit. All three Persons of the Godhead are eternally unique and distinct, yet only one God.

In a similar way, mankind is a trichotomy—the makeup of a human being is: 1) body, 2) soul, and 3) spirit. All three components of man are unique and distinct, yet only one man. Yes, mankind has been created with an image similar to that of his Creator.

This can help us understand some difficult concepts concerning the Trinity, such as, "If Jesus and the Father are the same God, then who was Jesus praying to, Himself?" The answer seems almost too simple: we all think, reason, debate, and at times even talk out loud to ourselves. If we commune within ourselves, and we are created in God's image, why is it so odd to think that the Triune God also communes within Himself?

## Typical Mormon Response

When an LDS person allows you to walk them completely through the *Trinity Diagram*, they will often respond positively and say something like this, "I have never heard anything like that before. You are the only person that has ever been able to explain the Trinity in a way that makes any sense to me. I don't necessarily agree with you, but for the first time I do understand why you believe in the Trinity."

## QUESTIONS FOR REVIEW

**What is the personal name of the Father, the Son, and the Holy Ghost/Spirit?**

**Where does the Bible teach that man is a trichotomy (a three-part being)?**

**What three unique and distinct components make up a human being?**

    **1.**

    **2.**

    **3.**

**How does the image of man help us understand the image of God?**

# Explaining the Trinity—Part 2

**LDS ARGUMENT #2**—The Bible Says the Father is 'greater' than Jesus!

> **John 14:28,** Jesus said, *"If ye loved me, ye would rejoice, because I said, I go unto the Father: for my Father is greater than I."*

Mormons will ask, "If Jesus and the Father are the same God, how do you explain the fact that Jesus said, 'My Father is greater than I'"?

## Christian Answer—The Ocean Illustration

Reply by using *The Ocean Illustration*—Let's say you take a trip to the ocean and you are very impressed! The ocean is awesome, magnificent, immense, powerful and majestic. You decide you want to share the experience with your friends and family who have never seen the ocean, so you take a few pictures and fill a bottle with ocean water—adding some sand, a sea shell, and a piece of seaweed.

When you arrive back home, you describe the ocean to your friends—you show them your pictures, and you show them your bottle of ocean water.

- You instruct your friends to smell it and explain, "That is what the ocean smells like."

- You tell them to taste the water—it's salty.

- You show them the sand, seashell, and the seaweed, things you found in the ocean.

Now ask your Mormon friend, "Was the ocean in the bottle?"

Yes, but no. Yes, a small portion of the ocean was in the bottle. But no, not all of the ocean can be contained in something so small.

And what about the ocean—was the majesty or power of the ocean altered in any way because you removed one small bottle of ocean water? Not in the least!

In a similar way, Jesus was God manifested to the world in a human body.

**1 Timothy 3:16,** *"And without controversy great is the mystery of godliness: God was manifest in the flesh."*

God the Son humbled Himself, leaving behind His glory, majesty, and power, which allowed mankind to see, touch, and experience God in a real and living way.

**Philippians 2:5-8,** *"Let this mind be in you, which was also in Christ Jesus: Who, being in the form of God, thought it not robbery to be equal with God: But made himself of no reputation, and took upon him the form of a servant, and was made in the likeness of men: and being found in fashion as a man, he humbled himself, and became obedient unto death, even the death of the cross."*

In His humanity, Jesus was the physical representation of the infinite, Almighty God. In relation to *The Ocean Illustration,* Jesus was like God in a bottle of human flesh.

## God Cannot Be Fully Contained in an Earthly Tabernacle

**1 Kings 8:27,** *"But will God indeed dwell on the earth? Behold, the heaven and heaven of heavens cannot contain thee; how much less this house that I have builded?"*

**Jeremiah 23:23-24,** *"Am I a God at hand, saith the LORD, and not a God afar off? Can any hide himself in secret places that I shall not see him? saith the LORD, do not I fill heaven and earth? saith the LORD."*

The ocean pales in comparison to the greatness of Almighty God who fills the heavens and earth. While a bottle of ocean water may illustrate this important concept, it does not convey the full impact of God humbling himself to become a man.

## QUESTIONS FOR REVIEW

**In your own words describe how the incarnation of Christ is similar to a bottle of ocean water.**

**What Biblical references would help to explain why Jesus said, 'My Father is greater than I?'**

# Explaining the Trinity—Part 3

**LDS ARGUMENT #3**—Humanly speaking, the Trinity does not make sense, so according to Mormonism, it must be wrong. Mormonism tries to bring the Godhead down to a human level. Joseph Smith reasoned, "Where was there ever a son without a father? And where was there ever a father without first being a son?" (*Teachings of the Prophet Joseph Smith*, Joseph Fielding Smith, p. 373.)

Joseph Smith is reasoning from a human perspective—trying to liken the Godhead to a human family here on earth. But God is not a human, and the Godhead is not a human family. This kind of simplistic humanistic reasoning just doesn't work with the Infinite, Almighty God.

The following Biblical passages cause Mormons to draw false conclusions about God.

**Matthew 3:16-17,** *"And Jesus, when he was baptized, when up straightway out of the water: and, lo, the heavens were opened unto him, and he saw the Spirit of God descending like a dove, and lighting upon him: and lo a voice from heaven, saying, 'This is my beloved Son, in whom I am well pleased.'"*

Mormons will ask, "Who said, 'This is my beloved Son', was Jesus being a ventriloquist? This is obviously two different persons, not one God!" (And, from a human non-Biblical perspective, that would appear to make sense.)

**Acts 7:55-56,** *"But he, being full of the Holy Ghost, looked up steadfastly into heaven, and saw the glory of God, and Jesus standing on the right hand of God, and said, 'Behold, I see the heavens opened, and the Son of Man standing on the right hand of God.'"*

Mormons will say, "Since Jesus is standing at the right hand of God, they must be two Gods! Think about it! Doesn't that interpretation make a lot more sense than believing they are one God?" (Again, from a human non-Biblical perspective, that appears to make sense.)

**Christian Response:** We cannot interpret these passages in contradiction to what God has said about Himself. God said,

**Isaiah chapters 43, 44, and 45,** *"I am the LORD; and there is none else... before me there was no God formed, neither shall there be after me... I am the first, and I am the last; and beside me there is no God... Is there a God beside me? yea, there is no God; I know not any... I am God, and there is none else."*

There is not one passage in the Bible that says there is more than one true God. You cannot insert your own thinking into the Bible, just because it makes sense to you. What you don't understand is that God is not bound by human limitations, and nothing is impossible for God.

**Matthew 19:26,** *"But Jesus beheld them, and said unto them, with men this is impossible; but with God all things are possible."*

Because Mormonism says God is an exalted man with a physical body of flesh and bones, Mormons do not believe God can be Omnipresent *(in more than one place at a time.)*

🛑 **Turn to the Glossary of Mormon Terms and read the LDS definitions of 'God' and 'Holy Ghost'.**

## But, God is Omnipresent

God fills the heavens and the earth.

**Psalm 139:7-10,** *"Whither shall I go from thy spirit? Or whither shall I flee from thy presence? If I ascend up into heaven, thou art there: if I make my bed in hell, behold, thou art there. If I take the wings of the morning, and dwell in the uttermost parts of the sea; Even there shall thy hand lead me, and thy right hand shall hold me." (See* **Jeremiah 23:23-24***.)*

The attribute of omnipresence allows God to be in Heaven in control of the universe while at the same time He is on earth in the person of Jesus Christ.

## Jesus Also Claimed to be Omnipresent

It is interesting to note that while Jesus was here on earth He claimed to be 'in heaven' at the same time.

**John 3:13,** *"And no man hath ascended up to heaven, but he that came down from heaven, even the Son of man which is in heaven."* ['Which is in heaven' is present tense.]

**Matthew 18:20,** *"For where two or three are gathered together in my name, there am I in the midst of them."*

## The Infinite, Almighty God

An infinite God is beyond the understanding of any finite human mind—we, as humans, cannot begin to comprehend the abilities of the Almighty.

- Can you honestly say you understand how God made Adam out of dust (**Genesis 2:7**)?

- Can you comprehend the fact that God spoke trillions of stars into existence and knows each one by name?

    **Genesis 1:16,** *"And God made two great lights; the greater light to rule the day, and the lesser light to rule the night: he made the stars also."*

    **Psalm 33:6, 8-9,** *"By the word of the LORD were the heavens made; and all the host of them by the breath of his mouth… Let all the earth fear the LORD: let all the inhabitants of the world stand in awe of him. For he spake, and it was done; he commanded, and it stood fast."*

    **Psalm 147:4-5,** *"He telleth the number of the stars; he calleth them all by their names. Great is our LORD, and of great power: his understanding is infinite."*

- Has mankind figured out how high the heavens are above the earth?

    **Isaiah 55:8-9,** *"For my thoughts are not your thoughts, neither are your ways my ways, saith the LORD. For as the heavens are higher than the earth, so are my ways higher than your ways, and my thoughts than your thoughts."*

## Do You, By Faith, Believe God?

COMPREHENDING God and UNDERSTANDING what the Bible says about God are two completely different things. No one can comprehend God—that is impossible. But we can read what the Bible tells us about God and believe Him—IF we have enough faith. Do you have enough faith to believe God even though He does not make sense humanly speaking?

    **Hebrews 11:3, 6,** *"Through faith we understand that the worlds were framed by the word of God, so that things which are seen were not made of things which do appear.… But without faith it is impossible to please him for he that cometh to God must believe that he is, and that he is a rewarder of them that diligently seek him."*

**Typical Mormon Response:** I bear you my testimony…

**Christian Answer**—See Chapter 4, 'Dealing With Feelings', Sections 13-16.

## QUESTIONS FOR REVIEW

**Why can't the human brain fully comprehend an infinite God?**

**How is it possible for Jehovah God to be in Heaven in control of the universe and, at the same time, be on the earth in the person of Jesus Christ?**

# SECTION 22
# The Back Door to The Trinity

This method is a fun way to SHOW the Trinity to an LDS person. What makes this fun is when the following questions are asked, it is impossible to give a wrong answer.

The following FIVE QUESTIONS and the Biblical answers will show that all three members of the Trinity (the Father, the Son, and the Holy Ghost) take credit for the exact same actions or creative acts.

## QUESTION #1: Whose 'Spirit' dwells in all believers?

- **Spirit of God – Romans 8:9a,** *"Ye are not in the flesh, but in the Spirit, if so be that the Spirit of God dwell in you."*

- **Spirit of Christ – Romans 8:9b-10,** *"Now if any man have not the Spirit of Christ, he is none of his. And if Christ be in you, the body is dead because of sin; but the Spirit is life because of righteousness."*

- **Spirit of the Father – Romans 8:11,** *"But if the Spirit of him that raised up Jesus from the dead dwell in you, he that raised up Christ from the dead shall also quicken [make alive] your mortal bodies by his Spirit that dwelleth in you."*

- **Holy Ghost – 1 Corinthians 6:19,** *"What? Know ye not that your body is the temple of the Holy Ghost which is in you, which ye have of God."*

### So, how many Spirits dwell in a believer?
- **One Spirit – 1 Corinthians 12:13,** *"By one Spirit are we all baptized into one body, whether we be Jews or Gentiles, whether we be bond or free; and have been all made to drink into one Spirit."*

## QUESTION #2: Who raised Jesus from the dead?
- **The Father – Galatians 1:1,** *"Paul, an apostle, (not of men, neither by man, but by Jesus Christ, and God the Father, who raised him from the dead.)"*

- **Jesus Raised Himself – John 2:19-21,** *"Jesus answered and said unto them, 'Destroy this temple, and in three days I will raise it up'. Then said the Jews, 'Forty and six years was this temple in building, and wilt thou rear it up in three days?' But he spoke of the temple of his body."*

- **The Holy Spirit/Ghost – 1 Peter 3:18,** *"For Christ also hath once suffered for sins, the just for the unjust, that he might bring us to God, being put to death in the flesh, but quickened [made alive] by the Spirit."*

### So, did one God or several Gods raise Jesus from the dead?
- **One God - Acts 2:32,** *"This Jesus hath God raised up, whereof we all are witnesses."*

## QUESTION #3: Who created our world?
- **God – Genesis 1:1,** *"In the beginning God [In Hebrew – Elohim] created the heaven and the earth."*

- **The Holy Spirit/Ghost – Genesis 1:2,** *"And the earth was without form, and void; and darkness was upon the face of the deep. And the Spirit of God moved upon the face of the waters."*

- **The LORD – Genesis 2:4,** *"These are the generations of the heavens and of the earth when they were created, in the day that the LORD [In Hebrew – Jehovah] God made the earth and the heavens."*

- **The Entire Godhead – Genesis 1:26,** *"And God said, Let us make man in our image, after our likeness."*

- **The Word/Jesus – John 1:1-3, 14,** *"In the beginning was the Word, and the Word was with God, and the Word was God. The same was in the beginning with God. All things were made by him; and without him was not any thing made that was made… And the Word was made flesh, and dwelt among us."*

### So, did one God or three Gods create our world?
- **One God – Isaiah 44:24,** *"Thus saith the LORD, thy redeemer, and he that formed thee from the womb, 'I am the LORD that maketh all things; that stretcheth forth the heavens alone; that spreadeth abroad the earth by myself.'"*

**STOP** **Turn to the Glossary of Mormon Terms and read the LDS definition of 'Creation'.**

## QUESTION #4: Who is the Father of Jesus Christ?

- **Heavenly Father – John 3:16,** *"For God so loved the world, that he gave his only begotten Son, that whosoever believeth in him should not perish, but have everlasting life."*

- **The Holy Ghost/Spirit – Matthew 1:18, 20,** *"Now the birth of Jesus Christ was on this wise: When as his mother Mary was espoused to Joseph, before they came together, she was found with child of the Holy Ghost… The angel of the LORD appeared unto him in a dream, saying, 'Joseph, thou son of David, fear not to take unto thee Mary thy wife: for that which is conceived in her is of the Holy Ghost.'"*

- **The LORD [Jehovah] – Psalm 2:7,** *"I will declare the decree: the LORD [Jehovah] hath said unto me [to Jesus], 'Thou art my Son; this day have I begotten thee.'"*

## QUESTION #5: How many true Gods exist?

- **ONLY ONE GOD – Isaiah 44:6, 8,** *"Thus saith the LORD the King of Israel, and his redeemer the LORD of hosts; 'I am the first, and I am the last; and beside me there is no God… Fear ye not, neither be afraid: have not I told thee from that time, and have declared it? Ye are even my witnesses. Is there a God beside me? Yea, there is no God; I know not any.'"*

### Typical Mormon Response
This is so confusing. I just don't understand the Christian Trinity.

### Christian Answer
Explain the Trinity to your Mormon friend using the Trinity Diagram *(see Section 21.)*

👁 **Go to: TriGrace.org**
**Under 'Resources' find and print the free PDF download of *Back Door to the Trinity*. Then watch the TGM Tutorial explaining how to use this Visual Aid with Mormon people.**

## QUESTIONS FOR REVIEW

**What is the Biblical answer to ALL of the questions above?**

**According to the Bible, can there be more than one true and living God?**

# SECTION 23
# Is God An Exalted Man?

🛑 **Turn to the Glossary of Mormon Terms and read the LDS definitions for 'God', 'Kolob', and 'Mankind'.**

The LDS Church teaches that God was once a mortal human being who lived on another planet similar to earth and by obedience to LDS gospel principles became an 'exalted man' or a God. LDS doctrine states that God, today, is an exalted man with a physical body of flesh and bones as tangible as our human bodies.

### A Good Question to Ask your LDS Friend
"Where in the Bible or the Book of Mormon does it state that God is a man with a physical body of flesh and bones?" [Answer: Neither the Bible nor the Book of Mormon state that God is a man with a physical body of flesh and bones.]

### God Is Not a Man
**Hosea 11:9,** *"I will not execute the fierceness of mine anger, I will not return to destroy Ephraim: for I am God, and not man, the Holy One in the midst of thee."*

**Numbers 23:19,** *"God is not a man, that he should lie; neither the son of man, that he should repent."*

**1 Samuel 15:29,** *"the Strength of Israel will not lie nor repent: for he is not a man."*

## Mormon Response

First, your Mormon friend may respond by saying, "The Bible says God made man in his own image, if I am made in the image of God, and I have a body of flesh and bones, then God must have a body of flesh and bones, too."

## Christian Answer

Although the word 'image' can be used in reference to a physical image, it does not always refer to the physical. Consider the following passages from the Bible and the Book of Mormon:

### The Bible

**Romans 8:29,** *"For whom he did foreknow, he also did predestinate to be conformed to the image of his Son."* Jesus was a human being just like us, so what would this mean?

### The Book of Mormon

**Alma 5:19,** *"Can ye look up to God at that day with a pure heart and clean hands? I say unto you, can you look up, having the image of God engraven upon your countenances?"* (See also **Alma 5:14** and **Ether 3:12-16**.)

[Use the *Trinity Diagram* to explain the Biblical concept of the term 'image'.]

## A Second Mormon Response

A Mormon might respond by saying, 'Joseph Smith saw God Father and his Son, Jesus Christ, and they were two separate personages who had physical bodies'.

## Christian Response

Do you know there are at least 9 different accounts of Joseph Smith's 'First Vision' and they don't all support the idea that Joseph Smith saw God the Father and Jesus Christ?

[See Section 49, Varying Accounts of 'The First Vision'.]

## QUESTIONS FOR REVIEW

Is there one place in the Bible or the Book of Mormon where it says that God is a man with a physical body of flesh and bones?

Why is the concept that God is an exalted man illogical and unbiblical?

# S E C T I O N 24
# God Does Not Change

**STOP** Turn to the Glossary of Mormon Terms and read the LDS definition of 'Eternal Progression'.

In the LDS religion there are no Gods that have eternally been God. All LDS Gods are bound by the LDS law of eternal progression and as such had to become Gods. According to LDS theology there is not a 1st God or any truly eternal Gods.

## God has Eternally Been God

The LDS 'Law of Eternal Progression' contradicts the Bible and the Book of Mormon which both state God has eternally been God.

### The Bible

**Psalm 90:1-2,** *"LORD, thou has been our dwelling place in all generations. Before the mountains were brought forth, or ever thou hadst formed the earth and the world, even from everlasting to everlasting, thou art God."* (See **Deuteronomy 33:27** and **Isaiah 57:15**.)

## Book of Mormon

**2 Nephi 26:12,** *"And as I spake concerning the convincing of the Jews, that Jesus is the very Christ, it must needs be that the Gentiles be convinced also that Jesus is the Christ, the Eternal God."*

## God Never Changes

Both the Bible and the Book of Mormon teach that God never changes; therefore, God cannot be subject to the 'Law of Eternal Progression'.

## The Bible

**Malachi 3:6,** *"For I am the LORD, I change not; therefore ye sons of Jacob are not consumed."* (This verse is quoted in **3 Nephi 24:6**.)

## Book of Mormon

**Moroni 8:18,** *"For I know that God is not a partial God, neither a changeable being; but he is unchangeable from all eternity to all eternity."* (See **Moroni 7:22** and **Mormon 9:9-10, 19**.)

## Mormon Response

Mormons will sometimes say this refers only to God's character which has not changed throughout his eternal progression.

## Christian Answer

The scriptures we just read refer not only to God's unchanging character but also to his eternal position as the Almighty God. If God has eternally been God, then 'eternal progression' does not apply to Him.

## Another Possible Mormon Response

Mormons may try to explain away the words 'everlasting' and 'eternal'. They may try to convince you that these words are simply descriptive 'name titles' for God and should not be taken literally. They will tell you that even though God is sometimes called 'the Eternal God' or 'the Everlasting God', these name titles do not suggest that God existed eternally as God.

**NOTE**: Don't feel badly if you don't totally get this. Neither do I. The following definitions in the Glossary of Mormon Terms will help you understand this illogical concept.

🛑 **Turn to the Glossary of Mormon Terms and examine the LDS definitions of 'Eternal Damnation' and 'Eternal Punishment'.**

## Christian Answer

As Christians, we don't have to change the definitions of common words to make them fit our theology. It makes more sense to take God at his word and believe what he says. Do you have enough faith to just believe what God says?

👁 **Go to: TriGrace.org**
Under 'Resources' find and print the free PDF download of the *4-Step Moroni 8:18 Visual.* Then watch the TGM Tutorial explaining how to use this Visual Aid with Mormon people.

## QUESTIONS FOR REVIEW

In your own words explain the LDS law of eternal progression.

How would this LDS law eliminate any possibility of an eternal God?

# C H A P T E R 7
# THE LORD GOD

# S E C T I O N 25
# Jehovah and Elohim

🛑 **Turn to the Glossary of Mormon Terms and read the LDS definitions of 'Elohim', 'Heavenly Father', and 'Jehovah'.**

As you discuss the doctrine of God with your LDS friends, it will be profitable for you to understand the following information relating to the Hebrew word 'YHWH' and 'Elohim'.

'YHWH', known as the Hebrew tetragrammaton, is translated 'LORD' (small capitals) or 'Jehovah' in the Old Testament.

'Elohim' is the Hebrew word translated 'God' or 'gods' in the Old Testament.

## Biblical Background

**LORD /JEHOVAH**—the word 'LORD' (small capitals in the KJV) appears over 6,000 times in the Old Testament. 'LORD' is a translation from the Hebrew word 'YHWH' (it was translated 'Jehovah' a few places in the King James Bible.)

If you own an LDS Bible, this fact can be supported by going to the LDS Bible Dictionary and reading the definition for 'Jehovah'—midway through the definition it says, *"In the KJV, the Jewish custom has been followed, and the name is generally denoted by LORD or GOD, printed in small capitals."*

**God/Elohim**—the word 'God' appears about 3,000 times in the Old Testament. There are four closely-related words for God that all stem from the same basic root; 'el', 'elah', 'eloah', and 'elohim'. All of these titles denote deity and are

rightly translated as 'God', 'god', or 'gods'. Depending upon the context, these titles may be used to denote the true God of the Bible, false gods, or human rulers.

Of the nearly 3,000 times the word God appears in the KJV, 87% of the time it is the Hebrew word 'elohim'.

The remaining 13% of the time, 'el', 'elah', and 'eloah' are used. These titles are found only in unique books or used in unique ways in the Hebrew Old Testament.

- The vast majority of the time, 'el' and 'eloah' appear in the poetic books of Job, Psalms, and Isaiah and are used interchangeably to fit the poetic style.

- In Old Testament times, Aramaic was the common trade language, so 'elah' is found only in the Aramaic passages of the Old Testament: Daniel and certain sections of Ezra and Jeremiah.

- Scattered throughout the Old Testament are instances when adjectives are tied to the noun El—such as El Shaddai [God Almighty], El Elyon [God Most High], El Kehdem [God Eternal], El Yeshua [God of Salvation], etc.

## Title vs. Name

To understand the identity of 'Jehovah', you first need to understand the difference between His title and His name.

🛑 **Before going any further: Take your Bible and turn to Exodus 3:1-15—read this passage substituting 'Elohim' for the word 'God', and 'Jehovah' for the word 'LORD'.**

When you finish, note the question asked by Moses in **Exodus 3:13,**

*"And Moses said unto God [Elohim], Behold, when I come unto the children of Israel, and shall say unto them, the God [Elohim] of your fathers hath sent me unto you and they shall say to me, 'What is his name?' what shall I say unto them?"*

The question asked by Moses would make no sense if God's personal name was 'Elohim'. (Keep in mind, 'Elohim' is a title, not a personal name. It would be like asking the President of the United States, "Mr. President, what is your name?" You have addressed him by his title, but you still do not know his personal name.) Notice how God [Elohim] answered Moses' question.

> **Exodus 3:15** *"And God [Elohim] said moreover unto Moses, Thus shalt thou say unto the children of Israel, the L*ORD *[Jehovah] God [Elohim] of your fathers, the God [Elohim] of Abraham, the God [Elohim] of Jacob, hath sent me unto you: this is my name for ever, and this is my memorial unto all generations."*

God [Elohim] is his title. LORD [Jehovah] is his personal name.

## 'YHWH'

The Hebrew word 'YHWH' translated 'LORD' *(or 'JEHOVAH')* is God's personal name.

> **Exodus 6:2-3** *"And God [Elohim] spake unto Moses, and said unto him, I am the L*ORD *[Jehovah]: And I appeared unto Abraham, unto Isaac, and unto Jacob, by the name of God Almighty [El Shaddai], but by my name JE-HO-VAH was I not known to them.[?]"*

> **Isaiah 42:8,** *"I am the L*ORD *[Jehovah]: that is my name: and my glory will I not give to another..."* (See also **Deuteronomy 28:58; Psalm 29:2, Jeremiah 16:21,** and **Amos 4:13**.)

'YHWH' or 'Jehovah' means 'I self-exist'. The name Jehovah is eternally unique and cannot be claimed by any other being because Jehovah God is the only self existent Being. When the Hebrew letters 'YHWH' are broken down to their root meanings, they mean 'I was, I AM, I will be', or very simply, 'I exist'. 'I AM' means Jehovah is the self-existent One.

In Exodus 3:14, when God told Moses, "I AM THAT I AM", he was literally saying to Moses, 'I exist because I exist'. Jehovah is the only Being that had no beginning and will have no end.

## QUESTIONS FOR REVIEW

**In the King James Bible, L**ORD **(small capitals) is always what Hebrew word?**

**Where is the Hebrew word 'YHWH' translated 'JEHOVAH' in the King James Bible? (List as many references as you can find.)**

**To LDS people, who is Jehovah?**

If you don't know, <kbd>STOP</kbd> Turn to the Glossary of Mormon Terms and read 'Jesus Christ'.

**To LDS people, who is Elohim?**

If you don't know, <kbd>STOP</kbd> turn to the Glossary of Mormon Terms and read 'Elohim' and 'Heavenly Father'.

**What does the name L**ORD **/Jehovah mean?**

**Why is the meaning of Jehovah God's name important as you witness to LDS people?**

# Jehovah is the Only True God

🛑 **Turn to the Glossary of Mormon Terms and read the LDS definitions of 'Elohim' & 'Jehovah'.**

Because the LDS Church teaches Elohim *[God the Father]* and Jehovah *[Jesus, His Son]* are two distinct Gods, the following Biblical passages are a huge problem for Mormons. In all of the verses in this section, LORD = 'Jehovah' and God = 'Elohim'.

**I Kings 8:60,** *"That all the people of the earth may know that the LORD [Jehovah] is God [Elohim], and that there is none else."*

- **FACT:** The books of the Old Testament are the only scriptures recognized by both Christians and Mormons that were originally written in Hebrew.

- **FACT:** Jehovah and Elohim are Hebrew words.

- **THEREFORE:** Correct Understanding of these Hebrew terms must be derived from the Hebrew Old Testament. The interpretation of these words cannot contradict what is taught in the Bible.

## The LORD *[Jehovah]* is God *[Elohim]*

**Deuteronomy 4:35, 39,** *"Unto thee it was shewed, that thou mightiest know that the LORD [Jehovah] he is God [Elohim]; there is none else beside him…Know therefore this day, and consider it in thine heart, that the LORD [Jehovah] he is God [Elohim] in heaven above, and upon the earth beneath: there is none else."*

**Isaiah 44:6** *"Thus saith the LORD [Jehovah] the King of Israel, and his redeemer the LORD [Jehovah] of hosts; I am the first, and I am the last; and beside me there is no God [Elohim]."*

**Isaiah 45:5,** *"I am the LORD [Jehovah], and there is none else, there is no God [Elohim] beside me…"*

**Psalm 100:3,** *"Know ye that the LORD [Jehovah] he is God [Elohim]: it is he that hath made us, and not we ourselves…"*
*(See also **Numbers 27:16, Deuteronomy 14:1, 2 Samuel 7:22, 1 Kings 8:23, Isaiah 40:28 & 45:18, and Jeremiah 10:10 & 23:23-24**.)*

## Search the Old Testament

- Never is Elohim the Father of Jehovah
- Never is Jehovah the son of Elohim
- Never are Jehovah and Elohim referred to as separate Gods.
- Always Jehovah is Elohim, the one and only true and living God.

## False Gods

Not only are LDS people troubled to discover Jehovah is the only true Elohim, it is also shocking for them to learn that the Hebrew word 'elohim' is at times used to denote false gods.

You will recall from the previous section that 'elohim' is not a personal name—it is a title. As a title, it is quite often tied to idols.

**I Kings 18:26-27,** *"O Baal, hear us. But there was no voice, nor any that answered. And they leaped upon the altar which was made. And it came to pass at noon, that Elijah mocked them, and said, Cry aloud: for he is a god [elohim]; either he is talking, or he is pursuing, or he is in a journey, or peradventure he sleepeth, and must be awaked."*

**1 Chronicles 10:8-10,** *"The Philistines… found Saul and his sons fallen in mount Gilboa… they took his head, and his armour… And they put his armour in the house of their gods [elohim], and fastened his head in the temple of Dagon."*

## There are many false 'gods' [elohim]

**Exodus 12:12,** *"And against all the gods [elohim] of Egypt I will execute judgment: I am the LORD."*

**Psalm 96:4-5,** *"For the LORD [Jehovah] is great, and greatly to be praised: he is to be feared above all gods [elohim]. For all the gods [elohim] of the nations are idols: but the LORD [Jehovah] made the heavens."*

## Typical Mormon Response

It's all a matter of interpretation. You interpret it your way and we interpret it our way.

## Christian Answer

Have the LDS person re-read some of the above verses and ask for their interpretation. Do not let them get away with changing what a verse actually says unless they can support their interpretation with other Biblical or Book of Mormon passages. *(See **Deuteronomy 4:35, 39, 1 Kings 8:60, Isaiah 44:6, etc.**)*

## QUESTIONS FOR REVIEW

**Why are Deuteronomy 4:35, 39; Psalm 100:3; Isaiah 44:6; and Isaiah 45:5 a problem for LDS people?**

**What idol gods in the Bible are called 'elohim?'**

**How do the verses in this section support the idea that 'elohim' is a title and not a personal name?**

**Who is the only true and living 'Elohim?'**

# Elohim is Plural

LDS people will sometimes say, "The Hebrew word 'Elohim' is a plural noun, so it should always be translated plural—Gods!"

Though the Hebrew word 'Elohim' is a plural noun, 'Elohim' does not indicate that there is more than one God simply because of its plural ending. In the Old Testament scriptures, Elohim is directly tied to singular pronouns such as I, He, Me, His, My, Himself, and Myself—99% of the time. It would violate Hebrew grammar to force Elohim to be translated 'Gods' simply because of its plural ending. Consider only a few of the examples *(from the book of Genesis)* where Elohim has a singular pronoun attached to it.

> **Genesis 1:27** *"So God [Elohim] created man in **his** own image, in the image of God [Elohim} created **he** him; male and female created **he** them"*

> **Genesis 2:2** *"And on the seventh day God [Elohim] ended **his** work which **he** had made; and **he** rested on the seventh day from all **his** work which **he** had made."*

> **Genesis 6:13** *"And God [Elohim] said unto Noah, The end of all flesh is come before **me**; for the earth is filled with violence through them; and behold, **I** will destroy them with the earth."*

> **Genesis 22:8** *"And Abraham said, 'My son, God [Elohim] will provide **himself** a lamb for a burnt offering': so they went both of them together."*

*(See also **Genesis 1:10, 29, 31; 2:3, 8, 18, 21-22; 5:1; 9:1-6; 8-17; 17:3-22; 20:6; 21:12-13, 18-19; 22:1-2; 26:24; 35:10-13; 46:2-4**, and 100's more.)*

These passages illustrate why, according to Hebrew grammar, Elohim cannot be translated 'Gods' simply because of its plural ending.

Throughout recorded history *(over 3,500 years)*, Hebrew-speaking Jewish scholars have never translated Elohim as 'Gods' simply because of its plural ending. Rather, Hebrew scholars see Elohim as a 'plural of majesty' a special title of glory fit only for the LORD God.

## Joseph Smith's Interpretation of Elohim

In contrast to the Bible, read the following passage from The Pearl of Great Price which supports the LDS belief in a plurality of Gods.

*"And then the Lord said: Let us go down. And they went down at the beginning, and they, that is the Gods organized and formed the heavens and the earth. And the earth, after it was formed, was empty and desolate, because they had not formed anything but the earth; and the darkness reigned upon the face of the deep, and the Spirit of the Gods was brooding upon the face of the waters. And they (the Gods) said: Let there be light; and there was light. And they (the Gods) comprehended the light, for it was bright; and they divided the light, or caused it to be divided, from the darkness. And the Gods called the light Day and the darkness they called Night... And the Gods also said: Let there be an expanse in the midst of the waters, and it shall divide the waters from the waters. And the Gods ordered the expanse, so that it divided the waters which were under the expanse from the waters which were above the expanse; and it was so, even as they ordered..."* **(The Pearl of Great Price, Abraham 4:1-7.)**

## Typical Mormon Response

If Elohim is not plural, then why does God say, 'Let us make man in our image' in **Genesis 1:26**?

## Christian Answer

The simple answer to this question is that the God of the Bible is a 'plural' Being. He is the Father, the Son, and the Holy Spirit, all of which are unique and distinct yet only one God. The LORD God of the Bible is Three-in-One or a Triune Being known to all of Christianity as the Trinity.

An example of this can be found by opening your Bible and showing your LDS friend **Genesis 1:26 and 1:27**. Genesis 1:26 is a plural statement, but 1:27 is completely singular. Why is Genesis 1:26 plural and 1:27 singular? Use *The Trinity Diagram* to answer this question. *[See Chapter 6, Section 21, Explaining the Trinity.]*

## QUESTIONS FOR REVIEW
**True or False? Elohim is a plural word.**

**Why is 'elohim', a Hebrew noun with a plural ending, not translated 'Gods' 99% of the time?**

**Give a few examples**

**Is Joseph Smith's translation of 'Elohim' as 'Gods' found in Abraham 4:1-7 correct?**

**Why not?**

# S E C T I O N 28
# Is Jesus Christ Really God?

🛑 **Turn to the Glossary of Mormon Terms and read the LDS definition of 'Jesus Christ'.**

LDS doctrine does state that Jesus is a God. Due to conflicting and confusing statements within Mormonism, however, LDS people are often unsure of Jesus Christ's deity.

If you ever speak with a Mormon who doubts the deity of Christ, the following verses from both the Bible and the Book of Mormon state that Jesus is God.

## The Bible

**Isaiah 9:6,** *"For unto us a child is born, unto us a son is given: and the government shall be upon his shoulder: and his name shall be called Wonderful, Counselor, The mighty God, The everlasting Father, The Prince of Peace."*
*(This is identical to* **2 Nephi 19:6** *in the Book of Mormon.)*

**Matthew 1:22-23,** *"Now all this was done that it might be fulfilled which was spoken of the Lord by the prophet, saying, Behold, a virgin shall be with child, and shall bring forth a son, and they shall call his name Emmanuel, which being interpreted is, God with us." (See also* **Isaiah 7:14.***)*

**Jude 1:24-25,** *"Now unto him that is able to keep you from falling, and to present you faultless before the presence of his glory with exceeding joy, to the only wise God our Saviour, be glory and majesty, dominion and power, both now and ever. Amen."*

**1 Timothy 3:16,** *"Without controversy great is the mystery of godliness: God was manifest in the flesh, justified in the Spirit, seen of angels, preached unto the Gentiles, believed on in the world, received up into glory."*

## The Book of Mormon

**Mosiah 5:15,** *"Therefore, I would that ye should be steadfast and immovable, always abounding in good works, that Christ, the Lord God Omnipotent, may seal you his, that you may be brought to heaven, that ye may have everlasting salvation and eternal life, through the wisdom and power, and justice, and mercy of him who created all things, in heaven and in earth, who is God above all. Amen."*

**2 Nephi 11:7,** *"For if there be no Christ there be no God; and if there be no God we are not, for there could have been no creation. But there is a God, and he is Christ, and he cometh in the fulness of his own time."*

**2 Nephi 26:12,** *"And as I spake concerning the convincing of the Jews, that Jesus is the very Christ, it must needs be that the Gentiles be convinced also that Jesus is the Christ, the Eternal God."*

## QUESTION FOR REVIEW

Write a reference from both the Bible and the Book of Mormon that state Jesus is God.

From what you have learned about the Mormon concept of the Godhead, why do you think some LDS people might be confused about the deity of Christ?

How might the LDS Law of Eternal Progression create doubt in the mind of an LDS person as to whether or not Jesus is actually a God?

🛑 See the Glossary of Mormon Terms, 'God', and 'Eternal Progression'.

# CHAPTER 8

# LDS 'PROOF TEXTS' FOR PLURAL GODS?

## SECTION 29

## "Ye Are Gods" —John 10:34

(STOP) **Turn to the Glossary of Mormon Terms and read the LDS definition of 'Mankind'.**

In an effort to support the LDS doctrine that men are genetically 'little gods in the making', some Mormons will use John 10:34. Here is the verse in its context.

> **John 10:33-36** *"The Jews answered him, saying, For a good work we stone thee not; but for blasphemy; and because that thou, being a man, makest thyself God. Jesus answered them, Is it not written in your law, I said, Ye are gods? If he called them gods, unto whom the word of God came, and the scripture cannot be broken; Say ye of him, whom the Father hath sanctified, and sent into the world, Thou blasphemest; because I said, I am the Son of God?"*

Taken out of context, John 10:34 might appear to support the Mormon doctrine of a plurality of gods; but in context, the opposite is true.

To whom was Jesus talking in this chapter? He was addressing the Jewish religious rulers, the judges of Israel. These were the judges who would later condemned Jesus to death. Does anyone

want to maintain that the murderers of our Lord were actually 'gods' (present tense) as Jesus inferred in John 10:34?

## Why Did Jesus Call Jewish Religious Rulers 'gods'?

John 10:34 is a quote from Psalm 82 where the LORD God is talking to the judges of Israel.

(STOP) **Turn to Psalm 82 in your Bible and read it before continuing.**

In Psalm 82, God is angered by the 'gods' who are judging 'unjustly'. He tells these 'gods' they will 'die like men'. Question, can true 'gods' die like men? Do true 'gods' judge unjustly? What is going on in this passage? Is God actually reprimanding other gods? NO WAY!

Psalm 82 refers back to the Old Testament law and the regulations given to the 'judges' of Israel. In the following passages, the words 'gods' and 'judges' are translated interchangeably from the same Hebrew word, 'elohim'.

> **Exodus 21:6** *"Then his master shall bring him unto the judges [elohim]; he shall also bring him to the door, or unto the door post; and his master shall bore his ear through with an awl; and he shall serve him for ever."*

In this verse, the word 'judges' is the same Hebrew word as 'gods' in Psalm 82.

**INTERESTING NOTE**: Joseph Smith supposedly corrected the King James Bible. This literary work is recognized by LDS scholars as the 'Joseph Smith Translation' *(JST)* or 'Inspired Version'. If you own a Bible printed by the LDS Church, some of these changes will appear as (JST) footnotes at the bottom of the page. Joseph's inspired version of Exodus 21:7 does not change the word 'judges' to the more literal translation 'gods', why not?

> ***The JST says,*** *"Then his master shall bring him unto the judges; he shall also bring him to his door, or unto the door post; and his master shall bore his ear through with an awl; and he shall serve him for ever."* (**Exodus 21:6 JST.**) *(Joseph Smith's "New Translation" of the Bible, Herald Publishing House.)*

**Exodus 22:8-9,** *"If the thief be not found, then the master of the house shall be brought unto the judges [elohim], to see whether he have put his hand unto his neighbour's goods. For all manner of trespass, whether it be for ox, for ass, for sheep, for raiment, or for any manner of lost thing, which another challengeth to be his, the cause of both parties shall come before the judges [elohim]; and whom the judges [elohim] shall condemn, he shall pay double unto his neighbor."*

**Exodus 22:28,** *"Thou shalt not revile the gods [elohim], nor curse the ruler [or judge] of thy people."*

## Why did God Call Israelite judges—'gods'?

God called the judges of Israel 'elohim/gods' because they were His representatives. They stood in His place judging His people. In Deuteronomy 1, God warns these men not to judge unjustly and bring disgrace upon His name.

**Deuteronomy 1:15-17,** *"So I took the chief of your tribes, wise men, and known, and made them heads over you, captains over thousands, and captains over hundreds, and captains over fifties, and captains over tens, and officers among your tribes. And I charged your judges at that time, saying, Hear the causes between your brethren, and judge righteously between every man and his brother, and the stranger that is with him. Ye shall not respect persons in judgment; but ye shall hear the small as well as the great; ye shall not be afraid of the face of man; for the judgment is God's: and the cause that is too hard for you, bring it unto me, and I will hear it."*

## Elohim Can Also Refers to False Gods

Remember, in the Bible, 'elohim' is a title and as a title it can also denote false gods.

**Psalm 96:4-5** *"For the LORD [Jehovah] is great, and greatly to be praised: he is to be feared above all gods [elohim]. For all the gods [elohim] of the nations are idols: but the LORD [Jehovah] made the heavens."*

## One True God

There is only one true God, the LORD God, so the judges who were called 'gods' (little 'g') were not really Gods (big 'G'.)

**Isaiah 44:6** *"Thus saith the LORD the King of Israel, and his redeemer the LORD of hosts; I am the first, and I am the last; and beside me there is no God."*

## QUESTIONS FOR REVIEW

**From the context of John 10:33-36, give some reasons why Jesus was not saying these men were true Gods.**

**Why did God call the judges of Israel 'elohim/gods?'** *(See Deuteronomy 1.)*

**Who is the one and only true living God?**

S E C T I O N **30**

# One God in Purpose —John 17:11

🛑 **Turn to the Glossary of Mormon Terms and read the LDS definition of 'Godhead'.**

Mormon people like to use John chapter 17 to support the LDS theology that Jesus and the Father are two separate and distinct Gods, united only in purpose. They will sarcastically ask, "What does it mean when Jesus prayed for the disciples to be one with the Father just as He and the Father were one? Does it mean the disciples, Jesus, and the Father were all going to be rolled up into one big God?"

**John 17:11,** *"Holy Father, keep through thine own name those whom thou hast given me, that they may be one, as we are."* (See **also John 17:20-23.**)

John 17 is a prayer offered by the Lord on behalf of all who would believe in Him. Jesus prayed that all Christians would be united in the same way that He and the Father were united. This prayer was answered in a wonderful way.

While Jesus was on this earth, the Spirit of God indwelt his mortal body, and he enjoyed intimate fellowship and perfect unity with the Father. In like manner, the Spirit of God indwells each believer. All believers are privileged to enjoy the same intimate relationship with God that Jesus experienced as a man.

John 17 contains no statements discussing the plurality of gods. When John 17 is used in an attempt to prove Jesus and Father are two separate Gods united only in purpose, the passage has been taken completely out of context. The Bible teaches there is only one God. The LDS interpretation is not consistent with the rest of the Bible.

## Jesus Was United with the Father

**John 14:7-11,** *"If ye had known me, ye should have known my Father also: and from henceforth ye know him, and have seen him. Philip saith unto him, Lord, shew us the Father, and it sufficeth us. Jesus saith unto him, Have I been so long time with you and yet has thou not known me, Philip? He that hath seen me hath seen the Father; and how sayest thou then, Shew us the Father? Believest thou not that I am in the Father, and the Father in me? The words that I speak unto you I speak not of myself: but the Father that dwelleth in me, he doeth the works. Believe me that I am in the Father, and the Father in me: or else believe me for the very works' sake."*

**2 Corinthians 5:19,** *"To wit, that God was in Christ, reconciling the world unto himself, not imputing their trespasses unto them; and hath committed unto us the word of reconciliation."*

## Believers Are Also United with the Father

Just as Jesus, when He was on earth, was united with the Father by the indwelling Spirit of God, all believers are united in like manner with the Father by the indwelling of the Holy Spirit.

**Romans 8:11,** *"But if the Spirit of him that raised up Jesus from the dead dwell in you, he that raised up Christ from the dead shall also quicken your mortal bodies by his Spirit that dwelleth in you."*

**Romans 8:14-16,** *"For as many as are led by the Spirit of God, they are the sons of God. For ye have not received the spirit of bondage again to fear; but ye have received the Spirit of adoption, whereby we cry, Abba, Father. The Spirit itself beareth witness with our spirit, that we are the children of God."*

**1 Corinthians 3:16,** *"Know ye not that ye are the temple of God, and that the Spirit of God dwelleth in you?"*

Yes, the prayer of Jesus in John 17 was answered. All believers do experience the same intimate relationship with the Father that Jesus experienced while in his humanity here on this earth.

## QUESTIONS FOR REVIEW

**Read John 17 and briefly summarize the prayer of Jesus—are there any statements that might suggest Jesus and the Father are two Gods?**

**Explain how we are united with the Father in the same way Jesus, in his humanity, was united with the Father?**

# The Council of Nicea: Right or Wrong?

🛑 **Turn to the Glossary of Mormon Terms and read the LDS definition of 'Great Apostasy, The'.**

Mormon people are taught that the Council of Nicea was one of the key factors leading to the great apostasy of the Christian Church. The LDS Church would have you believe the Roman Emperor Constantine greatly influenced the outcome of the Council of Nicea which defined the traditional Christian view of the Trinity. A close examination of the Nicene Creed as it compares with the message of the Bible, however, proves exactly the opposite to be true.

## Arius, Athanasius, & the Council of Nicea

The council of Nicaea was a response to the challenge of Arianism which denied the full deity of Christ.

Arius, presbyter of the Baucalis Church in Alexandria (about A.D. 318), taught that God is eternal, unbegotten, and without beginning. Christ, however, could not be God in the same sense as the Father because he was 'begotten'. Arius taught the Son did not exist from all eternity but was created out of nothing like all other created beings. Arianism maintained the Son was not consubstantial (Latin 'homoousios', of the same substance) with the Father, but rather he existed by the will of the Father.

Athanasius, patriarch of the Holy See of Saint Mark, also in Alexandria, stood against Arianism and argued, Christ was consubstantial ('Homoousios', of the same substance) with the Father and was, therefore, co-equal and co-eternal with the Father.

The teaching of Arius was condemned in A.D. 325 at the Council at Nicea. The 318 assembled bishops drafted a creed based upon clear Biblical teachings which tell us that the Son of God is consubstantial (Latin 'homoousios', of the same substance) with the Father. In other words, the Son is a coequal and coeternal member of the Trinity and not simply a part of creation.

Of the 318 bishops in attendance, all but two voted in favor of the Nicene Creed which defined the deity of Jesus Christ and brought clarity to the doctrine of the Trinity.

## Is the Nicene Creed Right or Wrong?

It is significant to note that both the Bible and the Book of Mormon agree with the central truths of the creed drawn at the Council of Nicea: Jesus is 'homoousios', of the same substance, with God the Father.

## Jesus is God
## The Bible

**Matthew 1:22-23,** *"Behold, a virgin shall be with child, and shall bring forth a son, and they shall call his name Emmanuel, which being interpreted is, God with us."*

**1 Timothy 3:16,** *"And without controversy great is the mystery of godliness. God was manifest in the flesh."*

## The Book of Mormon

**2 Nephi 26:12,** *"And as I spake concerning the convincing of the Jews, that Jesus is the very Christ, it must needs be that the Gentiles be convinced also that Jesus is the Christ, the Eternal God." (See also **Mosiah 15:1-4**.)*

## Jesus and the Father are 'Homoousios'
## The Bible

**John 14:7-11,** *"If ye had known me ye should have known my Father also: and from henceforth ye know him, and have seen him. Philip saith unto him, Lord, shew us the Father, and it sufficeth us. Jesus saith unto him, Have I been so long time with you, and yet has thou not known me, Philip? He that hath seen me hath seen the Father; and how sayest thou then, Shew us the Father? Believest thou not that I am in the Father, and the Father in me? The words that I speak unto you I speak not of myself: but the Father that dwelleth in me, he*

*doeth the works. Believe me that I am in the Father, and the Father in me: or else believe me for the very works' sake."*
*(See also Isaiah 9:6.)*

## The Book of Mormon

**Mosiah 15:1-4,** *"And now Abinadi said unto them: I would that ye should understand that God himself shall come down among the children of men, and shall redeem his people. And because he dwelleth in flesh he shall be called the Son of God, and having subjected the flesh to the will of the Father, being the Father and the Son; the Father, because he was conceived by the power of God; and the Son, because of the flesh; thus becoming the Father and Son; And they are one God, yea, the very Eternal Father of heaven and of earth." (See also **2 Nephi 19:6**.)*

## Scriptural Identity of the Trinity: One God
## The Bible

**Matthew 28:19,** *"Go ye therefore, and teach all nations, baptizing them in the name of the Father, and of the Son, and of the Holy Ghost."*

**John 10:30,** *"I and my Father are one."*

## The Book of Mormon

**2 Nephi 31:21,** *"Behold, my beloved brethren, this is the way; and there is none other way nor name given under heaven whereby man can be saved in the kingdom of God. And now, behold, this is the doctrine of Christ, and the only and true doctrine of the Father, and of the Son, and of the Holy Ghost, which is one God, without end. Amen." (See also **Alma 11:44** and The Testimony of the Three Witnesses.)*

**NOTE:** The LDS Church also teaches the Council of Nicea was the time in history when the Bible lost many of its 'plain and precious truths'. Mormons believe Emperor Constantine and the Christian bishops chose which books of the Bible to keep and which to eliminate. The LDS Church teaches the Bible was utterly corrupted by the great and abominable Church. *(see **1 Nephi 13:21-29**.)*

## The Content of the Bible at Nicea

No discussions about the canonization of the Christian scriptures took place at the Council of Nicea. No decisions were made to keep or eliminate any Old Testament or New Testament books nor were any parts of the Bible changed or removed. The current books of both the Old and the New Testaments were already established and being used in the early Christian churches by the time of the Council of Nicea.

## QUESTIONS FOR REVIEW

**Do the Bible and Book of Mormon, agree or disagree with the Creed formed at the Council of Nicea?**

**Why or why not?**

**What does the key word of the Council of Nicea, 'consubstantial/homoousios', mean?**

**Are Jesus and the Father 'homoousios?'**
**Give one Bible reference and one Book of Mormon reference to support your answer.**

**Were any books of the Bible removed or any changes made to the Christian Bible at the Council of Nicea?**

# The 'Most High' and the 'Lᴏʀᴅ'

### The 'Most High' and the 'Lᴏʀᴅ' (Jehovah) —Are They Different Gods?

It has been argued by some LDS scholars that Deuteronomy 32:8-9 is proof for two separate Gods in the Old Testament. Let's consider this passage:

**Deuteronomy 32:8-9,** *"When the most High divided to the nations their inheritance, when he separated the sons of Adam, he set the bounds of the people according to the number of the children of Israel. For the Lᴏʀᴅ's portion is his people; Jacob is the lot of his inheritance."*

The LDS argument goes something like this—it is always the Father who leaves an inheritance to his children. And, in this passage, the 'most High' *(or Heavenly Father)* is dividing his inheritance amongst his children, named in this passage as 'the sons of Adam'. A portion of the inheritance is allotted to the Lᴏʀᴅ or Jehovah, who according to LDS theology, is the first born Son of God. Therefore, the most High and the Lᴏʀᴅ (Jehovah) must be different Gods.

This challenge is easily answered by simply asking the following questions:

1) According to the Bible, who is the 'most High' God?

2) How many 'most High' Gods can there be?

Read these Bible verses:

**Psalm 91:1-2,** *"He that dwelleth in the secret place of the **most High** shall abide under the shadow of the Almighty I will say of the Lᴏʀᴅ [Jehovah], He is my refuge and my fortress: my God; in him will I trust."*

**Psalm 91:9,** *"Because thou has made the Lᴏʀᴅ [Jehovah], which is my refuge, even the **most High**, thy habitation; There shall no evil befall thee."*

**Psalm 92:1,** *"It is a good thing to give thanks unto the Lᴏʀᴅ [Jehovah], and to sing praises unto thy name, O **most High**."*

Who is the 'most High' in all of these verses? The Lᴏʀᴅ God is the most High, and how many 'most High' Gods can there be?

### What is the correct interpretation of Deuteronomy 32:8-9?

It really is very simple—when the 'most High' *(Jehovah God)* divided to the nations their inheritance, He *(Jehovah)* chose Israel as His inheritance. And so, from ancient times, the sons of Jacob or the Israelites have been commonly known as the Lᴏʀᴅ God's chosen people.

### <u>QUESTIONS FOR REVIEW</u>
**What passages in the Bible can be used to show that the 'most High' is the Lᴏʀᴅ *(Jehovah God)*?**

**How many most High God's can there be?**

# CHAPTER 9
# THE DOCTRINE OF SALVATION

## SECTION 33
## The LDS Plan of Salvation

LDS Salvation is first and foremost a universal gift to all of mankind, meaning that virtually all human beings *(except 'sons of perdition')* will go to one of the three LDS Heavens. The Atonement of Jesus Christ guarantees a kingdom of glory to every person who ever lived *(again, except sons of perdition'.)*

**STOP** **Turn to the Glossary of Mormon Terms and read the LDS definitions of 'Heaven', 'Celestial Kingdom', & 'Sons of Perdition'.**

The greatest deception within Mormonism is the terminology used by the LDS Church to define its plan of salvation. The LDS Church has redefined virtually every Biblical term relating to this topic so discussing 'the gospel' with LDS people becomes a frustrating experience for the person who does not understand Mormon terminology. Do not be deceived into thinking Biblical salvation and Mormon 'salvation' have anything in common. The importance of understanding LDS terms cannot be overemphasized!

**STOP** **Turn to the Glossary of Mormon Terms and read the LDS definitions of 'Gospel, The LDS', 'Salvation', 'Redemption', 'Salvation by Grace Alone'.**

## Book of Mormon 'Salvation'

While the Book of Mormon does agree in principle with the Bible in regard to the doctrine of God, it does not agree with Biblical teachings concerning salvation. Although isolated passages may appear to support salvation by grace alone, DO NOT USE the Book of Mormon to support the Biblical concept of salvation. Specifically, Book of Mormon salvation is a system of faith plus works. Consider the following verses which typify this doctrine in the Book of Mormon. The terms used in these passages may be Biblical, but the message has been twisted, resulting in heretical doctrine.

**2 Nephi 9:23-24,** *"And he commandeth all men that they must repent, and be baptized in his name, having perfect faith in the Holy One of Israel, or they cannot be saved in the kingdom of God. And if they will not repent and believe in his name, and be baptized in his name, and endure to the end, they must be damned; for the Lord God, the Holy One of Israel, has spoken it."* (See also **3 Nephi 27:16-22**.)

**Moroni 10:32,** *"Yea, come unto Christ, and be perfected in him; and deny yourselves of all ungodliness; and if ye shall deny yourselves of all ungodliness, and love God with all your might, mind and strength, then is his grace sufficient for you."*

**2 Nephi 25:23,** *"For we labor diligently to write, to persuade our children, and also our brethren, to believe in Christ, and to be reconciled to God; for we know that it is by grace that we are saved, after all we can do."*

**Mosiah 2:41,** *"I would desire that ye should consider on the blessed and happy state of those that keep the commandments of God. For behold, they are blessed in all things, both temporal and spiritual; and if they hold out faithful to the end they are received into heaven, that thereby they may dwell with God in a state of never-ending happiness. O remember, remember that these things are true; for the Lord God hath spoken it."*

## QUESTIONS FOR REVIEW

**Why is the LDS gospel so deceptive and hard for Christians to grasp?**

**Which Christian doctrine should you NOT USE the Book of Mormon to support?**

**What can you see in these Book of Mormon passages that would contradict the Christian/Biblical doctrine of salvation?**

# SECTION 34
# Traditional Witnessing Approaches

Traditional witnessing approaches are often not effective when trying to share the gospel with Mormon people. The 'Four Spiritual Laws' is a tried and true witnessing method that has led multitudes into a relationship with Jesus Christ. However, when an LDS person is presented the Four Spiritual Laws, a problem caused by LDS terminology comes into play, consider how LDS people might view each point.

## The Four Spiritual Laws

**1. God LOVES you and offers a wonderful PLAN for your life (John 3:16; 10:10.)**

**Mormon thinking:** Of course God loves us! He is our Heavenly Father. He and our Heavenly Mother gave birth to us in the preexistence, and God love His children as much as we love our children. God's wonderful plan for mankind enables us to be like Him and become gods someday if we obey all of his commandments.

**2. Man is SINFUL and SEPARATED from God; therefore, he cannot know and experience God's love and plan for his life (Romans 3:23 and 6:23.)**

**Mormon thinking:** Yes, we are all in a state of mortality and testing because of Adam's transgression. Thanks to Adam and Eve, who made the right decision in the Garden of Eden when they partook of the forbidden fruit, we all have the knowledge and experience we need to become gods in eternity future and to fulfill God's wonderful plan for our lives. But we needed a Savior in order for that plan to be set in motion.

🛑 **Turn to the Glossary of Mormon Terms and read the LDS definition of 'Fall, The'.**

**3. Jesus Christ is God's ONLY provision for man's sin. Through Him you can know and experience God's love and plan for your life (Romans 5:8, 1 Corinthians 15:3-6; John 14:6.)**

**Mormon thinking:** Yes, Jesus Christ, God's firstborn spirit child and our literal spirit brother, was chosen in the preexistence to be the one to atone for the original sin of Adam. Because of the great atonement of Christ, every person will be resurrected and given the free gift of immortality. Due to this free gift, we all have the opportunity to experience one of three Heavens and may even become gods someday if we obey all the laws and ordinances of the LDS gospel.

🛑 **Turn to the Glossary of Mormon Terms and read the LDS definition of 'Atonement of Christ'.**

**4. We must individually receive Jesus Christ as Savior and Lord; then we can know and experience God's love and plan for our lives (John 1:12; Ephesians 2:8-9; John 3:1-8.)**

**Mormon thinking:** Yes, only those who recognize Jesus as the Savior will have the opportunity to completely fulfill God's greatest plan, which is for us to reach a place of exaltation and become gods just like our Heavenly Father.

Can you see how the terminology barrier may hinder LDS people from understanding the message you are trying to present? To the unwary, the way Mormons respond may sound 'Christian', but there is no connection between LDS theology and Biblical truth. LDS people may even appear receptive to your message, and occasionally a Mormon might even agree to pray the sinner's prayer with you. You may walk away rejoicing that they have been saved, while they walk away still steeped in Mormonism and believing they are little gods in the making.

## Evangelism Explosion International®

The traditional EE 'diagnostic questions' are also a tried and true witnessing method, but once again the terminology barrier may interfere when witnessing to Mormons. Consider these questions and how a Mormon might respond.

**Question One:** Have you come to the place in your spiritual life where you know for certain you will go to Heaven, or is that something you would say you're still working on?

**Mormon thinking:** To a Mormon, salvation by grace *(which is resurrection or immortality)* is a free gift from God. Almost every person who ever lived, regardless of belief, will enter one of the three Mormon Heavens at the resurrection. So a Mormon could honestly answer the first question, "Yes, I know for sure that I will go to Heaven some day as a result of the atonement of Jesus Christ."

**Question Two:** Suppose you were to die today and stand before God and He were to ask you, 'Why should I let you into My Heaven?' What would you say?

**Mormon thinking:** I would be allowed to go to Heaven because of the atonement of Jesus Christ. Through repentance and obedience to the gospel of Jesus Christ, I know for certain that I will go to Heaven (one of the three LDS Heavens) when I die.

The Christian may walk away marveling that this Mormon appears to be a true believer. The Mormon may walk away still steeped in false doctrine, believing they will be a god some day.

## QUESTIONS FOR REVIEW
**Why is it often a problem to use traditional witnessing approaches with LDS people?**

**Why is it vitally important for Christians to fully understand LDS terminology before witnessing to LDS people?**

# S E C T I O N 35
# Eternal Life

🛑 **Turn to the Glossary of Mormon Terms and read the LDS definitions of 'Eternal Life', 'Exaltation', and 'Immortality'.**

The Biblical topic of eternal life is a crucial subject to discuss with your Mormon friends. According to the LDS Church, eternal life is earned by obedience to all the laws and ordinances of the gospel. Mormon people, therefore, can never know for sure if they have done enough. Eternal life only comes after the final judgment, if they have done sufficient works to earn this privilege.

👁 Go to: TriGrace.org
**Under 'Resources' find and print the free PDF download of *The Gospel Truth* visual. Read this handout before proceeding.**

## A Slightly Altered 'EE' Approach

By slightly altering the traditional Evangelism Explosion® questions, it is possible to get into a great discussion about eternal life with a Mormon.

**Altered 'EE' Question 1:** If you were to die today do you know for certain that you have eternal life and would live forever with Heavenly Father in His Celestial Kingdom?

If the LDS person you are talking with understands Mormon doctrine, they should respond by saying something like this, "No one can know for certain that they have earned eternal life until after the final judgment."

**Altered 'EE' Question 2:** If Heavenly Father were to ask you, 'Why should I let you into My Celestial Kingdom?' What would you say?

If a Mormon thinks he is going to make it to the Celestial Kingdom, he will respond by saying something like this, "I would tell Heavenly Father that he should let me into the Celestial Kingdom because I have done my best to kept all the laws and ordinances of the gospel."

**NOTE:** If a Mormon responds this way, use The 'Impossible Gospel' witnessing approach which is explained in Section 41 of this book.

The vast majority of LDS people, however, rightly understand that it is impossible for them to have any assurance of eternal life. In fact the official teaching of the LDS Church says this,

"If we use the word *salvation* to mean eternal life, none of us can say that we have been saved in mortality. That glorious gift can come only after the Final Judgment." *(True to the Faith, by the LDS Church, 2004, pg. 153.)*

LDS doctrine teaches you must earn eternal life by doing good works. The Bible teaches eternal life is a free gift of grace and a gift is not earned but is received. The Bible also teaches we can know for sure that we have *(present tense)* eternal life. Use the following passages to show LDS people the Biblical gift of eternal life.

### 'Jesus Christ's Testimony of Eternal Life'

**John 3:14-18, 36,** *"And as Moses lifted up the serpent in the wilderness, even so must the Son of man be lifted up: That whosoever believeth in him should not perish, but have eternal life (present tense.) For God so loved the world, that he gave his only begotten Son, that whosoever believeth in him should not perish but have everlasting (in Greek: eternal) life (present tense.) For God sent not his Son into the world to condemn the world; but that the world through him might be saved. He that believeth on him is not condemned (present tense), but he that believeth not is condemned already, because he hath not believed in the name of the only begotten Son of God... He that believeth on the Son hath everlasting (in Greek: eternal) life (present tense): and he that believeth not the Son shall not see life; but the wrath of God abideth on him."*

### 'Heavenly Father's Testimony of Eternal Life'

**1 John 5:9-13,** *"If we receive the witness of men, the witness of God is greater: for this is the witness of God which he hath testified of his Son. He that believeth on the Son of God hath the witness in himself: he that believeth not God hath made him a liar; because he believeth not the record that God gave of his Son. And this is the record, that God hath given to us eternal life, (present tense) and this life is in his Son. He that hath the Son hath life (present tense); and he that hath not the Son of God hath not life. These things have I written unto you that believe on the name of the Son of God that ye may know that ye have eternal life (present tense), and that ye may believe on the name of the Son of God."*

The next group of passages clearly present Jesus Christ's simple gospel. These passages are 'Good News' for Mormons who are under the bondage of an impossible works based religion.

## The Only Biblical Requirement

**John 6:27-29,** *"Labour not for the meat which perisheth, but for that meat which endureth unto everlasting (in Greek: eternal) life, which the Son of man shall give unto you: for him hath God the Father sealed. Then said they unto him, What shall we do, that we might work the works of God? Jesus answered and said unto them, This is the work of God, that ye believe on him whom he hath sent."*

## Eternal Life Is a Gift

Eternal life is freely offered and freely given to all who will believe in Jesus Christ; but eternal life was not cheaply purchased. Jesus died in our place, paying sin's penalty for us, so he could buy this priceless gift for mankind.

**Romans 6:23,** *"For the wages of sin is death; but the gift of God is eternal life through Jesus Christ our Lord."*

## Missing God's Righteousness

Like the Jews of Paul's day, the LDS people have been deceived into believing they can earn their own righteousness by keeping the law.

**Romans 10:1-4,** *"Brethren, my heart's desire and prayer to God for Israel [and for the LDS people] is, that they might be saved. For I bear them record that they have a zeal of God, but not according to knowledge. For they being ignorant of God's righteousness, and going about to establish their own righteousness, have not submitted themselves unto the righteousness of God. For Christ is the end of the law for righteousness to every one that believeth."*

## Becoming Righteous Through Faith

We become right with God (righteous) when we believe in Jesus and receive Him as our Lord and Savior. Notice that it says it is 'with the heart' that we 'believe' not 'work' unto righteousness.

**Romans 10:9-10,** *"That if thou shalt confess with thy mouth the Lord Jesus, and shalt believe in thine heart that God hath raised him from the dead, thou shalt be saved. For with the heart man believeth unto righteousness; and with the mouth confession is made unto salvation."*

## Salvation is by Grace Through Faith— Not of Works

**Ephesians 2:8-9,** *"For by grace are ye saved through faith; and that not of yourselves: it is the gift of God: Not of works, lest any man should boast."*

**2 Corinthians 9:15**, *"Thanks be unto God for His unspeakable gift."*

## ◉ Go to: TriGrace.org

**Under 'Resources' find and print the free PDF download of the *Eternal Life Diagram*. Then watch the TGM Tutorial explaining how to use this Visual Aid with Mormon people.** [We offer two options for the *Eternal Life Diagram*—with slightly different information. One challenges Mormons with *'Lucifer's gospel'* which is more confrontational; the other has *'Paul's explanation of the gospel'* and is less confrontational.]

## The Eternal Life Diagram

In spite of the clarity of God's word, the Biblical topic of eternal life is often very confusing for a Mormon. Most LDS people truly don't get it. They think Mormons and Christians all *(pretty much)* believe the same things—they just think Latter-day Saints approach salvation with more 'zeal' than most Christians.

It is not uncommon to hear a Mormon say, "Look, you believe faith in Jesus is important and so do we. You believe in repentance and we believe in repentance. We both believe good works are important. I don't understand why you think we are so wrong just because we place a greater emphasis on keeping the commandments than you do."

This is where *The Eternal Life Diagram* will help. When the 'Biblical Gift of Eternal Life' is compared with the 'LDS Law of Eternal Life', the differences become obvious—they are completely different gospels.

The 'Biblical Gift of Eternal Life' is the gospel taught by Jesus Christ and 'LDS Law of Eternal Life' follows what we would say is Lucifer's gospel. The *Eternal Life Diagram* is a graphic visual for any Mormon and will plant a seed that will not be easily forgotten.

## QUESTIONS FOR REVIEW

**Write out the slightly altered Evangelism Explosion® questions.**

    **Question #1:**

    **Question #2:**

**Explain the differences between Biblical Eternal Life and LDS Eternal Life.**

**Explain why Romans 10:1-4 and 10:9-10 are great passages to share with LDS people.**

**After studying 'The Eternal Life Diagram'—what are the most significant contrasts between these two belief systems?**

# SECTION 36
# Born Again

🛑 **Turn to the Glossary of Mormon Terms and read the LDS definition of 'Baptism'.**

## A Witnessing Opportunity

Asking the simple question, 'Have you been born again?' can present a wonderful opportunity to share the gospel with LDS people.

## Possible LDS Response

Some LDS people are not familiar with the term 'born again' and may, like Nicodemus, ask, 'What do you mean?' In this case, show them **John 3:3** where Jesus says,

> *"Verily, verily, I say unto thee, Except a man be born again, he cannot see the kingdom of God."*

Ask if they want to know what it means to be born again. Use John 3 to share the gospel with them. Be sure to show them *'Jesus Christ's Testimony of Eternal Life'* (**John 3:14-18, 36**.)

## Another Possible Response

If an LDS person answers the question by saying, "I was born again when I was baptized into the LDS Church", use the following discussion ideas to show them water baptism is not what Jesus meant when he said, "You Must be Born Again"—read the story,

> **John 3:1-7,** *"There was a man of the Pharisees named Nicodemus, a ruler of the Jews. The same came to Jesus by night, and said unto him, Rabbi, we know that thou art a teacher come from God: for no man can do these miracles that thou doest, except God be with him. Jesus answered and said unto him, Verily, verily, I say unto thee, Except a man be born again, he cannot see the kingdom of God. Nicodemus saith unto him, How can a man be born when he is old? Can he enter the second time into his mother's womb, and be born? Jesus answered, Verily, verily, I say unto thee, Except a man be born of water and of the Spirit, he cannot enter into the kingdom of God. That which is born of the flesh is flesh; and that which is born of the Spirit is spirit. Marvel not that I said unto thee, Ye must be born again."*

The phrase, *"Except a man be born of water and of the Spirit"*, is interpreted by the LDS Church to mean you must be water baptized to be born again. But is this what Jesus meant?

In this passage, Jesus was talking about being born 'again', or being born twice. All men experience the first birth—physical birth, but if you hope to see the kingdom of God, you must also experience a second birth—spiritual birth. You must be 'born again'.

In verse 5, the first birth is described as being born of water and the second birth being born of the Spirit. Jesus interpreted these two births for us in vs. 6, *"That which is born of the flesh is flesh; and that which is born of the Spirit is spirit."*

The first birth *(of the flesh)* takes place when a mother's water membrane ruptures and the child is born. This is the physical/water birth.

The second birth *(of the Spirit)* takes place when a person is born of the Spirit into God's family. This is what it means to be 'born again'.

Jesus Christ's explanation of the two births makes it clear that water baptism and being born again are not synonymous terms. A person is born again when he believes Jesus *(John 3:14-18, 36.)*

## The Conversion of Alma 'the Younger'

In the Book of Mormon, the conversion of Alma supports the Biblical idea of 'born again'.

**NOTE**: It is interesting to note that Alma 'the Younger' was converted or 'born again' in this passage, yet nowhere in the account of his conversion does he get water baptized. Water is never mentioned—check it out for yourself.

> **Mosiah 27:24-26,** *"For, said he [Alma 'the Younger'], I have repented of my sins, and have been redeemed of the Lord; behold I am born of the Spirit. And the Lord said unto me: Marvel not that all mankind, yea, men and women, all nations, kindreds, tongues and people, must be born again; yea, born of God, changed from their carnal and fallen state, to a state of righteousness, being redeemed of God, becoming his sons and daughters; And thus they become new creatures; and unless they do this, they can in nowise inherit the kingdom of God."*

## Baptism and the Holy Ghost

Reception of the Holy Ghost is also not synonymous with water baptism. There are at least two examples in the Bible where people were filled with the Holy Ghost apart from or before water baptism.

> **Acts 2:1-4,** *"And when the day of Pentecost was fully come, they were all with one accord in one place. And suddenly there came a sound from heaven as of a rushing mighty wind, and it filled all the house where they were sitting. And there appeared unto them cloven tongues like as of fire, and it sat upon each of them. And they were all filled with the Holy Ghost, and began to speak with other tongues, as the Spirit gave them utterance."*

> **Acts 10:44-48,** *"While Peter yet spake these words, the Holy Ghost fell on all them which heard the word. And they of the circumcision which believed were astonished, as many as came with Peter, because that on the Gentiles also was poured out the gift of the Holy Ghost. For they heard them speak with tongues, and magnify God. Then answered Peter, Can any man forbid water, that these should not be baptized, which have received the Holy Ghost as well as we? And he commanded them to be baptized in the name of the Lord."*

At this point, you might ask your Mormon friend, 'May I tell you when I was born again?' and share your personal testimony with them.

## QUESTIONS FOR REVIEW

**Explain in your own words what it means to be born again. (Support your answer with the Bible.)**

**Explain why the LDS interpretation of 'born again' is not what Jesus was teaching?**

# CHAPTER 10
# THINKING ABOUT SALVATION

## SECTION 37
## Knowing the Biblical Jesus

**STOP** Turn to the Glossary of Mormon Terms and read the LDS definitions of 'Jesus Christ', and 'Satan'.

After you show a Mormon several Bible passages which prove that salvation/eternal life is a free gift to those who believe in Jesus, they may respond by saying, "So, I believe in Jesus. According to your definition, I'll be okay, right?"

LDS people believe in the historical person the world knows as Jesus. Their Jesus was born in Bethlehem, miraculously healed the sick, had 12 disciples, died on a cross and rose again.

### Is the LDS Jesus Different?

While it may be argued that the Mormon and Christian Jesus is the same historical person, the similarities end there. The eternal nature or the essence of the LDS and Christian Jesus is totally different. The eternal nature of the LDS Jesus is human by nature. The eternal nature of the Biblical Jesus is God (or Deity) by nature.

**STOP** Go to FIGURE 10.1 on the following page and compare the LDS Jesus with the Biblical Jesus.

This theological problem is bigger than just Jesus because the LDS Church also denies the eternal nature of God himself. Each of the false statements about the LDS Jesus listed in FIGURE 10.1 can also be applied to Heavenly Father and all the other gods of Mormonism. LDS doctrine excludes any possibility of a God who existed as God *"from everlasting to everlasting"* (**Psalm 90:2**.) Yes, the eternal nature/essence of the LDS and Biblical Jesus is very different.

### Biblical Warning About Believing in a Different Jesus

**2 Corinthians 11:3-4,** *"But I fear, lest by any means, as the serpent beguiled Eve through his subtlety, so your minds should be corrupted from the simplicity that is in Christ. For if he that cometh preacheth another Jesus, whom we have not preached, or if ye receive another spirit, which ye have not received, or another gospel, which ye have not accepted, ye might well bear with him."*

Each warning voiced by Paul in 2 Cor. 11:3-4 applies to Mormonism. The LDS Church preaches a different Jesus, promotes another spirit, and teaches a different gospel. As the serpent beguiled Eve through his subtlety, even so many people today are being led astray by the deceptions of Mormonism.

### How Important Is It?

According to Jesus, a person cannot put their trust in a different Jesus and be saved.

**John 8:24,** *"I [Jesus] said therefore unto you, that ye shall die in your sins: for if ye believe not that I am he, ye shall die in your sins."* (See also **John 8:28, 58.**)

### Who Did Jesus Claim to Be?

In John 8, Jesus claimed to be the 'I AM' or the LORD *(Jehovah God of the Old Testament.)*

**John 8:58,** *"Jesus said unto them, Verily, verily, I say unto you, Before Abraham was, I am."*

Consider the LORD's inspired comments as recorded by the prophet Isaiah.

| THE MORMON JESUS/JEHOVAH | THE BIBLICAL JESUS/JEHOVAH |
|---|---|
| • Is one god among many gods (Jesus is just one god in a long succession of gods) | • Jesus/Jehovah is the only God (Isaiah 43:10, 44:6-8, and Jude 1:24-25, John 8:58) |
| • Is not really the Most High or the Almighty God (Jesus is not as powerful as the Gods above him) | • Jesus/Jehovah is the Most High, the Almighty God (Psalm 91:1-2, 9; Revelation 1:7-8, 4:8) |
| • He has not eternally been God (Jesus had to earn godhood by keeping the LDS gospel laws) | • Jesus/Jehovah has eternally been God (John 1:1-2, Micah 5:2, & Psalm 90:1-2) |
| • He is our oldest brother (Jesus is the firstborn of our Heavenly Father & Mother in the pre-mortal existence) | • Jesus/Jehovah is our creator and our God (John 1:3, Revelation 4:8-11) |
| • He is the spirit brother of Lucifer (Jesus is Satan's spirit brother in the LDS pre-mortal existence) | • Jesus/Jehovah is the Creator of Lucifer (John 1:3, Colossians 1:16-17, Ezekiel 28:12-16) |
| • He created only this earth and with the assistance of others (Many of God's noble sons assisted Jesus in creation) | • Jesus/Jehovah created everything that exists—alone, by himself (John 1:3, Colossians 1:16-17, Isaiah 44:24) |
| • He didn't really create anything, he only organized existing matter (All matter is eternal so nothing was created 'ex nihilo'—out of nothing) | • Jesus/Jehovah spoke all of creation into existence—'ex nihilo'—from nothing (Genesis 1, Psalm 33:6-9, Hebrews 11:3) |
| • He cannot be omnipresent—everywhere present (Because he is a man and has a physical body, he cannot be omnipresent) | • Jesus/Jehovah is omnipresent— everywhere present (John 3:13; Matthew 18:20, 28:20; Hebrews 13:5, Jeremiah 23:23-24) |
| • He was not born of a virgin (Jesus was begotten naturally by an exalted man, Heavenly Father) | • Jesus/Jehovah was born of a virgin miraculously (Isaiah 7:14, Matthew 1:18-23) |

**FIGURE 10.1**

**Isaiah 43:10-12,** *"Ye are my witnesses, saith the LORD, and my servant whom I have chosen: that ye may know and believe me, and understand that I am he: before me there was no God formed, neither shall there be after me. I, even I, am the LORD; and beside me there is no Saviour. I have declared, and have saved... therefore ye are my witnesses, saith the LORD, that I am God."*

**Isaiah 44:6, 8,** *"Thus saith the LORD the King of Israel, and his redeemer the LORD of hosts; I am the first, and I am the last; and beside me there is no God ... Fear ye not, neither be afraid: have not I told thee from that time, and have declared it? Ye are even my witnesses. Is there a God beside me? Yea, there is no God; I know not any."*

These statements, made by the LORD God Himself make it clear that He is the only true God. Mormonism denies what Jesus is claiming in John 8:24, 28, 58—they do not believe He is the 'I AM' of the Old Testament, the one and only true God.

The LDS Jesus is NOT the Jesus of the Bible. The LDS Jesus is not the only true and living God. According to Jesus, unless you believe He is who he claimed to be, you will die in your sins.

### Does Jesus Know You?

If you do not know the Jesus of the Bible, then it follows, He does not know you. One of the most horrifying statements in the Bible is found in Matthew chapter 7.

**Matthew 7:21-23,** *"Not every one that saith unto me, Lord, Lord, shall enter into the kingdom of heaven; but he that doeth the will of my Father which is in heaven. Many will say to me in that day, Lord, Lord, have we not prophesied in thy name? And in thy name have cast out devils? And in thy name done many wonderful works? And then will I profess unto them, I never knew you: depart from me, ye that work iniquity."*

It is vitally important that you know the Jesus of the Bible and that He knows you!

**QUESTIONS FOR REVIEW**

In your opinion, can an LDS person be saved by placing their faith in the Jesus of Mormonism?

What do you consider to be the most important differences between the LDS Jesus and the Biblical Jesus from Figure 10.1.

STOP and THINK about the message of Jesus in Matthew 7:21-23.

What were these people putting their trust in for their salvation?

What were these people missing?

How do we obey Jesus and do *"the will of [His] Father in heaven?"* (See *John 6:27-29*.)

# SECTION **38**
# Are We All Children of God?

🛑 Turn to the Glossary of Mormon Terms and read the LDS definitions of 'Heavenly Father', 'Heavenly Parents', and 'Pre-Mortal Life or Preexistence'.

### God Is the Father of All Creation

God is the Father of creation in much the same sense as George Washington is the father of our country or Henry Ford is the father of the Model T

Ford. George did not literally give birth to the USA and Henry did not literally give birth to the Model T Ford. Even so, God is the Father of all created things in a figurative but not literal sense.

## The Bible

**Malachi 2:10,** *"Have we not all one father? Hath not one God created us?"*

## The Book of Mormon

**1 Nephi 17:36,** *"Behold, the Lord hath created the earth that it should be inhabited; and he hath created his children that they should possess it."*

## God Does Not Regard All Of Mankind As His Children

In the Bible, God views rebellious creatures as children of wrath or children of the Devil, who is the father of rebellion. Neither Christians nor Mormons would take the following statements literally, as if Satan actually gave birth to human beings. These individuals are figuratively children of the Devil by choice.

**John 8:44,** *"Ye are of your father the devil, and the lusts of your father ye will do. He was a murderer from the beginning, and abode not in the truth, because there is no truth in him. When he speaketh a lie, he speaketh of his own: for he is a liar, and the father of it."*

**Hebrews 12:7-8,** *"If ye endure chastening, God dealeth with you as with sons; for what son is he whom the father chasteneth not? But if ye be without chastisement, whereof all are partakers, then are ye bastards, and not sons."*

## Becoming Children of God

As you study the scriptures, you will find that being recognized as a child of God is a granted privilege. The LDS religion, however, states all people are the genetic offspring of Deity in a literal sense. The obvious question to ask a Mormon would then be, 'Why do we have to become children of God if you believe we already are children of God?'

## The Bible

**John 1:12,** *"But as many as received him, to them gave he power to become the sons of God, even to them that believe on his name."*

**1 John 3:1,** *"Behold, what manner of love the Father hath bestowed upon us, that we should be called the sons of God."*

## The Book of Mormon

**Moroni 7:26, 48,** *"And after that he came men also were saved by faith in his name; and by faith, they become the sons of God... Wherefore, my beloved brethren, pray unto the Father with all the energy of heart, that ye may be filled with this love, which he hath bestowed upon all who are true followers of his Son, Jesus Christ; that ye may become the sons of God."*

## Believers Are Adopted By God Into His Eternal Family

The Bible tells us all believers are adopted into God's family. Once again, the question could be asked, "If we are literal children of God, why does God adopt those who believe?" Parents do not need to adopt their own children!

**Romans 8:9, 14-16,** *"But ye are not in the flesh, but in the Spirit, if so be that the Spirit of God dwell in you. Now if any man have not the Spirit of Christ, he is none of his... For as many as are led by the Spirit of God, they are the sons of God. For ye have not received the spirit of bondage again to fear; but ye have received the Spirit of adoption, whereby we cry, Abba, Father, The Spirit itself beareth witness with our spirit, that we are the children of God."*

**Ephesians 1:3-5,** *"Blessed be the God and Father of our Lord Jesus Christ, who hath blessed us with all spiritual blessings in heavenly places in Christ: According as he hath chosen us in him before the foundation of the world, that we should be holy and without blame before him in love: Having predestinated us unto the adoption of children by Jesus Christ to himself, according to the good pleasure of his will."*

**Are all people children of God figuratively or literally?**

**What Biblical doctrines would be compromised if we were literally the genetic children of God, little gods in the making?**

**Does God recognize all human beings as his children?**

**How do people become children of God?**

# SECTION 39
# We will be like Him, But will we be Gods?

🛑 **Turn to the Glossary of Mormon Terms and read the LDS definitions of 'Godhood' and 'Endowment'.**

LDS people try to use the Biblical phrase, *'We will be like Him'* to say we will someday become Gods, just like the LDS Heavenly Father. They will say, "We are all children of God. Don't you expect your children to grow up to be like you?"

To support these thoughts they may ask:

- What does a kitten grow up to be? A cat.

- What does a puppy grow up to be? A dog.

- So, sons of God will grow up to be? Gods.

While this argument might sound logical, it is humanistic idea that does not agree with either the Bible or the Book of Mormon.

## We Shall Be Like Him
## The Bible

**1 John 3:1-3,** *"Behold, what manner of love the Father hath bestowed upon us, that we should be called the sons of God: therefore the world knoweth us not, because it knew him not. Beloved, now are we the sons of God, and it doth not yet appear what we shall be: but we know that, when he shall appear, we shall be like him; for we shall see him as he is. And every man that hath this hope in him purifieth himself, even as he is pure."*

First, it should be noted in verse 1 that it is an honor which God has bestowed upon mankind to be called the sons of God. We are not naturally sons of God, we become sons of God when we receive Jesus Christ as our Savior (see **John 1:12**.)

Secondly, the context of this passage does not say we will become gods just like our Heavenly Father. In accordance with the context, becoming like Him is in reference to one day becoming sinlessly perfect so we can stand in the presence of God and look upon his perfect holiness.

## The Book of Mormon

Interestingly, the Book of Mormon supports this interpretation perfectly.

**Moroni 7:48,** *"Wherefore, my beloved brethren, pray unto the Father with all the energy of heart, that ye may be filled with this love, which he hath bestowed upon all who are true followers of his Son, Jesus Christ; that ye may become the sons of God; that when he shall appear we shall be like him, for we shall see him as he is; that we may have this hope; that we may be purified even as he is pure. Amen."*

## No New Gods

And remember, according to God, there will never be any new gods.

**Isaiah 43:10,** *"Ye are my witnesses, saith the* LORD, *and my servant whom I have chosen: that ye may know and believe me, and understand that I am he: before me there was no God formed, neither shall there be after me."*

## QUESTIONS FOR REVIEW

**In your own words, explain what the Apostle John meant when he said, 'We will be like Him'.**

**According to the Bible, why can't John's statement, 'We will be like Him', mean that we will become Gods just like God the Father?**

# SECTION 40

# Is God Fair?

🛑 **Turn to the Glossary of Mormon Terms and read the LDS definitions of 'Baptism for the Dead', 'Millennium, The' and 'Spirit World'.**

## The LDS Question

Mormons will often ask, "Would God be fair to send people to hell if they never had a chance to hear the gospel?" This question has in mind the justice of God. The LDS implication is, "Our Heavenly Father would never do that!"

## LDS Solutions

- **Three Heavens/Degrees of Glory**

LDS doctrine tries to solve this moral dilemma in two ways. First, according to Mormonism, due to the universal atonement of Christ, virtually all of humanity will spend eternity in one of three Mormon Heavens. Mormons will ask, "What kind of a God would send his children to a fiery Hell?"

🛑 **Turn to the Glossary of Mormon Terms and read the LDS definition of 'Heaven'.**

- **Temple Works for the Dead**

Secondly, for those who did not have the opportunity to accept Mormonism in this life and are now being held in the LDS 'Spirit Prison'—all is not lost. There is still hope for those who are dead because of the LDS practice of 'temple works for the dead'.

LDS people are required to search for the names of departed non-Mormons in their genealogy centers. Each year millions of proxy baptisms and temple ordinances are performed by Mormons in LDS temples for these departed souls. If the dead persons in spirit prison accept the temple works performed in their behalf they can then begin their work toward exaltation and godhood in the afterlife.

## The LDS Religion Makes Their God Fair

In the mind of a Mormon, these LDS solutions make God fair. In Mormonism, everyone has a chance, if not in this life, then in the next. And virtually everyone goes to a wonderful Heaven that God has prepared for all of His children.

The LDS religion hates the idea of eternal punishment. Mormon people will sometimes say, "Our God is much more merciful than your God. Our Heavenly Father loves all of his children and He would never send them to an eternal hell!"

## What About the 'Sons of Perdition?'

The LDS 'Sons of Perdition' are problematic for Mormons who don't want to believe in a literal, eternal, fiery hell.

68

What most Mormons never consider is the fact that, according to LDS doctrine, one-third of God's spirit children were judged to be 'sons of perdition' and destined for 'Outer Darkness' *(the LDS version of hell)* before this earth was created.

According to LDS theology, in the pre-mortal life, when Lucifer rebelled against God's decision to make Jesus the Savior of this world, all the spirit children that sided with Lucifer in 'the great war in Heaven' were cast out and never given a chance to repent. Before the world began, the LDS God judged and condemned one-third of his children to eternal 'Outer Darkness'.

## Is God Fair—The Biblical Answer

Is the God of Christianity fair? The Biblical answer is that God is indeed fair. If you are willing to believe by faith what the Bible says about God and His dealings with human beings, all of mankind does indeed have a chance. Consider the following Biblical statements that speak of God's justice and mercy.

## God is Not Responsible for Man's Sin

All men were created with a free will *(LDS free agency)* and the choices of man are not God's fault. In keeping with God's character, God has placed within man the knowledge he needs to understand the truths about God. God is faithful to reveal truth in spite of man's rebellious heart.

> **Romans 1:18-23,** *"For the wrath of God is revealed from heaven against all ungodliness and unrighteousness of men, who hold the truth in unrighteousness; **Because that which may be known of God is manifest in them; for God hath shewed it unto them**. For the invisible things of him from the creation of the world are clearly seen, being understood by the things that are made, even his eternal power and Godhead; so that they are without excuse: Because that, when they knew God, they glorified him not as God, neither were thankful; but became vain in their imaginations, and their foolish heart was darkened. Professing themselves to be wise,*

*they became fools, and changed the glory of the uncorruptible God into an image made like to corruptible man."*

## The Spirit of God Reproves the World

**John 16:8-11,** *"And when he [the Holy Ghost/Spirit] is come, **he will reprove the world of sin, and of righteousness, and of judgment**: Of sin, because they believe not on me; Of righteousness, because I go to my Father, and ye see me no more; Of judgment, because the prince of this world is judged."*

## God Placed 'Faith' Within Every Man

**Romans 12:3,** *"For I say, through the grace given unto me, to every man that is among you, not to think of himself more highly than he ought to think; but to think soberly, according as **God hath dealt to every man the measure of faith**."*

## God's Will is that All Men be Saved

**2 Peter 3:9,** *"The Lord is not slack concerning his promise, as some men count slackness; but is longsuffering to us-ward, **not willing that any should perish**, but that all should come to repentance."*

## Jesus Christ Draws All Men

**John 12:32,** *"And I, if I be lifted up from the earth, **will draw all men unto me**."*

## Jesus is Knocking

**Revelation 3:20,** *"Behold I stand at the door, and knock: **if any man hear my voice, and open the door,** I will come in to him, and will sup with him, and he with me."*

## God's Promise—All Who Seek Will Find

**Matthew 7:7-8,** *"Ask, and it shall be given you; seek, and ye shall find; knock, and it shall be opened unto you: For every one that asketh receiveth; and he that seeketh findeth; and to him that knocketh it shall be opened."*

**Acts 17:27-28,** *"They should seek the Lord, if haply they might feel after him, and find him, though he be not far from every one of us: For in him we live, and move, and have our being."*

**Proverbs 8:17,** *"I love them that love me; and those that seek me early shall find me."*

**Jeremiah 29:12-14,** *"Then shall ye call upon me, and ye shall go and pray unto me, and I will hearken unto you. And ye shall seek me, and find me, when ye shall search for me with all your heart. And I will be found of you, saith the LORD..."*

**Deuteronomy 4:29,** *"Thou shalt seek the LORD thy God, thou shalt find him, if thou seek him with all thy heat and with all thy soul."*

## Whosoever Means You!

**Romans 10:13,** *"For whosoever shall call upon the name of the Lord shall be saved."*

## God's Plan is Sufficient

God has been at work with mankind since the beginning of time. No one is—or ever has been—outside of God's reach. God's plan of salvation has always been available to mankind because GOD IS FAIR! God brings circumstances (crisis' of belief) into everyone's life so as to cause them to question their direction in life. God's Spirit convicts the world (every person in the world) of their sins of rebellion against Him. Anyone who responds to the patient draw of God in their life and seeks for Him will find him.

Based on these facts, you can lovingly share the following invitation with your Mormon friend—According to God's word, those who have lived and died have had their opportunities. Right now God is giving you a chance to accept the gospel of Jesus Christ as recorded in the Bible. Will you accept it or reject it? After today, you can't say, "I never had a chance."

## The Biblical Gospel in a Nutshell

- Man's universal problem (**Romans 3:10-12, 23**)

- God's grace (**Romans 5:8, Romans 6:23**)

- God's way (**Romans 10:1-4,9-10; John 6:28-29**)

- God's free gift (**John 3:14-18; 1 John 5:9-13**)

- Only one way (**John 14:6, Acts 4:12**)

- Nothing can be added (**Ephesians 2:8-9; Romans 3:27-28; Galatians 2:16, 21**)

- Good works do not earn salvation (**Titus 3:8; John 15:1-5, 8; James 2:17-20**)

## QUESTIONS FOR REVIEW

**Why is it problematic for a Mormon to say the LDS Heavenly Father is so loving he would never send His children to eternal punishment in hell?**

**Why is it a matter of faith to believe that God will be fair to everyone?**

**Why can we say with confidence that no one will be able to stand in the judgment and tell God, "You never gave me a chance?"**

**Write out the plan of salvation using Biblical references to support each point.**

# CHAPTER 11
# GOSPEL TOPICS

# SECTION 41
# The 'Impossible Gospel'

🛑 **Turn to the Glossary of Mormon Terms and read the LDS definitions of 'Forgiveness', 'Perfection', and 'Repentance'.**

### The Impossible Gospel of Mormonism

The plan of salvation, as taught in the LDS scriptures, can be described as the 'Impossible Gospel'. As you will see, 'Impossible' is the perfect word to describe the 'restored gospel' of Mormonism. The Impossible Gospel witnessing method is an effective approach to use with LDS people. It is also a very complex approach and will require time and effort on your part to master it.

The best way to use the 'Impossible Gospel' method is to first have the Mormon read the pertinent passages from the LDS scriptures, then ask questions allowing them to define their own scriptures. This approach will take time, so don't rush it. Continue to ask leading questions until you are certain the person understands the full impact of each passage.

When Mormon people realize the direction you are leading them, they will attempt to change the subject. Do not let them sidetrack you! As they begin to feel the full weight of the LDS gospel law, they will often become noticeably uncomfortable—don't let up. Keep laying it on thick! Mormons must first come to realize that the LDS gospel is BAD NEWS before they will be ready to hear and accept the GOOD NEWS, the true gospel of Jesus Christ.

The 'Impossible Gospel' is presented in outline form and uses Mormon scriptures as discussion starters, followed by questions to ask your LDS friend. Probable LDS objections are listed as well as appropriate answers that lead to the next point in your discussion.

The Impossible Gospel witnessing method follows this basic outline:

1. **Sinless perfection is required (Moroni 10:32, 2 Nephi 25:23, Alma 11:37.)**

2. **You can do it! You can stop sinning (1 Nephi 3:7.)**

3. **True repentance means you have stopped sinning (Doctrine and Covenants 58:42-43 D&C 1:31-33, D&C 82:7.)**

4. **You must stop sinning in this life (Alma 34:30-35.)**

**NOTE:** It is not always necessary to use every verse in every discussion, and at times you may want to alter the order in which these verses are used. Every person is unique so don't hesitate to adjust your approach to fit the person with whom you are talking.

A Special 'Impossible Gospel' reference guide has been created by TGM which features the key LDS scriptures and quotes from LDS sources which support the literal interpretation of each passage.

👁 **Go to: TriGrace.org**
**Under 'Resources' find and print the free PDF download of *Miracle of Forgiveness Reference Guide*. Then watch the TGM Tutorial explaining how to use this Visual Aid with Mormon people.**

**BEFORE YOU BEGIN:** It does not take a rocket scientist to understand the 'Impossible Gospel' witnessing method, but it does require a tenacious evangelist to implement this approach effectively with LDS people. We intentionally did not try to shorten or simplify what an 'Impossible Gospel' discussion might look like because we want you to have a view of how this witnessing method works in the real world.

Everyone who has a desire to evangelize Mormons should at least understand this approach; but if you want to use this approach effectively, you will need to study through the details of the following discussion in depth. Don't become discouraged—this is well worth the effort for those who are serious about winning LDS people to the Lord.

For those who choose to invest the time and energy it takes to master this approach, the rewards will be very satisfying.

## Moroni 10:32

*"Yea, come unto Christ, and be perfected in him, and deny yourselves of all ungodliness; and **if** ye shall deny yourselves of **all ungodliness**, and love God with all your might, mind and strength, **then** is his grace sufficient for you, that by his grace ye may be perfect in Christ."*

**KEY POINTS** are: the 'IF/THEN' statement and 'ALL UNGODLINESS'.

## Questions and Possible LDS Responses:

A.  Do you see the if/then statement? Can you read it for me?
**Mormon Response:** If you deny yourselves of all ungodliness, and love God with all your might, mind and strength, then is his grace sufficient for you.

B.  What is required if you hope to receive Christ's grace?
**Mormon Response:** We need to deny ungodliness and love God.

C.  How much ungodliness must you deny? What does the passage say?
**Mormon Response:** (hesitates) All ungodliness?

D.  How fully are you to love God?
**Mormon Response:** (hesitates again) With all your might, mind and strength.

E.  How are you doing with that?
**Mormon Response:** What do you mean?

F.  Well, if you are required to 'deny yourself of all ungodliness and love God with all your might

mind and strength', I am curious how you are doing. Have you denied yourself of all ungodliness?
**Mormon Response:** (hesitates again) Well, I am trying.

G.  Does that mean you have or you haven't denied yourself of all ungodliness?
**Mormon Response:** I don't know what you mean. I said I am trying.

H.  Okay, answer this for me: If you denied yourself of all ungodliness, what would your life look like? I mean, if you had no ungodliness in your life, what would you be?
**Mormon Response:** Well, I guess I would be perfect?

I.  Right, so how are you doing? Have you denied yourself of all ungodliness? Is your life perfect?
**Mormon Response:** No one is perfect!

J.  But this passage says you must deny yourself of all ungodliness which would mean you must perfect your life.
**Mormon Response:** That is impossible, no one is perfect!

K.  So, are you telling me this verse is not true?
**Mormon Response:** No, this verse is true; we need to try to deny ourselves of all ungodliness.

L.  Oh, I didn't realize the verse said that. Let's read it again together, *"If ye shall deny yourselves of all ungodliness, and love God with all your might, mind and strength, then is his grace sufficient for you."* It looks to me like you first must deny yourself of all ungodliness. I don't see where it says you merely try to do this.
**Mormon Response:** Well, that's what I think it means.

M.  Think about it this way. When you were a kid, and your mom said, "If you eat all your vegetables, then you will get your desert" what did you have to do to get your desert?
**Mormon Response:** I had to eat my vegetables.

N.  How many of your vegetables?
**Mormon Response:** All my vegetables.

O. I think you see my point. This verse says if you deny yourself of all ungodliness, then you will receive Christ's grace.

*(At this point you can show them a quote from an LDS source that supports your interpretation. See 'The Miracle of Forgiveness Reference Guide'—or move on to the next LDS scripture passage.)*

**Christian:** If you will humor me for a minute, I think there is another verse in the Book of Mormon which seems to support the idea that you must do something before you receive Christ's grace. Will you read **2 Nephi 25:23** with me?

## 2 Nephi 25:23

> *"We labor diligently to write, to persuade our children, and also our brethren, to believe in Christ, and to be reconciled to God; for we know that it is by grace that we are saved, **after all we can do.**"*

**KEY POINT:** 'AFTER ALL WE CAN DO'.

## Questions and Possible LDS Responses:

A. So, when does the saving grace apply to your life?
**Mormon Response:** It says, 'after all we can do'.

B. Right, so Christ's grace doesn't apply until after you have done all you can do first?
**Mormon Response:** Well, I guess it depends on how you interpret it. One of my professors at BYU said this verse could be interpreted to say, "We know that it is by grace that we are saved, in spite of all we can do." I believe if we do our best, Christ will do the rest.

C. So you think 'after' means 'in spite of'? When your mom said, "After you eat all of your vegetables, then you get your desert" did she mean, 'In spite of the fact that you are not eating your vegetables, I will still give you your desert'.
**Mormon Response:** Well, umm, I don't know...

D. So, you think **2 Nephi 25:23** should say, *"We know that it is by grace that you are saved, in spite of the fact that you are still an unclean sinner."*

**Mormon Response:** We are supposed to do our best. God knows if we are doing all we can do.

E. The real question is, what is all you can do?
**Mormon Response:** I already told you, I am only required to do my best.

F. I don't want to sound like a broken record, but you remember that **Moroni 10:32** said, *"If you deny yourself of all ungodliness... then is his grace sufficient"*, and this verse says we are saved by Christ's grace *"after all we can do."*
**Mormon Response:** I already told you I am trying. You are just picking out a couple of passages and trying to make me look bad.

*(When you feel certain the point has been made you can either show them a quote from an LDS source that supports your interpretation—see The 'Miracle of Forgiveness Reference Guide'—or move on to the next LDS scripture passage.)*

**Christian:** Please forgive me. I really am not trying to judge you. I am trying to understand how this all works for an LDS person. I did find another passage that I think says basically the same thing. Will you read Alma 11:37 with me?

## Alma 11:37

> *"And I say unto you again that he cannot save them **in their sins**; for I cannot deny his word, and he hath said that **no unclean thing** can inherit the kingdom of heaven; therefore, how can ye be saved, except ye inherit the kingdom of heaven? Therefore, ye cannot be saved **in your sins.**"*

**KEY POINTS:** 'NO UNCLEAN THING' and 'IN YOUR SINS'.

## Questions and Possible LDS Responses:

A. This verse says God cannot save you in your sins, so what do you think that means?
**Mormon Response:** As I said before, I think it means that we are supposed to do the best we can.

B. But if you are still 'in your sins', wouldn't that make you 'unclean'? This verse says 'no unclean thing' can inherit the kingdom of Heaven.

73

**Mormon Response:** Like I said, we do our best and Christ does the rest.

C.   I am not sure you understand my point. Will you read this verse again with me? *"And I say unto you again that he cannot save them in their sins; for I cannot deny his word, and he hath said that no unclean thing can inherit the kingdom of heaven; therefore, how can ye be saved, except ye inherit the kingdom of heaven? Therefore, ye cannot be saved in your sins."* What do you think 'in your sins' means?

**Mormon Response:** I guess it means you are still sinning.

D.   I have to ask again, how are you doing? Have you stopped sinning?

**Mormon Response:** This is crazy! What you are requiring is impossible! No one is perfect!

E.   You know the difference between IN and OUT, don't you? If you are IN your sins you are still sinning; if you are OUT—you are not sinning. So are you IN or OUT of your sins?

**Mormon Response:** What you are implying would be impossible.

*(Again, if you think a quote from an LDS source would strengthen your case there are some amazing quotes in the 'Miracle of Forgiveness Reference Guide'. Be sure to check them out. Or you can move on to the next LDS scripture passage.)*

F.   It sounds like you believe it is impossible to do what God requires. I have another verse I would like for you to explain to me.

**INTERESTING NOTE:** The next verse, 1 Nephi 3:7, is an LDS SCRIPTURE MASTERY VERSE, so all active Mormons should have this verse memorized. Challenge them to quote the verse for you. If they need some help, give them the first line to get them started. This is a fun exercise that will help to loosen up your conversation.

## 1 Nephi 3:7

*"And it came to pass that I, Nephi, said unto my father: I will go and do the things which the Lord hath commanded, for I know that the*

*Lord giveth no commandments unto the children of men, save **he shall prepare a way** for them that they may **accomplish the thing which he commandeth** them'.*

**KEY POINT:** 'HE SHALL PREPARE A WAY and ACCOMPLISH the thing which he COMMANDETH'.

## Questions and Possible LDS Responses:

A.   According to this verse, has God given you any commandments that you cannot keep?

**Mormon Response:** (hesitates) No.

B.   Then why do you keep insisting that it is impossible for you to keep God's commandments? If God commands you to 'deny yourself of all ungodliness', can you?

**Mormon Response:** (hesitates) I already told you, I think you are misinterpreting that passage.

C.   I have some questions for you: If you are tempted to lie, do you have to lie or could you tell the truth?

**Mormon Response:** I could tell the truth.

D.   If you are tempted to steal, do you have to steal or could you do the right thing and not steal?

**Mormon Response:** I could do the right thing.

E.   If you are tempted to commit adultery, do you have to sin or could you refrain?

**Mormon Response:** I could refrain.

F.   Is there any commandment you cannot keep?

**Mormon Response:** No, I guess not. If I try really hard, I can keep the commandments.

G.   If you can keep God's commandments, it should be possible for you to stop sinning, right?

**Mormon Response:** Yeah, I guess it might be theoretically possible.

H.   So, how are you doing?

**Mormon Response:** I already told you that I am trying. God knows I am doing the best that I can.

I.   When you say you are trying, it sounds to me like you are admitting you are still sinning. It seems like you don't really believe it is possible to keep God's commandments.

**Mormon Response:** There is a doctrine in our church called repentance, and because God knows we are not perfect he allows us to repent. Like I said, we do our best and Christ does the rest.

(**NOTE:** This is the point in the conversation where you NEED to start using some of the quotes outlined in the *'Miracle of Forgiveness Reference Guide'*. LDS prophets have eliminated all the loopholes Mormon people like to use to justify their sins. Using these quotes will greatly strengthen your position. Several of these quotes are outlined under **D&C 58:42-43**.)

## Doctrine and Covenants 58:42-43

*"Behold, he who has repented of his sins, the same is forgiven, and I, the Lord, remember them no more. By this ye may know if a man repenteth of his sins—behold, he will confess them and forsake them'.*

**KEY POINT:** 'He will confess them and FORSAKE THEM'.

## Questions and Possible LDS Responses:

A.  According to this verse, how can you tell when a person has truly repented?
**Mormon Response:** It says you will confess your sins and forsake them.

B.  What do you think 'forsake them' means?
**Mormon Response:** Well, I guess it means that you need to stop sinning.

C.  Stop sinning? Do you mean like stop sinning permanently?
**Mormon Response:** (hesitates) Yes, I guess, but we are only expected to try our best.

D.  When a person says their wedding vows, they promise to be faithful to their spouse, 'forsaking all others'—MOST OF THE TIME? Would it be okay to spend one night each year with an old boyfriend/girlfriend? NO WAY! They are expected to forsake all others all of the time, right?
**Mormon Response:** Okay yes, we are expected to stop sinning permanently.

E.  So, I have to ask you again, how are you doing? Have you stopped sinning permanently?

**Mormon Response:** All I can say is that I am doing my best; but I am human and occasionally I mess up, so I repent. If I mess up again, I just repent again. God knows how hard I am trying.

F.  Can I show you something I read in *Gospel Principles (LDS Church Manual)*, chapter 19?
It says, "'We Must Forsake Our Sins'—*Our sincere sorrow should lead us to forsake (stop) our sinning... If we truly repent of our sins, we will do them no more... The Lord said to the Prophet Joseph Smith: 'By this ye may know if a man repents of his sins—behold. he will confess them and forsake them'* (**D&C 58:43**.)"

President Kimball said this about the "'Abandonment of Sin'—And the Lord said: 'By this ye may know if a man repenteth of his sins—behold, he will... forsake them'. (D&C 58:43.) The forsaking of sin must be a permanent one. True repentance does not permit making the same mistake again." *(Repentance Brings Forgiveness, Spencer W. Kimball, published by the LDS Church, 1984.)*

If this is true, there really is no such thing as 'repent again'—you either truly repent, which means you stop sinning, or you don't repent, and you keep sinning.
**Mormon Response:** You are completely misinterpreting what the LDS Church teaches. God knows we are not perfect so he allows us to repent, and if we are trying, God will forgive us.

Can I show you a story I read in the *The Miracle of Forgiveness, by Spencer Kimball*? On page 163, the title of the chapter is, 'Abandonment of Sin', and **D&C 58:43** is quoted. Then on page 164 it says,
**"Trying Is Not Sufficient**... A story will perhaps illustrate this. An army officer called a soldier to him and ordered him to take a message to another officer. The soldier saluted and said, "I'll try, sir! I'll try!" To this the officer responded: *"I don't want you to try*, I want you to deliver this message." The soldier, somewhat embarrassed, now replied: "I'll do the best I can, sir." At this the officer, now disgusted, rejoined with some vigor: *"I don't want you to try* and I don't want you to 'do the

best you can'. I want you to deliver this message." Now the young soldier, straightening to his full height, approached the matter magnificently, as he thought, when he saluted again and said: "I'll do it or die, sir." To this the now irate officer responded: "I don't want you to die, and I don't want you merely to do the best you can, and I don't want you to try. Now, the request is a reasonable one; the message is important; the distance is not far; you are able-bodied; you can do what I have ordered. Now get out of here and accomplish your mission."

Spencer Kimball followed this story with, "To "try" is weak. To "do the best I can" is not strong. We must always do *better* than we can. This is true in every walk of life."

If what Spencer Kimball says is true, it is not okay to just try or to merely do the best you can, you need to truly repent which means you must stop sinning. This agrees with **Moroni 10:32**, *"Deny yourself of all ungodliness"*, and **Alma 11:37**, *"You cannot be saved in your sins."*
**Mormon Response:** I don't care what you show me. I know what my Church teaches, and I can repent every day if I need to.

H. When you tell me that you can repent every day—have you thought about what that really means? If you need to repent every day, then what are you doing every day?
**Mormon Response:** (hesitates) I guess it means I am sinning.

I. Right, do you think it pleases God when you sin every day? Joseph Smith said this,
> *"Repentance is a thing that cannot be trifled with every day. Daily transgression and daily repentance is not that which is pleasing in the sight of God." (Teachings of the Prophet Joseph Smith, Joseph Fielding Smith, p. 148.)*
**Mormon Response:** I don't care what you say, I know Heavenly Father loves us, and I think he will demonstrate mercy because he knows I am trying my hardest.

**Christian:** It sounds to me like you don't really take your sins very seriously. It sounds like you don't think God takes your sins very seriously, like He can just overlook your sins. I think you need to see **D&C 1:31-33**.

## Doctrine and Covenants 1:31-33

> *"For I the Lord cannot look upon sin with **the least degree of allowance;** Nevertheless, he that repents and does the commandments of the Lord shall be forgiven; And he that repents not, from him shall be taken even the light which he has received; for my Spirit shall not always strive with man, saith the Lord of Hosts."*

**KEY POINT:** 'The Lord cannot look upon sin with THE LEAST DEGREE OF ALLOWANCE'.

## Questions and Possible LDS Responses:

A. What do you think the Lord means when he says, *"I the Lord cannot look upon sin with the least degree of allowance?"* If you believe the Lord is going to demonstrate mercy while you are still 'in your sins', what sins do you think he will allow?
**Mormon Response:** I see where you are going with this. You are trying to put a huge guilt trip on me, aren't you? So, do you think you are perfect?

B. First, NO, I am not trying to 'put a guilt trip on you'. All I am showing you is what your Church teaches. If that makes you feel guilty, it's not my fault. Your scriptures and the teachings of your prophets make you feel guilty—not me. Second, NO, I am not perfect; but I am also not a Mormon, so these scriptures don't apply to me.
**Mormon Response:** Why are you using the LDS scriptures if you don't believe them?

C. Because you are LDS, and you are supposed to believe your scriptures. But you don't sound like you believe what your Church teaches at all.
**Mormon Response:** You are wrong. I know my Church is the only true Church, and I know Joseph Smith was a prophet of God, and I know the scriptures of my Church were inspired by God.

D. If what you just said is true, then why are you fighting against your scriptures and the teachings

76

of your prophets? If you truly believe what your Church teaches, you will humble yourself and admit that you are not doing what has been commanded. You are a sinner!

**Mormon Response:** You are right. I am a sinner and I need to try harder. If I try really hard I will be able to stop sinning. I just have to try harder!

E.   Thank you for being honest with me.

**Christian:** I only have a couple more passages that I have questions about. Will you look at D&C 82:7 with me?

## Doctrine and Covenants 82:7

*"And now, verily I say unto you, I, the Lord, will not lay any sin to your charge; go your ways and sin no more; but unto that soul who sinneth shall **the former sins return**, saith the Lord your God."*

**KEY POINT:** 'The former sins RETURN'.

## Questions and Possible LDS Responses:

A.   So, what happens when you think you have repented and then you sin again?
**Mormon Response:** I guess my former sins come back on me.

B.   So every time you mess up, all of your former sins get added to your account again?
**Mormon Response:** Yeah, I guess so.

C.   I have heard this idea described like a ladder. As you obey the commandments, it is like you are climbing a ladder. The only way you will be saved to the highest degree is if you climb to the top of the ladder. But when you mess up, you slip—and you don't just slip down one rung on the ladder—you slip all the way to the bottom and have to start over. Have you ever heard that story?
**Mormon Response:** (very sober) Yes.

D.   So if what you have been telling me is true, every time you sin, you slip to the bottom of the ladder and have to start repentance all over again.
**Mormon Response:** Yeah, I guess so.

E.   Will you ever make it to the top of the ladder?
**Mormon Response:** I just have to try harder.

F.   So, whose fault is it that you keep messing up?
**Mormon Response:** Mine, but I don't have to completely perfect myself in this life. I can always repent in the Spirit World.

G.   Can you tell me about that?
**Mormon Response:** Yeah, it is a place we go after we die where we can complete our repentance. I should try my hardest in this life; but if I have done my best and I still fall short, I can always repent in the Spirit World.

**Christian:** I only have one more scripture to show you. Are you up for one more passage?

**NOTE:** Christian evangelists call this passage 'THE HAMMER' because its implications are horrific for Mormon people. I have watched the blood literally drain from LDS people's faces as they come to understand the consequences of delaying their repentance until death.

## Alma 34:32-35

*"Behold, **this life** is the time for men to prepare to meet God; yea, behold **the day of this life** is the day for men to perform their labors. And now, as I said unto you before, as ye have had so many witnesses, therefore, I beseech of you that ye **do not procrastinate** the day of your repentance until the end; for after **this day of life**, which is given us to prepare for eternity, behold, if we do not improve our time while **in this life**, then cometh the night of darkness wherein there can be no labor performed. Ye cannot say, when ye are brought to that awful crisis, that I will repent, that I will return to my God. Nay, ye cannot say this; for that same spirit which doth possess your bodies at the time that ye go out of **this life**, that same spirit will have power to possess your body in that eternal world. For behold, **if ye have procrastinated** the day of your repentance even until death, behold, ye have become subjected to the spirit of the devil, and he doth seal you his; therefore, the Spirit of the Lord hath withdrawn from you, and hath no place in you, and the devil hath all power over you; and this is the final state of the wicked."*

**KEY POINTS:** 'IN THIS LIFE', and
'PROCRASTINATE the day of YOUR REPENTANCE'

## Questions and Possible LDS Responses:

A.   This passage sounds like you have to complete your repentance in 'this life'. Count with me how many times the author emphasizes this point—four times he says you must complete your repentance in 'this life'.

**Mormon Response:** *(a bit desperate)* I know what my Church teaches, and my Church teaches that we can repent in the spirit world!

B.   Let me show you another quote from *The Miracle of Forgiveness*,

> *"Repent in Mortality – I have referred previously to the significance of this life in the application of repentance but will emphasize it here in relation to the eventual judgment. One cannot delay repentance until the next life, the spirit world, and there prepare properly for the day of judgment… Men and women who live in mortality and who have heard the gospel here have had their day, their seventy years to put their lives in harmony, to perform the ordinances, to repent and to perfect their lives… It is true that repentance is always worth while. But spirit world repentance cannot recompense for that which could and should have been done on earth" (The Miracle of Forgiveness, pg. 313-315.)*

This seems very clear—Latter-day Saints, who know better, must repent now. They must 'Repent in Mortality' in 'this life'.

**Mormon Response:** Prophets can have their own opinions, not everything spoken by a prophet was necessarily inspired by God.

C.   I don't get it—Every Mormon says the most wonderful thing about the LDS Church is the fact that you have living prophets. Yet you don't seem to believe what your prophets tell you.

**Mormon Response:** We do believe our prophets! I just don't understand why Spencer Kimball said what he did.

D.   You know what it means to 'procrastinate' don't you? Why do you think it says, "I beseech of you that ye do not procrastinate the day of your repentance until the end?" Read it for yourself. 'The end' means the end of this life, doesn't it?

**Mormon Response:** *(unsure)* That is what it looks like.

E.   What happens to people who 'procrastinate their repentance even until death'?

> *"For behold, if ye have procrastinated the day of your repentance even until death, behold, ye have become subjected to the spirit of the devil, and he doth seal you his; therefore, the Spirit of the Lord hath withdrawn from you, and hath no place in you, and the devil hath all power over you; and this is the final state of the wicked."*

What do you think it means when it says the devil 'doth seal you his?'

**Mormon Response:** I don't know.

F.   Don't check out on me here! This is important. All night long you have been telling me that you are trying to repent, which really means you are giving in to your sins and not truly repenting—you are 'procrastinating your repentance'! Look at this passage again and tell me what happens to people who procrastinate their repentance until death.

**Mormon Response:** I don't know!

G.   You don't know or you don't want to say?

**Mormon Response:** I said, I don't know!

**CHRISTIAN EVANGELIST, STOP HERE:** At this point your conversation can only go two directions.

**MORMON RESPONSE #1.**

The first possibility is VERY SAD—The Mormon may say, "Well I guess I need to try harder. I know I can repent if I try really hard, so that is what I am going to do. I know my Church is true, and I know Joseph Smith was a prophet, and I know the Book of Mormon is true. I am going to do what the prophets tell me to do. I don't want to talk anymore!"

**YOUR RESPONSE:** At this point you must leave your Mormon friend in the hands of God. The Holy

Spirit will never let them forget your conversation, and He will continue to convict them of their sins.

What you can do is attempt to **PRAY** with them and attempt to **SWAP CONTACT** information with them. No matter how hard they try, they will never perfect themselves. If you can stay in touch with them, you may have more chances to invest in their lives. The other thing you can do is to continue to pray for your new Mormon friend.

**MORMON RESPONSE #2.**

This possibility is VERY ENCOURAGING—The Mormon may say, "I will never make it! No matter how hard I try, I will never be able to perfect myself. It is hopeless."

**YOUR RESPONSE:** When a Mormon says this, you can smile and say, "I have some very good news for you; it is called the gospel of Jesus Christ. Jesus did not teach the things we have been discussing today. Jesus Christ's message is a message of hope and forgiveness. Would you like to know that your sins have been forgiven?"

THEN SHARE THE TRUE GOSPEL WITH THEM. If possible, introduce them to Jesus by praying the sinner's prayer with them. If they don't want to pray with you, explain that they can come to Jesus any time! 'Whosoever calls upon the name of the Lord shall be saved'. GLORY!

Before they leave, be sure to **SWAP CONTACT INFORMATION** with them and attempt to **PRAY** with them. Then continually pray for your new friend. You can be certain that God WILL do His work in their lives.

## The 'Impossible Gospel' Reference Guides

There are three basic LDS sources where we gathered the LDS quotes used in the Impossible Gospel Witnessing Method.

👁 **Go to: TriGrace.org**
**Under 'Resources' find and print the free PDF downloads for *Miracle of Forgiveness Reference Guide; True to the Faith Reference Guide*; and *Gospel Principles Reference Guide*.**

These Guides will provide the quotes Christian evangelists like to use with LDS people when they use the 'Impossible Gospel' witnessing method.

**1. *The Miracle of Forgiveness***

**2. *True to the Faith***

**3. *Gospel Principles, 1979 edition***

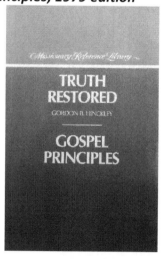

We strongly encourage you to purchase these resources for yourself @ Amazon.com – They are inexpensive and an invaluable resource when witnessing to LDS people.

## QUESTIONS FOR REVIEW

**What are the reasons for sharing the 'Impossible Gospel' with LDS people?**

**True or False? According to the LDS scriptures, is there such a phrase as 'repent again'?**

**Explain.**

**According to Mormon doctrine, before you are worthy to receive eternal life and enter the Celestial Kingdom, what must you do?**

# SECTION **42**
# 'The Miracle of Forgiveness' Quotes

🛑 **Turn to the Glossary of Mormon Terms and read the LDS definitions of 'Forgiveness', and 'Adultery' and 'Murder'.**

**NOTE**: For years the LDS book, *The Miracle of Forgiveness*, written by LDS Prophet Spencer W. Kimball, has been required reading for any Mormon who has been reprimanded for sinful behavior. I think you will be amazed by what you are about to read. I encourage you to purchase *The Miracle of Forgiveness*, mark the following quotes, and use them as you witness to LDS people. This book is supporting evidence for the 'Impossible Gospel' witnessing approach.

## *THE MIRACLE OF FORGIVENESS* QUOTES:

*"The Gospel Our Map*—The Lord Jesus Christ, our Redeemer and Savior, has given us our map—a code of laws and commandments whereby we might attain perfection and, eventually, godhood. This set of laws and ordinances is known as the gospel of Jesus Christ, and it is the only plan which will exalt mankind. The Church of Jesus Christ of Latter-day Saints is the sole repository of this priceless program in its fullness." (p. 6.)

### Sins of Commission

"While we lack recollection of our pre-mortal life, before coming to this earth all of us understood definitely the purpose of our being here… We were to eliminate sins of omission and of commission, and to follow the laws and commandments given us by our Father." (p. 5.)

### Scriptural List of Sins of Commission

"As we read the scriptures… we observe that they list virtually all the modern transgressions, though sometimes under ancient names. Let us review the lengthy list:
Murder, adultery, theft, cursing, unholiness in masters, disobedience in servants, unfaithfulness, improvidence, hatred of God, disobedience to husbands, lack of natural affection, high-mindedness, flattery, lustfulness, infidelity, indiscretion, backbiting, whispering, lack of truth, striking, brawling, quarrelsomeness, unthankfulness, inhospitality, deceitfulness, irreverence, boasting, arrogance, pride, double-tongued talk, profanity, slander [this is only about 1/3 of this lengthy list]… These are transgressions the Lord has condemned through his servants. Let no one rationalize his sins on the excuse that a particular sin of his is not mentioned nor forbidden in scripture." (p. 25.)

*"Sins of Omission* [failure to do what is right]—
'Therefore to him that knoweth to do good and doeth it not', warns James, 'to him it is sin'. (James 4:17.) And who 'knoweth to do good' better than Latter-day Saints?"(p. 91-92.)

**"Many Opportunities for Omission**—*Clearly the potential for sins of omission is as broad as the converse opportunity for righteousness. Let us consider some examples...*

*The home teacher... must not fail to teach...*

*Tithing is a law of God and is required...*

*The Sabbath is a holy day in which to do worthy and holy things...*

*To marry is an obligation...*

*To refuse to bear or refrain from the bearing of children is an error of omission...*

*To proselyte and warn our neighbors of the divinity of the gospel is a command...*

*Likewise, failing to fast is a sin...*

*Consider the Ten Commandments... One must actively love and serve the true and living God with total heart, might, mind and strength...*

*Excuses Irrelevant—Many and varied are the excuses for sins of omission, and they are all irrelevant...*

*Yes, sins of omission have much in common with those of commission. One common feature is their potential for damning the sinner."* (p. 96-101.)

**"As a Man Thinketh**—*Akin to Sins of Omission are 'Thought Sins'...*

*Even our thoughts will condemn us...*

*It is well for all of us to realize that our thought sins as well as all other sins are recorded in heaven...*

*The thought that stirred the look that provoked the lust was evil in its beginning. To want, to desire, to crave – that is to lust. So when the thought is born which starts a chain reaction, a sin has already been committed...*

*Man alone, of all creatures of earth, can change his thought pattern and become the architect of his destiny."* (p. 103-114.)

**"Abandonment of Sin**— *'By this ye may know if a man repenteth of his sins—behold, he will confess them and forsake them'. (Doctrine & Covenants 58:43.)*

*There is one crucial test of repentance. This is abandonment of the sin...*

**Desire Is Not Sufficient**—*In other words, it is not real repentance until one has abandoned the error of his way and started on a new path... The saving power does not extend to him who merely wants to change his life...*

**Trying Is Not Sufficient**—*[see the army officer story, p. 164]...*

*To 'try' is weak. To 'do the best I can' is not strong. We must always do better than we can. This is true in every walk of life...*

*The Lord's prophet Amulek had said emphatically: '...Ye cannot be saved in your sins'. (Alma 11:37.)"* (p. 163-165.)

**"Forgiveness Cancelled on Reversion to Sin**

*Old sins return, says the Lord in his modern revelations... 'Go your ways and sin no more', the Lord warned. And again, '...Unto that soul who sinneth shall the former sins return, saith the Lord your God'. (D&C 82:7.)...*

*Those who feel that they can sin and be forgiven and then return to sin and be forgiven again and again must straighten out their thinking. Each previously forgiven sin is added to the new one and the whole gets to be a heavy load.*

*Thus when a man has made up his mind to change his life, there must be no turning back... When one quits, he must quit."* (p. 169-170.)

**"Forgiveness by the church**—*Heavenly Father has promised forgiveness upon total repentance and meeting all the requirements, but that forgiveness is not granted merely for the asking. There must be works – many works – and an all-out, total surrender, with a great humility and 'a broken heart and a contrite spirit'.*

*It depends upon you whether or not you are forgiven, and when. It could be weeks, it could be years, it could be centuries before that happy day when you have the positive assurance that the Lord has forgiven you. That depends on your humility, your sincerity, your works, your attitudes."* (p. 324-325.)

## "Sanctification Through Overcoming—

**Alma 13:11-12**... indicates an attitude which is basic to the sanctification we should all be seeking, and thus to the repentance which merits forgiveness. It is that the former transgressor must have reached a 'point of no return' to sin wherein there is not merely a renunciation but also a deep abhorrence of the sin—where the sin becomes most distasteful to him and where the desire or urge to sin is cleared out of the life...

Impure people can perfect themselves and become pure." (p. 354-355.)

## "Faith and Works [The LDS view of Salvation by faith alone]—*It may be well to say a word about the idea of salvation by faith alone. Some people not of our Church like to quote, in support of that concept, the following words of Paul: 'For by grace are ye saved through faith; and that not of yourselves: it is the give of God: Not of works, lest any man should boast'. (Ephesians 2:8-9.)*

*One of the most fallacious doctrines originated by Satan and propounded by man is that man is saved alone by the grace of God; that belief in Jesus Christ alone is all that is needed for salvation...*

*Church members are fortunate indeed to have scriptures brought forth in this age which clarify this and other doctrinal questions beyond all doubt...*

*For we know that it is by grace, that we are saved, after all we can do. (2 Nephi 25:23.)*

*...However good a person's works, he could not be saved had Jesus not died for his and everyone else's sins. And, however powerful the saving grace of Christ, it brings exaltation to no man who does not comply with the works of the gospel."* (p. 206-207.)

## "Repentant Life Seeks Perfection—*One could multiply references almost indefinitely but enough has been said to establish the point that the repentant life, the life which constantly reaches for perfection, must rely on works as well as on faith. The gospel is a program of action—of doing things... Immortality has been accomplished by the Savior's sacrifice. Eternal life hangs in the balance awaiting the works of men.*

*This progress toward eternal life is a matter of achieving perfection. Living all the commandments guarantees total forgiveness of sins and assures one of exaltation through that perfection which comes by complying with the formula the Lord gave us. In his Sermon on the Mount he made the commandment to all men: 'Be ye therefore perfect, even as your Father which is in heaven is perfect'. (Matthew 5:48.) Being perfect means to triumph over sin. This is a mandate from the Lord. He is just and wise and kind. He would never require anything from his children which was not for their benefit and which was not attainable. Perfection therefore is an achievable goal...*

*Perfection really comes through overcoming...*

*Christ became perfect through overcoming. Only as we overcome shall we become perfect and move toward godhood. As I have indicated previously, the time to do this is now, in mortality."* (p. 208-210.)

*"EXALTATION, THE PINNACLE OF THE PROPER DESIRE OF MAN, comes to him only if he is clean and worthy and perfected. Since man is weak and sinful, he must be cleansed before he can reach the exalted state of eternal life, and such cleansing from personal sins comes only through forgiveness following repentance."* (p. 261.)

## "Dangers of Delay—

*Because men are prone to postpone action and ignore directions, the Lord has repeatedly given strict injunctions and issued solemn warnings... And the burden of the prophetic warning has been that the time to act is now, in this mortal life. One cannot with impunity delay his compliance with God's commandments. Note Amulek's words, especially those forceful statements involving timing... Alma 34:21-34 [is quoted...]*

*Even if we leave aside the many scriptures which bear similar testimony, reading and prayerfully meditating upon this one brings an awe-inspiring conviction of the need to repent—now!*

*...It is true that a merciful Father makes special post-mortal provision for those who do not hear the gospel in this life, but for the Latter-day Saints the time is now...*

*Should one not have had opportunities to hear and understand the gospel in this mortal life, that privilege will be given him hereafter...*

*'But wo unto him that has the law given, yea, that has all the commandments of God, like unto us, and that transgresseth them, and wasteth the days of his probation, for awful is his state!'* **(2 Nephi 9:27.)**

*...Thus for us who know but do not comply, the opportunities for certain limitless blessings have an end when death closes our eyes.*

*...This is the state of those who knowingly fail to live the commandments in this life. They will bring upon themselves their own hell*

*...As we have seen, one can wait too long to repent. Many of the Nephites did. Of these, Samuel the Lamanite said:*

*'But behold, your days of probation are past; ye have procrastinated the day of your salvation until it is everlastingly too late, and your destruction is made sure...'* **(Helaman 13:38.)**

*...And let us not suppose that in calling the people to repentance the prophets are concerned only with the more grievous sins such as murder, adultery, stealing, and so on, nor only with those persons who have not accepted the gospel ordinances. All transgression must be cleansed, all weaknesses must be overcome, before a person can attain perfection and godhood."* (p. 9-16.)

## "Repent in Mortality—

*I have referred previously to the significance of this life in the application of repentance but will emphasize it here in relation to the eventual judgment. One cannot*

*delay repentance until the next life, the spirit world, and there prepare properly for the day of judgment while the ordinance work is done for him vicariously on earth. It must be remembered that vicarious work for the dead is for those who could not do the work for themselves. Men and women who live in mortality and who have heard the gospel here have had their day, their seventy years to put their lives in harmony, to perform the ordinances, to repent and to perfect their lives...*

*It is true that repentance is always worth while. But spirit world repentance cannot recompense for that which could and should have been done on earth."* (p. 313-315.)

## QUESTIONS FOR REVIEW

**After reading Spencer Kimball's quotations, what is your impression of** *The Miracle of Forgiveness*?

**How do you think this book makes LDS people feel when they read it?**

**Is** *The Miracle of Forgiveness* **'Good News?'**

**Explain:**

# SECTION 43
# Attaining Biblical Perfection

**STOP** Turn to the Glossary of Mormon Terms and read the LDS definition of 'Perfection'.

The goal of every devout Mormon is to reach a state of sinless perfection. Mormon people are taught that perfection is a requirement before a person can receive forgiveness of sins and enter the Celestial Kingdom. The 'perfection' doctrine of Mormonism can be used as a motivation to get your Mormon friends to study the gospel of the Bible with you. Consider the following verse.

**2 Timothy 3:16-17,** *"All scripture is given by inspiration of God, and is profitable for doctrine, for reproof, for correction, for instruction in righteousness. That the man of God may be **perfect**, throughly furnished unto all good works."*

The Greek word translated 'perfect' in this passage does not imply sinless perfection but could be translated 'thoroughly equipped', implying spiritual maturity. This verse says the written Word of God is the key to understanding God's righteousness. Take this opportunity to show a Mormon from the Bible how a person can become righteous, be forgiven, become **perfect** and know for sure they have eternal life.

## Becoming Righteous

The word 'righteous' means 'right in God's sight'. If you are not righteous you are not right with God. Consider what the following verses have to say about 'righteousness'.

**Romans 3:10, 23,** *"There is none **righteous**, no, not one… [because] …all have sinned, and come short of the glory of God."*

**Romans 10:1-4,** *"Brethren, my heart's desire and prayer to God for Israel [LDS people] is, that they might be saved. For I bear them*

*record that they have zeal of God, but not according to knowledge. For they being ignorant of God's **righteousness**, and going about to establish their own **righteousness**, have not submitted themselves unto the **righteousness** of God. For Christ is the end of the law for **righteousness** to every one that believeth."*

**Romans 10:9-10, 13,** *"That if thou shalt confess with thy mouth the Lord Jesus, and shalt believe in thine heart that God hath raised him from the dead, thou shalt be saved. For with the heart man believeth unto **righteousness**; and with the mouth confession is made unto salvation… For whosoever shall call upon the name of the Lord shall be saved."*

**Romans 4:3, 5,** *"For what saith the scripture? Abraham believed God, and it was counted unto him for **righteousness**… But to him that worketh not, but believeth on him that justifieth the ungodly, his faith is counted for **righteousness**."* (See also **Romans 3:10-28** and **Galatians 3:1-14**.)

## Receiving Forgiveness of Sins

Forgiveness of sins, according the God's word is not a process, it is an event.

**Acts 10:42-43,** *"And he commanded us to preach unto the people, and to testify that it is he which was ordained of God to be the Judge of quick and dead. To him give all the prophets witness, that through his name whosoever believeth in him shall receive remission of sins."*

**Acts 13:38-39,** *"Be it known unto you therefore, men and brethren, that through this man [Jesus] is preached unto you the forgiveness of sins: And by him all that believe are justified from all things, from which ye could not be justified by the law of Moses."*

**1 John 1:9,** *"If we confess our sins, he is faithful and just to forgive us our sins, and to cleanse us from all unrighteousness."* (Read how Jesus forgave sins in **Luke 7:37-50.**)

## What It Means to Be Forgiven

**Psalm 103:10-12,** *"He hath not dealt with us after our sins; nor rewarded us according to our iniquities. For as the heaven is high above the earth, so great is his mercy toward them that fear him. As far as the east is from the west, so far hath he removed our transgressions from us."*

**Micah 7:19,** *"He will turn again, he will have compassion upon us; he will subdue our iniquities; and thou wilt cast all their sins into the depths of the sea."* [And, He puts up a 'No Fishing' sign.]

**Isaiah 38:17,** *"Behold, for peace I had great bitterness: but thou hast in love to my soul delivered it from the pit of corruption: for thou has cast all my sins behind thy back."*

**Hebrews 8:12,** *"For I will be merciful to their unrighteousness, and their sins and their iniquities will I remember no more."*

## Becoming Perfect

**Galatians 3:2-6,** *"This only would I learn of you, Received ye the Spirit by the works of the law, or by the hearing of faith? Are ye so foolish? Having begun in the Spirit, are ye now made **perfect** by the flesh? Have ye suffered so many things in vain? if it be yet in vain. He therefore that ministereth to you the Spirit, and worketh miracles among you, doeth he it by the works of the law, or by the hearing of faith? Even as Abraham believed God, and it was accounted to him for righteousness."*

**Hebrews 10:14,** *"For by one offering he hath **perfected** for ever them that are sanctified."*

## Receiving the Gift of Eternal Life

See 'Jesus Christ's testimony' of eternal life based upon belief found in **John 3:14-18, 36**; and 'Heavenly Father's testimony' of eternal life based upon belief in his Son found in **1 John 5:9-13**.

## What Does Jesus Ask You to Do?

**John 6:28-29,** *"Then said they unto him, What shall we do, that we might work the works of God? Jesus answered and said unto them, This is the work of God, that ye believe on him whom he hath sent."*

## Salvation is by grace, not works.

**Ephesians 2:8-9,** *"For by grace are ye saved through faith; and that not of yourselves: it is the gift of God: Not of works, lest any man should boast."*

**Galatians 2:16, 21,** *"Knowing that a man is not justified by the works of the law, but by the faith of Jesus Christ, even we have believed in Jesus Christ, that we might be justified by the faith of Christ, and not by the works of the law: for by the works of the law shall no flesh be justified... I do not frustrate the grace of God: for if righteousness come by the law, then Christ is dead in vain."*

## QUESTIONS FOR REVIEW

**What Bible verse can be used to get into a discussion on perfection with a Mormon?**

**How does a person become righteous (right) in God's sight?**

**On what basis does a person receive forgiveness of sins and eternal life?**

**What does it mean to be forgiven? How does God describe what happens to a person's forgiven sins?**

# SECTION 44

# Faith Without Works Is Dead

🛑 **Turn to the Glossary of Mormon Terms and read the LDS definition 'Justification' and 'Salvation by Grace Alone'.**

## LDS Gospel is Jesus + Good Works

Mormon 'salvation' is a works-based system. As you share the Biblical concept of salvation by grace through faith alone, Mormons will often comment, "But James says faith without works is dead! Do you believe you can accept Christ and then live any way you please?"

## James: Faith Without Works Is Dead

**James 2:17-20,** *"Even so faith, if it hath not works, is dead, being alone. Yea, a man may say, Thou hast faith, and I have works: shew me thy faith without thy works, and I will shew thee my faith by my works. Thou believest that there is one God; thou doest well; the devils also believe, and tremble. But wilt thou know, O vain man, that faith without works is dead?"*

LDS people interpret these verses to mean good works play a vital role in earning your salvation. This interpretation fits very well with the Book of Mormon but does not agree with the Biblical concept of salvation.

## Paul: Salvation is Not of Works

**Romans 3:20-22,** *"Therefore by the deeds of the law there shall no flesh be justified in his sight: for by the law is the knowledge of sin. But now the righteousness of God without the law is manifested, being witnessed by the law and the prophets; Even the righteousness of God which is by faith of Jesus Christ unto all and upon all them that believe..."*

**Galatians 2:16,** *"Knowing that a man is not justified by the works of the law, but by the*
*faith of Jesus Christ, even we have believed in Jesus Christ, that we might be justified by the faith of Christ, and not by the works of the law: for by the works of the law shall no flesh be justified."*

**Ephesians 2:8-9,** *"For by grace are ye saved through faith; and that not of yourselves: it is the gift of God: Not of works, lest any man should boast."*

These passages teach that salvation is by faith alone and good works play no part in the process.

## Did James and Paul Disagree?

At first glance, James, the writer of the Epistle of James, appears to contradict Paul, the author of Romans, Galatians, and Ephesians. Were James and Paul at odds with each other?

🛑 **Read Acts 15:1-29 before proceeding.**

This is the story of 'The First Jerusalem Council'. Several significant leaders of the early church—Peter, Paul, Barnabas, and James—all voiced their opinions in this chapter. Did you notice how Paul and James were in perfect agreement? In fact, the united decision of all the leaders involved was that people do not have to keep the law to be saved. Salvation is by grace through faith alone.

## Understanding James

The book of James was written to a group of people who were being deceived by a first century heresy called Gnosticism. These people mixed Greek philosophy with Christianity. As a result, great emphasis was placed on the intellect *(spirituality)* while little value was placed on the physical *(practical, godly living.)* James informed his readers that 'pretend spirituality' that did not produce good works was no faith at all. It was dead faith. The key verse of the passage is:

**James 2:18,** *"Yea, a man may say, Thou hast faith, and I have works: shew me thy faith without thy works, and I will shew thee my faith by my works."*

If true faith is present in a person's life, good works will be the evidence. If there are no good works, then there is no real faith. A person does not do good works to get saved; a person does good works as a result of salvation.

## Proof of Saving Faith = Godly Living

No, Paul did not teach that we can be saved by faith alone and then live any way we please.

**Romans 6:1-2,** *"What shall we say then? Shall we continue in sin, that grace may abound? God forbid. How shall we, that are dead to sin, live any longer therein?"*

**Ephesians 2:8-10,** *"For by grace are ye saved through faith; and that not yourselves: it is the gift of God: Not of works, lest any man should boast. For we are his workmanship, created in Christ Jesus unto good works, which God hath before ordained that we should walk in them."*

**Galatians 6:7-9,** *"Be not deceived; God is not mocked: for whatsoever a man soweth, that shall he also reap. For he that soweth to his flesh shall of the flesh reap corruption; but he that soweth to the Spirit shall of the Spirit reap life everlasting. And let us not be weary in well doing: for in due season we shall reap, if we faint not."*

## QUESTIONS FOR REVIEW

**What part do good works play in obtaining our salvation?**

**How do good works relate to our salvation?**

**Will good works be a part of every true believer's life?**

# CHAPTER 12
# OTHER IMPORTANT LDS TOPICS

# SECTION 45
# The 'Restored Gospel' of Mormonism

🛑 **Turn to the Glossary of Mormon Terms and read the LDS definitions of 'Restoration, The' and 'Celestial Marriage'.**

## The 'Restoration' of the Gospel

The LDS Church believes the true gospel of Jesus Christ was totally lost during the time called the 'Great Apostasy' of the Christian church.

The word 'restored' implies bringing something back to its original condition. Joseph Smith is believed to be the 'Prophet of the Restoration'. The LDS Church claims to be the only Church on earth with the 'restored gospel' as originally taught by Jesus Christ and his apostles. The following approach will challenge this claim.

This argument will be most effective if you ask leading questions and allow the LDS person to define their own scriptures. Don't rush through this. Continue to ask questions until you are sure they understand the full impact of each passage.

## Galatians 1:6-9 the Apostle Paul said,

*"I marvel that ye are so soon removed from him that called you into the grace of Christ unto another gospel: Which is not another; but there be some that trouble you, and would pervert the gospel of Christ. But though we, or an angel from heaven, preach any other gospel unto you than that which we have preached unto you, let him be accursed. As we said before, so say I now again, If any man preach any other gospel unto you than that ye have received, let him be accursed."*

### QUESTIONS

- What is the problem Paul is addressing in this passage?

- Who is the 'we' in this passage?
  *"...though **we**, or an angel from heaven, preach any other gospel unto you than that which **we** have preached unto you."*

- What is the warning to anyone who alters the gospel message that was received from the Lord's apostles?

According to Galatians chapter 1, no one can alter the New Testament Gospel as taught by Jesus Christ and the Lord's Apostles.

## 3 Nephi 11—Jesus Christ (supposedly) Visits the Americas

**NOTE:** In the Book of Mormon, Jesus Christ comes to the New World after his death and resurrection to visit the Nephites and Lamanites (the LDS Native Americans.)

When Jesus arrived, the Book of Mormon claims He started His Church (the Christian Church) in the Americas. It teaches that Christianity became the universal religion of the New World from about AD 34 to 201. The teachings of Jesus in the book of 3 Nephi line up with the doctrines taught in the 4 Biblical Gospels. Why? BECAUSE they were copied from the King James Bible by Joseph Smith.

## 3 Nephi 11:39-40 Jesus said,

*"Verily, verily, I say unto you, that this is my doctrine, and whoso buildeth upon this buildeth upon my rock, and the gates of hell shall not prevail against them. And whoso shall*

*declare more or less than this, and establish it for my doctrine, the same cometh of evil, and is not built upon my rock; but he buildeth upon a sandy foundation, and the gates of hell stand open to receive such."*

## QUESTIONS

- Who is speaking in this passage?

- What does Jesus mean when he says, *"Whoso shall declare more or less than this?"*

- What is the warning to anyone who adds to or takes away from the Lord's gospel doctrine as taught in the book of 3 Nephi?

According to 3 Nephi 11 *(in agreement with Galatians 1)*, NO ONE can add anything to or take anything away from the gospel as taught by Jesus!

## INTRODUCTION to the Book of Mormon

According to Mormonism, both the Bible and the Book of Mormon are supposed to contain the 'fullness of the everlasting gospel' of Jesus Christ. The 1ˢᵗ paragraph of the 'INTRODUCTION' says:

*"The Book of Mormon is a volume of holy scripture comparable to the Bible. It is a record of God's dealings with the ancient inhabitants of the Americas and contains, as does the Bible, the fulness of the everlasting gospel."* (See also **D&C 42:12.**)

The 6ᵗʰ paragraph says:

*"Concerning this record the Prophet Joseph Smith said: 'I told the brethren that the Book of Mormon was the most correct of any book on earth, and the keystone of our religion, and a man would get nearer to God by abiding by its precepts, than by any other book."*

## QUESTIONS

- Do you believe these statements are true?

- How would you define 'fulness of the gospel' as used in the Book of Mormon 'Introduction'?

**QUOTATION**—LDS President Joseph Fielding Smith in *Doctrines of Salvation*, Vol. 1, says,

*"By fulness of the gospel is meant all the ordinances and principles that pertain to the exaltation in the celestial kingdom."* (p. 160.)

According to Joseph Fielding Smith, both the Bible and Book of Mormon contain the fulness of the gospel of Jesus Christ—or the complete LDS gospel.

## Gospel Principles *[LDS Church Manual]*

This LDS Church manual explains in detail the fulness of the 'Restored Gospel' of Mormonism.

**IMPORTANT NOTE**—Encourage the Mormon you are talking with to examine the following quote. Ask if they agree that this is the 'Restored Gospel' of Jesus Christ as taught in the LDS Church.

## "REQUIREMENTS FOR EXALTATION—

*Latter-day Saints are taught that now is the time to fulfill the requirements for exaltation (see Alma 34:32-34.) President Joseph Fielding Smith said, 'In order to obtain the exaltation we must accept the gospel and all its covenants; and take upon us the obligations which the Lord has offered; and walk in the light and understanding of the truth; and 'live by every word that proceedeth forth from the mouth of God'. (Doctrines of Salvation 2:43.)*

***There are specific ordinances we must have received to be exalted:***
1. *We must be baptized and confirmed a member of the Church of Jesus Christ.*
2. *We must receive the Holy Ghost.*
3. *We must receive the temple endowment.*
4. *We must be married for time and all eternity.*

***In addition to the required ordinances, there are also many laws we have to obey to qualify for exaltation. We must—***
1. *Love God and worship him.*
2. *Have faith in Jesus Christ.*
3. *Live the law of chastity.*
4. *Repent of our wrong doings.*
5. *Pay honest tithes and offerings.*
6. *Be honest in our dealings with others and with the Lord.*
7. *Speak the truth always.*

8. *Obey the Word of Wisdom.* 🛑 *[Turn to the Glossary of Mormon Terms and read the LDS definition of 'Word of Wisdom'.]*
9. *Search out our kindred dead and perform the saving ordinances of the gospel for them.*
10. *Keep the Sabbath day holy.*
11. *Attend our Church meetings as regularly as possible to renew our baptismal covenants. This is done as we partake of the sacrament.*
12. *Love and strengthen our family members in the ways of the Lord.*
13. *Have family and individual prayers every day.*
14. *Honor our parents.*
15. *Teach the gospel to others by word and example.*
16. *Study the scriptures.*
17. *Listen to and obey the words of the prophets of the Lord.*
18. *Develop true charity in our lives.*

*In other words, each person must endure in faithfulness, keeping all the Lord's commandments until the end of his life on earth." (Gospel Principles, LDS Church, 1979/1990, Chapter 47, 'Exaltation'.)*

### QUESTION
- Is this an accurate representation of the 'restored gospel' of Jesus Christ as taught in the LDS Church?

## The LDS Law of Celestial Marriage
QUOTATION—Consider this statement:
*"The prophets have uniformly taught that the consummate and culminating element of God's great plan for the blessing of his children is eternal marriage... President Howard W. Hunter described celestial marriage as 'the crowning gospel ordinance.'" (Ensign, May 2003, 'Eternal Marriage', Elder F. Burton Howard of the Seventy, p. 92.)*

### QUESTION
- Is being married in an LDS Temple, for time and all eternity, the 'Crowning Ordinance' of the 'Restored Gospel' of Jesus Christ?

**PROBLEM:** The 'Restored Gospel' of the Church of Jesus Christ of Latter-day Saints was never taught by Jesus Christ—not in the Bible or in the Book of Mormon!

### QUESTIONS
- Can you show me any place in the Bible or the Book of Mormon where marriage for time and all eternity is taught?

- Can you show me any place in the Bible or the Book of Mormon where anyone was married in a Jewish temple?

It seems inconceivable that in over 1,400 years of Bible history and 1,000 years of Book of Mormon history this doctrine is never mentioned. How could the crowning ordinance of the gospel not be mentioned in the Bible or Book of Mormon if they both contain 'the fulness of the gospel?'

If this doctrine was added by modern day LDS leaders, it would seem the Mormon Church and all who follow its teachings would be under the condemnation of God for changing/adding to the gospel *(Remember – Galatians 1:6-9, 3 Nephi 11:39-40.)* Is this a problem for you?

👁 **Go to: TriGrace.org**
**Under 'Resources' find and print the free PDF download of the *Truth About the Restored Gospel* visual. Then watch the corresponding TGM Tutorial explaining how this visual is used with LDS people.**

### QUESTIONS FOR REVIEW
**What passage from the Bible does NOT allow LDS prophets to change the gospel of Jesus Christ in any way?**


**What passage in the Book of Mormon tells the LDS prophets they cannot add to or remove anything from the gospel as taught by Jesus Christ?**

# SECTION 46

# The Pre-mortal Life or The Preexistence

🛑 **Turn to the Glossary of Mormon Terms and read the LDS definitions of 'Intelligences', 'Pre-mortal Life or Preexistence', and 'Council of the Gods'.**

The pre-mortal life (sometimes referred to as the preexistence) is a foundational belief of the Mormon Church which leads to heretical doctrine. The greatest heresy of this false doctrine is the LDS reasoning that since mankind is the literal offspring of deity, genetically little gods, human beings can one day become Gods/Goddesses just like our Heavenly Parents.

One difficulty we face when attempting to discuss this topic with LDS people are the verses in the Bible that might appear to support the idea of a preexistence of spirits. Mormons will use the following verses to defend this belief.

> **Jeremiah 1:5,** *"Before I formed thee in the belly I knew thee; and before thou camest forth out of the womb I sanctified thee, and I ordained thee a prophet unto the nations."*

> **Hebrews 12:9,** *"We have had fathers of our flesh which corrected us, and we gave them reverence: shall we not much rather be in subjection unto the Father of spirits, and live?"*

> **Acts 17:28-29,** *"For in him we live, and move, and have our being; as certain also of your own poets have said, For we are also his offspring. Forasmuch then as we are the offspring of God, we ought not to think that the Godhead is like unto gold, or silver, or stone, graven by art and man's device."*

## CHRISTIAN RESPONSES:

### Jeremiah 1:5—Yes, God knew us, but did we know Him?

Neither the Bible nor the Book of Mormon ever state, 'Before I formed you in the belly, you knew me'. But, God's foreknowledge is certain. God knew all about Jeremiah and the plan He had for his life before Jeremiah was ever created.

### God knows the future. Isaiah 46:9-10 says,

*"I am God, and there is none else; I am God, and there is none like me, declaring the end from the beginning, and from ancient times the things that are not yet done, saying, My counsel shall stand, and I will do all my pleasure."*

Yes, God knew all about each of us and the plans he had for us long before we ever existed.

### Hebrews 12:9—God, the Father of our spirits?

Because God is the Creator of everything in the heavens and on earth, He is symbolically the 'Father' of all creation.

> **Malachi 2:10,** *"Have we not all one father? Hath not one God created us?"*

The real question is this, did God 'create' or 'give birth to' our spirits?

> **Zechariah 12:1,** *"The burden of the word of the LORD for Israel, saith the LORD, which stretcheth forth the heavens, and layeth the foundation of the earth, and formeth the spirit of man within him."*

The evidence we have from the Bible is that God created everything, including our spirits. He did not give birth to us, we are not genetically deity, little gods in the making. The next argument will define this topic further.

### Acts 17:28-29—We are His offspring?

The Biblical word 'offspring' can refer to literal or symbolic offspring. A modern day example of this concept is Henry Ford, who is considered the 'father' of the Model T Ford, though no one would believe Henry literally gave birth to a car!

The following passages are Biblical examples of how the Biblical word 'offspring' can be used in a symbolic way. Both the Hebrew and Greek words for 'offspring' simply mean, 'what comes out from'.

> **Isaiah 42:5,** *"Thus saith God the LORD, he that created the heavens, and stretched them out; he that spread forth the earth, and **that which cometh out of it** [Hebrew, 'offspring']; he that giveth breath unto the people upon it, and spirit to them that walk therein." (See also **Isaiah 34:1**.)*

> **1 Corinthians 14:9-11,** *"Except ye utter by the tongue words easy to be understood, how shall it be known what is spoken? for ye shall speak into the air. There are, it may be, so many **kinds** [Greek, 'offspring'] of voices in the world, and none of them is without signification. Therefore if I know not the meaning of the voice, I shall be unto him that speaketh a barbarian, and he that speaketh shall be a barbarian unto me."*

Another interesting point in regard to **Acts 17** is that the Apostle Paul is quoting a pagan source. Paul was using terminology with which the gentile people in Athens were familiar. There is not one other place in the Bible where the word 'offspring' is used to describe our relationship to God. This would be a foreign concept to the Jewish people who did not consider themselves to be literal 'offspring' of deity.

**NOTE**: The Preexistence is a difficult topic to discuss with LDS people because this topic is emotionally charged. LDS people really like the doctrine of the pre-mortal life. If the preexistence is not true, the entire worldview of Mormonism crumbles. When the topic comes up in a conversation with LDS people, you might ask the following questions:

- Can you remember the preexistence? (Their answer will be 'No' since they believe God put a veil over their memory at birth.)
- Is there a Bible or Book of Mormon passage that defines the preexistence of spirits? (Other than the references mentioned above, there is not one passage that defines this doctrine.)

- Must a person believe in the pre-mortal life to go to Heaven? (No.)
- Have you ever considered what Jesus had to say about the pre-mortal life? (I have never met a Mormon who has considered this idea.)

## Use the Words of Jesus

The best way to disprove this LDS doctrine is to show them what Jesus had to say about the preexistence. Jesus said over and over again that He was the only person who had preexisted with the Father. Consider the words spoken by Jesus himself in the gospel of John.

> **John 17:24-25,** Jesus prayed, *"Father, I will that they also, whom thou hast given me, be with me where I am; that they may behold my glory, which thou hast given me: for thou lovedst me before the foundation of the world. O righteous Father, the world hath not known thee: but I have known thee, and these have known that thou hast sent me."*

> **John 5:37-38,** *"The Father himself, which hath sent me, hath borne witness of me. Ye have neither heard his voice at any time, nor seen his shape. And ye have not his word abiding in you: for whom he hath sent, him ye believe not."*

> **John 6:46,** *"Not that any man hath seen the Father, save he which is of God, he hath seen the Father."*

> **John 7:28-29,** *"Then cried Jesus in the temple… saying, Ye both know me, and ye know whence I am: and I am not come of myself, but he that sent me is true, whom ye know not. But I know him: for I am from him, and he hath sent me."*

> **John 8:54-55,** *"Jesus answered… it is my Father that honoureth me; of whom ye say, that he is your God: Yet ye have not known him; but I know him: and if I should say, I know him not, I shall be a liar like unto you: but I know him, and keep his saying."*

> **John 8:23,** *"And he said unto them, Ye are from beneath; I am from above: ye are of this world; I am not of this world."*

All of these verses are problematic for LDS people! Why does the Church of Jesus of Latter-day Saints conflict with the teachings of Jesus Christ?

## QUESTIONS FOR REVIEW

**What heretical doctrine arises from the LDS concept of the Preexistence of Spirits?**

**Why is the topic of the 'Pre-mortal Life' a difficult topic to discuss with Mormons?**

**What is the best way to challenge this heretical doctrine?**

# SECTION 47
# 'Total Apostasy' Problems

🛑 Turn to the Glossary of Mormon Terms and read the LDS definitions of 'Great Apostasy, The' and 'Bible'.

LDS people pride themselves in their belief that the LDS Church is the only religion on the face of the earth that has God's priesthood authority. The doctrines of modern day Christianity are considered by Mormons to be nothing more than a conglomerate of pagan traditions passed on by the great and abominable church *(see 1 Nephi Chapters 13-14.)* Mormonism says the gospel doctrines, and priesthood authority of Christ's church were totally changed and completely lost during the dark ages.

The LDS concept of a total apostasy can easily be refuted. Following are two ways to challenge your LDS friends when this topic comes up.

## Problem #1—Jesus Christ's Proclamations

LDS people who believe in a total apostasy of Jesus Christ's Church have a big problem when they consider the promises/prophesies made by Jesus concerning His church and His gospel.

- **Matthew 16:18,** In regard to His church, Jesus said, *"I will build my church; and the gates of hell shall not prevail against it."*

- **Matthew. 24:35,** In regard to His gospel, Jesus said, *"Heaven and earth shall pass away, but my words shall not pass away."*

- **Matthew. 28:20,** Jesus promised the body of believers in His church, *"I am with you alway, even unto the end of the world. Amen."*

- **Hebrews 13:5,** According to the author of Hebrews, this promise extends to all believers in all ages, *"For he hath said, 'I will never leave thee nor forsake thee.'"*

- *Acts 1:8,* Jesus said, *"Ye shall receive power, after that the Holy Ghost is come upon you: and ye shall be witnesses unto me both in Jerusalem, and in all Judaea, and in Samaria, and unto the uttermost part of the earth."*

These verses are a dilemma for Mormons because their church claims to be to the Church of Jesus Christ; yet the LDS doctrine of the 'Total Apostasy' of Christ's church makes Jesus a false prophet. Mormon people would never want to say they believe Jesus was a liar—so this is a discussion that will challenge them to the max.

## Problem #2—The 'Three Nephites' & John

LDS people who believe in the 'Total Apostasy' have not considered what the Book of Mormon says about the 'Three Nephites' and the Apostle John. According to **3 Nephi 28:4-9, 17-23,** and **27-31,** three Nephite Apostles and John the Apostle never died. These four Apostles of the Lord Jesus have been roaming around on this earth since the 1st century.

### Mormon Doctrine, by Bruce R. McConkie

*"**Three Nephites**—Three of the Nephite disciples, desiring to continue their apostolic ministry of bringing souls unto Christ, received this promise from the Lord:*

*'Ye shall never taste of death; but ye shall live to behold all the doings of the Father unto the children of men, even until all things shall be fulfilled according to the will of the Father, when I shall come in my glory with the powers of heaven'. (**3 Nephi 28:7**.)*

*They were to be free from pain and sorrow (except for the sins of the world), and were to minister, 'as the angels of God', unto the Jews, Gentiles, scattered tribes of Israel, 'and unto all nations, kindred, tongues, and people...'*

*Unbeknowns to the world, they are continuing their assigned ministry at this time, and there have been occasions when they have appeared to members of the Church in this final dispensation."* (Mormon Doctrine, Bruce R. McConkie, p.793, 1966.)

According to Mormonism, the Apostle John and the Three Nephites were ordained apostles of Jesus Christ. These four men must have had the LDS priesthood authority *(the Aaronic and Melchizedek priesthoods.)* Their ongoing ministry was to proclaim the LDS gospel of Jesus to 'all nations, kindred, tongues, and people' and 'bring the souls of men unto Jesus, while the world shall stand'. If they were doing their job, they must have been proclaiming the principles of the LDS gospel to the world for the past 2,000 years.

**QUESTION:**

When Mormon missionaries go out to proclaim their message around the world, do they ever find established Mormon churches in areas untouched by modern-day Mormonism? The answer is **NEVER**!

Mormon people who believe the story of the three Nephites have a huge problem—if the story is true, there could not have been a total apostasy of Christ's Church!

**Why is the LDS belief in the 'total apostasy' Biblically wrong?**

**How does the LDS 'total apostasy' contradict Mormon teaching?**

# SECTION 48
# Priesthood Authority

🛑 **Turn to the Glossary of Mormon Terms and read the LDS definition of 'Priesthood'.**

LDS people take great pride in the fact that they have 'priesthood authority' and you do not!

Mormonism says, unless you hold the Aaronic and/or Melchizedek priesthoods, which were restored to the earth by Joseph Smith, you have no authority to serve God in any way. The topic of 'priesthood' is taught more than any other doctrine in the LDS Church and is considered by Mormons to be the most important doctrine of the 'restored gospel' of Jesus Christ.

As you discuss this topic with LDS people, it is interesting to challenge them with the fact that Jesus never once discussed priesthood with His disciples. This is problematic, because the LDS Church is supposed to be the 'restored church' of Jesus Christ.

**QUESTION:** Ask your Mormon friends, 'If priesthood authority was going to be such an important part of Jesus Christ's Church, why did Jesus never discuss the topic of priesthood with His Apostles?'

## The Biblical Source of Authority

The Bible clearly states that the Holy Ghost is the divine source of authority in Christ's Church.

### He gave authority to those who wrote the Bible.

**2 Peter 1:21,** *"The prophecy came not in old time by the will of man: but holy men of God spake as they were moved by the Holy Ghost."*

### He gave John the Baptist his authority.

**Luke 1:15,** *"For he [John the Baptist] shall be great in the sight of the Lord, and shall drink neither wine nor strong drink; and he shall be filled with the Holy Ghost, even from his mother's womb."*

### He gave the disciples their power/authority.

**Acts 1:8,** *"But ye shall receive power, after that the Holy Ghost is come upon you: and ye shall be witnesses unto me both in Jerusalem, and in all Judaea, and in Samaria, and unto the uttermost part of the earth."*

**1 Thessalonians 1:5,** *"For our gospel came not unto you in word only, but also in power and in the Holy Ghost, and in much assurance; as ye know what manner of men we were among you for your sake."*

## In The Book of Mormon—
## The Holy Ghost Gives Authority

**1 Nephi 10:22,** *"The Holy Ghost giveth authority that I should speak these things."*

**Mosiah 18:12-14,** *"Alma took Helam, he being one of the first, and went and stood forth in the water, and cried, saying: O Lord, pour out thy Spirit upon thy servant, that he may do this work with holiness of heart. And when he had said these words, the Spirit of the Lord was upon him, and he said: Helam, I baptize thee, having authority from the Almighty God, as a testimony that ye have entered into a covenant to serve him until you are dead as to the mortal body; and may the Spirit of the Lord be poured out upon you; and may he grant unto you eternal life, through the redemption of Christ, whom he has prepared from the foundation of the world. And after Alma had said these words, both Alma and Helam were buried in the water; and they arose and came forth out of the water rejoicing, being filled with the Spirit."*

## The Recipients of Authority

All true believers are sealed with Holy Ghost authority.

**Ephesians 1:13,** *"In whom ye also trusted, after that ye heard the word of truth, the gospel of your salvation: in whom also after that ye believed, ye were sealed with that holy Spirit of promise."*

**1 Corinthians 6:19,** *"What? Know ye not that your body is the temple of the Holy Ghost which is in you, which ye have of God, and ye are not your own?"*

**Romans 15:13,** *"Now the God of hope fill you with all joy and peace in believing, that ye may abound in hope, through the power of the Holy Ghost."*

Authority is given by God, not a church! Authority is power. Authority is the indwelling of the Holy Spirit/Ghost. If you are a believer in Jesus Christ and have received the gift of the Holy Spirit, you have God-given authority.

## About the Aaronic Priesthood

A probing question to ask your LDS friend (assuming he is an adult male) is, 'Do you hold the Aaronic priesthood?' If he is active in his church he will probably answer, 'Yes'.

Next ask him, 'According to your patriarchal blessing, to which tribe of Israel do you belong?' 99.9% of the time, he will tell you he belongs to one of the tribes of Joseph: Ephraim or Manasseh.

This is a problem because the regulations laid out by God in the O.T. law stated that no one can be a priest unless he is from the tribe of Levi.

In addition, he must be a direct descendent of Aaron if he hopes to qualify for the Aaronic priesthood. The Levitical and/or Aaronic priesthoods were not held by any other tribe of Israel, and those who wrongly claimed this authority and attempted to perform the duties of a priest were severely punished. Not just any Israelite could be an Aaronic priest (See **Numbers 3:10, 16:1-35, and 17:1-10**.)

## New Testament 'Priesthood'

If you want to study the topic of 'priesthood' in the New Testament go to the book of Hebrews. According to Hebrews:

- **Hebrews 8:13,** The Levitical/Aaronic priesthoods became obsolete with the coming of Jesus Christ.

- **Hebrews 7:13-14,** Jesus could not hold the Levitical/Aaronic priesthood because he was not from the right tribe of Israel—Jesus was born into the tribe of Judah, all Aaronic priests had to be from the tribe of Levi and all Aaronic priests were required to be in the direct lineage of Aaron.

- **Hebrews 4-9,** In regard to Melchizedek, Jesus is said to be the only high priest after the order of Melchizedek. In Hebrews, every time the word 'priest' is associated with the word 'Melchizedek' the grammar is singular—there is only ONE PRIEST after the order of Melchizedek, JESUS! Encourage your friend to study this out.

There are only two New Testament books that address those who are believers in Jesus as 'priests'—**1 Peter 2:5-10** and **Revelation 1:6 & 5:10.** In each of these passages, the emphasis is on the fact that _GENTILE_ believers are said to be a 'holy priesthood' to God.

This would be shocking information to anyone of Israelite nationality. In Christ Jesus, ALL believers, Jews and Gentiles, Men and Women, are said to be a 'royal priesthood' to God. In Jesus, Jews, Gentiles and females were now considered equals in God's sight.

_Galatians 3:28-29,_ In Jesus, _"There is neither Jew nor Greek, there is neither bond nor free, there is neither male nor female: for ye are all one in Christ Jesus. And if ye be Christ's, then are ye Abraham's seed, and heirs according to the promise."_

In Christ Jesus, we all have been elevated to the level of an Old Testament 'priest'. We are all members of a 'holy priesthood', which means we can all enter into the service of God, a level of service that was reserved only for the Israelite tribe of Levi in the Old Testament. But, New Testament 'priests' are never said to be Aaronic or Melchizedek priests.

## QUESTIONS FOR REVIEW

**What did Jesus teach His apostles concerning the priesthood?**

**Why is this problematic for Latter-day Saints?**

**As a Bible-believing Christian, do you have God-given authority? Prove it Biblically.**

**Why can't an LDS person claim to have Aaronic priesthood authority?**

## The '4 Step Eternal Marriage' Visual

The topics in Chapter 12, Sections 45-48, are summed up in one interactive tract for Mormons titled, _The 4 Step Eternal Marriage Visual_. This interactive tract exposes the fact that none of these foundational LDS doctrines (_Eternal Marriage, Pre-Mortal Existence, Total Apostasy, or Priesthood_) were taught by Jesus and are actually in conflict with Jesus Christ's gospel.

👁 Go to: TriGrace.org
**Under 'Resources' find and print the free PDF download of the _4-Step Eternal Marriage_ visual. Then watch the TGM Tutorial explaining how to us this visual with LDS people.**

# CHAPTER 13
# PROPHET PROBLEMS

# SECTION 49
# Differing Accounts of 'The First Vision'

🛑 **Turn to the Glossary of Mormon Terms and examine the LDS definition of 'First Vision'.**

Joseph Smith and his family moved to New York State when he was a young boy, and it was here that he claims to have experienced his 'First Vision'—an AMAZING story of a heavenly visitation. This story is hallowed amongst LDS people because this heavenly vision establishes Joseph Smith's claim as a true 'Prophet' of God.

The 10th president of the LDS Church, Joseph Fielding Smith, wrote this about Joseph Smith:

*"Mormonism, as it is called, must stand or fall on the story of Joseph Smith. He was either a prophet of God, divinely called, properly appointed and commissioned, or he was one of the biggest frauds this world has ever seen. There is no middle ground. If Joseph Smith was a deceiver, who willfully attempted to mislead the people, then he should be exposed; his claims should be refuted, and his doctrines shown to be false, for the doctrines of an imposter cannot be made to harmonize in all particulars with divine truth. If his claims and declarations were built upon fraud and deceit, there would appear many errors and contradictions, which would be easy to detect."* (Doctrines of Salvation, Joseph Fielding Smith, Vol. 1, p. 188.)

Joseph Smith's First Vision is the foundation upon which the LDS Church rests. The First Vision exposes the 'Total Apostasy' of all Christian denominations and establishes the need for a 'Restoration' of the Christian church and the true gospel. The First Vision is the basis for the LDS doctrine of the 'Godhead' being three Gods. These shocking revelations supposedly came from two celestial Beings, Heavenly Father and Jesus Christ, as they appeared to Joseph while he was praying in a grove of trees near Palmyra, New York.

At least 9 recorded accounts of the First Vision of Joseph Smith have been discovered. Joseph wrote or assigned scribes to write four of these accounts. In addition to the firsthand accounts, there are also five descriptions of Joseph's vision recorded by his contemporaries. All of these are discussed on the LDS Church website.

The Problem: an in-depth investigation of this 'vision' reveals serious discrepancies. If Joseph Smith's First Vision story was found to be unreliable, this would reflect very badly on the 'prophet'. So, which of Joseph's First Vision accounts is true, or are any of them true?

## (1838) The Official LDS First Vision Account, in the Pearl of Great Price

*"I was at this time in my fifteenth year... It was on the morning of a beautiful, clear day, early in the spring of eighteen hundred and twenty...*

*I kneeled down and began to offer up the desires of my heart to God. I had scarcely done so, when immediately I was seized upon by some power which entirely overcame me, and had such an astonishing influence over me as to bind my tongue so that I could not speak. Thick darkness gathered around me, and it seemed to me for a time as if I were doomed to sudden destruction.*

*But, exerting all my powers to call upon God to deliver me out of the power of this enemy which had seized upon me, and at the very moment when I was ready to sink into despair and abandon myself to destruction— not to an imaginary ruin, but to the power of* some actual being from the unseen world, who had such marvelous power as I had never before felt in any being—just at this moment of great alarm, I saw a pillar of light exactly over my head, above the brightness of the sun, which descended gradually until it fell upon me.

It no sooner appeared than I found myself delivered from the enemy which held me bound. When the light rested upon me **I saw two Personages**, whose brightness and glory defy all description, standing above me in the air. **One of them spake unto me, calling me by name and said, pointing to the other—This is My Beloved Son. Hear Him!**

My object in going to inquire of the Lord was to know which of all the sects was right, that I might know which to join... (for at this time it had never entered into my heart that all were wrong.).. I was answered that I must join none of them, for they were all wrong; and the Personage who addressed me said that all their creeds were an abomination in his sight; that those professors were all corrupt; that: 'they draw near to me with their lips, but their hearts are far from me, they teach for doctrines the commandments of men, having a form of godliness, but they deny the power thereof'. He again forbade me to join with any of them..." (The Pearl of Great Price, Joseph Smith History 1:7, 14-20.)

**QUESTIONS:**
- How old was Joseph Smith in this account?

- How many personages did Joseph see?

- By implication, who were those personages?

### (1832) Joseph Smith's Personal Journal
This is the earliest documented account of the First Vision. Keep in mind, this is from Joseph's own journal, so there are grammar and spelling mistakes as well as corrections made by the 'prophet' himself.

"...by searching the scriptures I found that ~~mand~~ <mankind> did not come unto the Lord but that they had apostatised from the true and liveing faith and there was no society or denomination that built upon the gospel of Jesus Christ as recorded in the new testament and I felt to mourn for my own sins and for the sins of the world...

Therefore I cried unto the Lord for mercy for there was none else to whom I could go and ~~to~~ obtain mercy and the Lord heard my cry in the wilderness and while in <the> attitude of calling upon the Lord <**in the 16th year of my age**> a piller of ~~fire~~ light above the brightness of the sun at noon day come down from above and rested upon me and I was filled with the spirit of god and the <Lord> opened the heavens upon me and **I saw the Lord and he spake unto me** saying Joseph <my son> thy sins are forgiven thee. go thy <way> walk in my statutes and keep my commandments behold I am the Lord of glory I was crucifyed for the world that all those who believe on my name may have Eternal life <behold> the world lieth in sin ~~and~~ at this time and none doeth good no not one they have turned asside from the gospel and keep not <my> commandments they draw near to me with their lips while their hearts are far from me and mine anger is kindling against the inhabitants of the earth to visit them according to th[e]ir ungodliness... and my soul was filled with love and for many days I could rejoice with great Joy and the Lord was with me but [I] could find none that would believe the hevnly vision nevertheless I pondered these things in my heart." (Personal Writings of Joseph Smith, Compiled and Edited by Dean C. Jessee, p. 10-12.)

**QUESTIONS:**
- How old was Joseph Smith in this account?

- How many Personages did Joseph see?

- Can you see any other significant differences between the 1832 and the 1838 Versions?

## Joseph Smith to Joshua, the Jewish Minister (1835)

"While setting in my house between the hours of ten & 11 this morning, a man came in, and introduced himself to me, calling <himself> by the name of Joshua the Jewish minister [Robert Matthias]...

We soon commenced talking upon the subject of religion and after I had made some remarks concerning the bible I commenced giving him a relation of the circumstances connected with the coming forth of the book of Mormon, as follows – being wrought up in my mind, respecting the subject of religion and looking at the different systems taught the children of men, I knew not who was right or who was wrong and I considered it of the first importance that I should be right, in matters that involve eternal consequ[e]nces;

being thus perplexed in mind I retired to the silent grove and bow[e]d down before the Lord, under a realising sense that he had said (if the bible be true) ask and you shall receive knock and it shall be opened seek and you shall find and again, if any man lack wisdom let him ask of God who giveth to all men libarally and upbradeth not;

information was what I most desired at this time, and with a fixed determination to obtain it, I called upon the Lord for the first time, in the place above stated or in other words I made a fruitless attempt to p[r]ay, my toung seemed to be swolen in my mouth, so that I could not utter, I heard a noise behind me like some person walking towards me, I strove again to pray, but could not, the noise of walking seemed to draw nearer, I sprung up on my feet, ~~and~~ and looked around, but saw no person or thing that was calculated to produce the noise of walking, I kneeled again my mouth was opened and my toung liberated, and I called on the Lord in mighty prayer, a pillar of fire appeared above my head, it presently rested down upon me ~~head~~, and filled me with Joy unspeakable, **a personage appeard in the midst of this pillar of flame** which was spread all around, and yet nothing consumed, **another personage soon appeard like unto the first**, he said unto me thy sins are forgiven thee, he testifyed unto me that Jesus Christ is the Son of God; **<and I saw many angels in this vision> I was about 14 years old when I received this first** communication." (Personal Writings of Joseph Smith, Compiled and Edited by Dean C. Jessee, p. 104-5)

### QUESTIONS:

* How old was Joseph Smith in this account?

* How many personages did Joseph see?

* Who were the personages that appeared to Joseph in this vision?

## Joseph Smith to Erastus Holmes (1835)

"A Gentleman called this after noon by the name of Erastus Holmes of Newbury Clemon [Newberry, Clermont] Co. Ohio, he called to make enquiry about the establishment of the church of the latter-day Saints and to be instructed more perfectly in our doctrine & I commenced and gave him a brief relation of my experience while in my juvenile years, say from six years old up to the time I received **the first visitation of Angels** which was when **I was about fourteen. years old** and also the visitations that I received afterwards, concerning the book of Mormon, and a short account of the rise and progress of the church, up to this, date..." (Personal Writings of Joseph Smith, Compiled and Edited by Dean C. Jessee, p. 112-113)

### QUESTIONS:

* How old was Joseph Smith in this account?

* Who appeared to Joseph in this account?

Heber J. Grant, the seventh prophet of the LDS Church, made this alarming statement:

"Either Joseph Smith did see God and did converse with him, and God himself did introduce Jesus Christ to the boy Joseph Smith, *and Jesus did tell Joseph Smith that he would be the instrument in the hands of God of establishing again upon the earth the true gospel of Jesus Christ—or Mormonism, so called, is a myth." (Discourses of the Prophet Joseph Smith, Alma P. Burton, p. 18.)*

## Use this Info to Challenge LDS people.

It is not difficult to challenge the First Vision of Joseph Smith which brings the trustworthiness of the 'prophet' himself into question.

👁 **Go to: TriGrace.org**
**Under 'Resources' find and print the free PDF download of *Joseph Smith's 'First Vision'*. Then watch the TGM Tutorial explaining how this Visual is used with LDS people.**

This challenge will be most effective if you actually purchase the LDS book, *Personal Writings of Joseph Smith*, by Dean C. Jesse, which contains facsimile reprints of Joseph's personal journal. One of the first entries in this book is Joseph's 1832 'First Vision' account—the earliest and only account written by Joseph Smith himself. LDS people are shocked when they realize Joseph's 1832 'First Vision' is TOTALLY different than the Official LDS 'First Vision'. This book may be purchased at Amazon.com for about $20.

**INTERESTING NOTE:** Until recent years the LDS Church suppressed the knowledge of multiple accounts of the First Vision. In the early 1960's, the LDS Church was forced to acknowledge at least 9 accounts of the First Vision due to people like Jerald and Sandra Tanner who discovered and published this information—Utah Lighthouse Ministry: *www.utlm.org*

Today, in an effort to appear 'transparent', the LDS Church not only acknowledges these accounts but has also made them available on the LDS Church website under: *GOSPEL TOPICS / First Vision Accounts.*

The LDS Church, however, tries to downplay the discrepancies in the First Vision Accounts claiming, "The various accounts of the First Vision tell a consistent story, though naturally they differ in emphasis and detail."

The LDS Church then tries to liken Joseph's differing accounts of the First Vision to the Biblical accounts of Paul's vision of Jesus Christ on the road to Damascus or to the accounts of Jesus Christ's transfiguration as recorded in the Biblical Gospels, implying that Joseph's First Vision accounts and these Biblical stories are exactly the same in that they contain additional information or details, but all tell a consistent story. Is the LDS Church justified in making this claim? NO WAY!

- Joseph Smith's accounts CONTRADICT.
- The Biblical accounts DO NOT CONTRADICT.

## QUESTIONS FOR REVIEW

**Joseph Smith claimed to be what three different ages when he experienced his first vision?**

**Who appeared to Joseph Smith in these various accounts?**

**Do Joseph Smith's accounts of the First Vision contradict each other?**

**Read the accounts of Paul's vision (Acts 9:3-6 and 22:6-11) and the transfiguration of Christ (Matthew 17:1-8, Mark 9:2-8, and Luke 9:28-36.) Do these accounts contradict each other?**

# S E C T I O N 50
# Polygamy Contradictions

🛑 **Turn to the Glossary of Mormon Terms and examine the LDS definition of 'Plural Marriage/ Polygamy'.**

Mormonism is infamous for its practice of POLYGAMY! Even today there are tens of thousands of polygamist Mormons living in the western United States. Numerous documentaries and TV sitcoms highlighting the lives of polygamist Mormons have been produced in recent years..

The mainstream Mormon Church *(The Church of Jesus Christ of Latter-day Saints or the LDS Church)*, however, has not officially condoned the practice polygamy since 1890 when the LDS *Manifesto* was issued which *(supposedly)* ended the practice of polygamy in the LDS Church.

We don't, therefore, bring up the topic of polygamy to discuss the pros and cons of the practice of polygamy. The topic of polygamy is mentioned here to illustrate contradictions within the LDS scriptures and LDS Church history.

## Book of Mormon

In the Book of Mormon, polygamy is strongly condemned as wickedness in God's sight.

**Jacob 2:23-28,** *"But the word of God burdens me because of your grosser crimes. For behold, thus saith the Lord: This people begin to wax in iniquity; they understand not the scriptures, for they seek to excuse themselves in committing whoredoms, because of the things which were written concerning David, and Solomon his son. Behold, David and Solomon truly had many wives and concubines, which thing was abominable before me, saith the Lord. Wherefore, thus saith the Lord, I have led this people forth out of the land of Jerusalem, by the power of mine arm, that I might raise up unto me a righteous branch from the fruit of the loins of Joseph. Wherefore, I the Lord God will not suffer that this people shall do like unto them of old. Wherefore, my brethren, hear me, and hearken to the word of the Lord: For there shall not any man among you have save it be one wife; and concubines he shall have none; For I, the Lord God, delight in the chastity of women. And whoredoms are an abomination before me; thus saith the Lord of Hosts."*

## (1835) Doctrine and Covenants

In 1835 when the first edition of the Doctrine and Covenants was published it contained—

Section CI *[101]* 'MARRIAGE' pg. 251, which stated,

> *"Inasmuch as this church of Christ has been reproached with the crime of fornication, and polygamy: we declare that we believe, that one man should have one wife; and one woman, but one husband, except in case of death, when either is at liberty to marry again."*

**INTERESTING NOTE:** both the Book of Mormon *(published in 1830)* and the Doctrine and Covenants *(published in 1835)* strictly condemned polygamy. Yet leaders in the LDS Church were actively practicing polygamy from as early as 1833 when we have documentation of Joseph marrying Fanny Alger, *(Joseph's 16 year old maid.)*

## (1876) Doctrine and Covenants

The 1876 edition of The D&C deleted Section CI *[101]*, 'Marriage', and added Section 132 which commanded the practice of polygamy.

**D&C 132:1-4,** *"Verily, thus saith the Lord unto you my servant Joseph, that inasmuch as you have inquired of my hand to know and understand wherein I, the Lord, justified my servants Abraham, Isaac, and Jacob, as also Moses, David and Solomon, my servants, as touching the principle and doctrine of their having many wives and concubines—Behold, and lo, I am the Lord thy God, and will answer thee as touching this matter. Therefore, prepare thy heart to receive and obey the instructions which I am about to give unto you; for all those who have this law revealed unto them must obey the same. For behold, I reveal unto you a new and an everlasting covenant; and if ye abide not that covenant, then are ye damned; for no one can reject this covenant and be permitted to enter into my glory."*

**D&C 132:38-39,** *"David also received many wives and concubines, and also Solomon and Moses my servants, as also many others of my servants, from the beginning of creation until this time; and in nothing did they sin save in those things which they received not of me.*

*David's wives and concubines were given unto him of me, by the hand of Nathan, my servant, and others of the prophets who had the keys of this power; and in none of these things did he sin against me save in the case of Uriah and his wife; and, therefore he hath fallen from his exaltation, and received his portion; and he shall not inherit them out of the world, for I gave them unto another, saith the Lord."*

## Did You Notice the Contradiction?

In the Book of Mormon, **Jacob 2:23-28**, David and Solomon are used as examples to show how abominable polygamy was to God.

In **D&C, Section 132**, David and Solomon are used as examples of how righteous the principle of polygamy was to God.

## Doctrine and Covenants, Official Declaration I, The 'Manifesto'

In the year 1890, due to political pressures placed upon the LDS Church by the United States government, LDS prophet Wilford Woodruff received a 'revelation' from God called the *Manifesto* which stopped the 'new and everlasting covenant' of plural marriage.

The following declaration is found on pages 291-292 in the Doctrine and Covenants *(1981 ed.)*

*"I, therefore, as President of The Church of Jesus Christ of Latter-day Saints, do hereby, in the most solemn manner, declare that these charges are false. We are not teaching polygamy or plural marriage, nor permitting any person to enter into its practice, and I deny that either forty or any other number of plural marriages have during that period been solemnized in our Temples or in any other place in the Territory.*

*One case has been reported, in which the parties allege that the marriage was performed in the Endowment House, in Salt Lake City, in the Spring of 1889, but I have not been able to learn who performed the ceremony; whatever was done in this matter was without my knowledge. In consequence of this alleged occurrence the Endowment House*

*was, by my instructions, taken down without delay.*

*Inasmuch as laws have been enacted by Congress forbidding plural marriages, which laws have been pronounced constitutional by the court of last resort, I hereby declare my intention to submit to those laws, and to use my influence with the members of the Church over which I preside to have them do likewise.*

*There is nothing in my teachings to the Church or in those of my associates, during the time specified, which can be reasonably construed to inculcate or encourage polygamy; and when any Elder of the Church has used language which appeared to convey any such teaching, he has been promptly reproved. And I now publicly declare that my advice to the Latter-day Saints is to refrain from contracting any marriage forbidden by the law of the land (Wilford Woodruff, President of The Church of Jesus Christ of Latter-day Saints.)*

## Did the Manifesto End LDS Polygamy?

It is Interesting to note that even after the *Manifesto*, LDS prophets continued to practice polygamy. Each of these LDS prophets cohabited with plural wives after 1890, after the *Manifesto*.

- Wilford Woodruff had 5 plural wives
- His successor Lorenzo Snow had 11 wives
- His successor Joseph F. Smith had 6 wives
- His successor Heber J. Grant had 3 wives

As late as 1906, sixth LDS President Joseph F. Smith "pleaded guilty before Judge M. L. Ritchie in the District Court... to the charge of cohabitating with four women in addition to his lawful wife." He was fined $300, the maximum allowed by law (*Salt Lake Tribune*, 11/24/1906.)

The last recorded case of polygamy within the LDS Church leadership was November, 1943, when LDS Apostle Richard R. Lyman was excommunicated for secretly practicing polygamy.

## The 34 Wives of Joseph Smith

The topic of polygamy also becomes a major concern for the LDS Church when the details of Joseph Smith's plural marriages are considered.

The historical facts surrounding Joseph's many marriages have, for the most part, been suppressed by the LDS Church. Many Mormons even today are surprised to learn that Joseph Smith entered into marriages with at least 34 different women.

And, when Joseph's choice in wives is exposed, this is shocking information for most if not all Mormons. The following facts will challenge the thinking of virtually any Mormon:

- Ten of Joseph Smith's wives were teenage girls –two 14 year old and two 16 year old girls.

- Joseph married a mother & daughter set– Patty Bartlett Sessions & Sylvia Sessions Lyon.
  **God said,** *"If a man take a wife and her mother, it is wickedness: they shall be burned with fire, both he and they; that there be no wickedness among you." (Leviticus 20:14, see also Lev.18:17.)*

- Joseph married sets of sisters: the Johnsons, Huntingtons, Partridges, & Lawrence sisters
  **God said,** *"Neither shalt thou take a wife to her sister… to uncover her nakedness, beside the other in her lifetime." (Leviticus 18:18.)*

- Eleven marriages were to women who had living husbands. All of these married women lived ongoing 'polyandrous' relationships with both their husbands and Joseph Smith.
  **God said,** *"The man that committeth adultery with another man's wife… the adulterer and the adulteress shall surely be put to death." (Leviticus 20:10.)*

**Marrying married women was also adultery according to Joseph's own teachings,**
> *"If any man espouse a virgin, and desire to espouse another, and the first give her consent… and they are virgins, and have vowed to no other man, then is he justified; he cannot commit adultery for they are given unto him; for he cannot commit adultery with that that belongeth unto him and to no one else… But if one or either of the ten virgins, after she is espoused, shall be with another man, she has committed adultery and shall be destroyed. " (D&C 132:61-63.)*

These and many more incriminating facts about Joseph's 34 wives are documented in the LDS book, *In Sacred Loneliness, The Plural Wives of Joseph Smith*, by Todd Compton, Signature Books, 1997. Todd Compton (as of 2014) is an active Latter-day Saint in good standing with the LDS Church. *[See also: www.WivesofJosephSmith.org]*

◉ **Go to: TriGrace.org**
**Under 'Resources' find and print the free PDF download of the *34 Wives of Joseph Smith* visual.**

## Source Fix/Living Hope Video Resource

*Lifting the Veil of Polygamy*—Jesus said, "By their fruits ye shall know them." This documentary examines the roots of Joseph Smith's polygamous legacy, and its modern-day fruit. It follows the compelling testimonies of nine former fundamentalists who shed light on this practice and lifestyle which has been shrouded in secrecy since the earliest days of Mormonism; but more importantly, they share the true freedom they have found in Jesus Christ of the Bible.

*Lifting the Veil of Polygamy* can be purchase at: *www.sourceflix.com*

## QUESTIONS FOR REVIEW

**How has the LDS Church waivered in its stance on polygamy?**
**Book of Mormon, Jacob chapter 2?**

**1835 D&C section CI [101]?**

**Modern-day D&C section 132?**

**Official Declaration I, the 'Manifesto?'**

**How are Joseph Smith's plural marriages a problem for the LDS Church today?**

# SECTION 51
# False Prophecies of Joseph Smith

🛑 **Turn to the Glossary of Mormon Terms and examine the LDS quotes under 'Joseph Smith'.**

One topic that most Mormons have never considered is the idea that 'prophets' can be tested. If you ask an LDS person, "Is there anything the LDS Prophet could do that would disqualify him from being a prophet?" they will look at you with a 'deer in the headlights' expression. LDS people have been told, "The prophet will never lead the Church astray", and with blind faith they follow him.

Consider the following Biblical truths about 'prophets' and how Joseph Smith stacks up when he is put to the test.

## There Will Be False Prophets

**Matthew 24:11, 24,** Jesus said, *"Many false prophets shall rise, and shall deceive many… For there shall arise false Christs, and false prophets, and shall shew great signs and wonders; insomuch that, if it were possible, they shall deceive the very elect."*

## How to Test a Prophet

God gives us a simple way to test prophets—If they ever lie by proclaiming a false prophesy, they are a false prophet.

**Deuteronomy 18:20-22,** *"But the prophet, which shall presume to speak a word in my name, which I have not commanded him to speak, or that shall speak in the name of other gods, even that prophet shall die. And if thou say in thine heart, How shall we know the word which the LORD hath not spoken? When a prophet speaketh in the name of the LORD, if the thing follow not, nor come to pass, that is the thing which the LORD hath not spoken, but the prophet hath spoken it presumptuously:*

*thou shalt not be afraid of him." (See also Deuteronomy 13:1-3.)*

The Biblical test is simple: prophecy that comes from God must always come to pass. If it does not come to pass, then it did not come from God. Any prophet that prophesies falsely is not a true prophet.

A similar test is found in the LDS scriptures:
**Doctrine and Covenants 1:37-39,** *"Search these commandments, for they are true and faithful, and the prophecies and promises which are in them shall all be fulfilled. What I the Lord have spoken, I have spoken, and I excuse not myself; and though the heavens and the earth pass away, my word shall not pass away, but shall all be fulfilled, whether by mine own voice or by the voice of my servants, it is the same. For behold, and lo, the Lord is God, and the Spirit beareth record, and the record is true, and the truth abideth forever and ever. Amen."*

The prophecies in the D&C must come to pass or they were not revelations that came from God.

## Testing the Prophecies of Joseph Smith

The following two prophecies of Joseph Smith are false because they never came to pass. There are numerous other false prophecies made by Joseph Smith, but these two are the best to use because they are found in the LDS Doctrine and Covenants.

## Prophesy #1—
## Doctrine and Covenants 114:1

*"Revelation given through Joseph Smith the Prophet at Far West, Missouri, April 17, 1838:*
*'Verily thus saith the Lord: It is wisdom in my servant David W. Patten, that he settle up all his business as soon as he possibly can, and make a disposition of his merchandise, that he may perform a mission unto me next spring, in company with others, even twelve including himself, to testify of my name and bear glad tidings unto all the world.'"*

This prophecy never came to pass for one simple reason, David W. Patten died on October 25, 1838, of wounds suffered from the battle of Crooked River. David Patten was in the grave when he was supposed to be on his mission to the world with 11 other men.

**EXCUSES**

One attempt to excuse this false prophecy is to claim David Patten was unfaithful, so the Lord allowed him to be killed. But, Joseph Smith said this about David Patten at his funeral,

*"Brother David Patten was a very worthy man, beloved by all good men who knew him. He was one of the Twelve Apostles, and died as he had lived, a man of God, and strong in the faith." (To examine this historical event, see History of the Church, Vol. 3, pp. 170-171.)*

**Prophesy #2—**
**Doctrine and Covenants 84:1-5, 31**

*"Revelation given through Joseph Smith the Prophet, at Kirtland, Ohio, September 22 and 23, 1832... 1–5, The New Jerusalem and the temple shall be built in Missouri...*

*A revelation of Jesus Christ unto his servant Joseph Smith, Jun., and six elders, as they united their hearts and lifted their voices on high. Yea, the word of the Lord concerning his church, established in the last days for the restoration of his people, as he has spoken by the mouth of his prophets, and for the gathering of his saints to stand upon Mount Zion, which shall be the city of New Jerusalem. Which city shall be built, beginning at the temple lot, which is appointed by the finger of the Lord, in the western boundaries of the State of Missouri, and dedicated by the hand of Joseph Smith, Jun., and others with whom the Lord was well pleased. Verily this is the word of the Lord, that the city New Jerusalem shall be built by the gathering of the saints, beginning at this place, even the place of the temple, which temple shall be reared in this generation. For verily this generation shall not all pass away until an house shall be built unto the Lord, and a cloud shall rest upon it, which*

*cloud shall be even the glory of the Lord, which shall fill the house... Therefore, as I said concerning the sons of Moses—for the sons of Moses and also the sons of Aaron shall offer an acceptable offering and sacrifice in the house of the Lord, which house shall be built unto the Lord in this generation, upon the consecrated spot as I have appointed."*

The cornerstone for this LDS Temple was laid by Joseph Smith on the appointed 'Temple Lot' in Independence Missouri, in 1832—but no temple has ever been built on this plot of ground. The problems surrounding this false prophecy are compounded as the following statements made by subsequent Prophets and Apostles of the LDS Church are examined. [According to LDS Church policy, the President, the counselors to the First Presidency, and the twelve LDS Apostles are all prophets, seers, and revelators of the LDS Church.]

### 38 years after the prophecy

LDS Apostle Orson Pratt stated, *"God promised in the year 1832 that we should, before the generation then living had passed away, return and build up the City of Zion in Jackson County; that we should return and build up the temple of the Most High where we formerly laid the corner stone... We believe in these promises as much as we believe in any promise ever uttered by the mouth of Jehovah. The Latter-day Saints just as much expect to receive a fulfillment of that promise during the generation that was in existence in 1832 as they expect that the sun will rise and set tomorrow. Why? Because God cannot lie. He will fulfill all His promises. He has spoken, it must come to pass. This is our faith." (Journal of Discourses, Vol. 13, p. 362.)*

### 58 years after the prophecy

The *1890 edition of the Doctrine and Covenants*, section 84, p. 289, contained a footnote that said, *"a generation does not all pass away in one hundred years."* [This footnote was deleted in later editions.]

## 68 years after this prophecy was made (in the year 1900)

LDS prophet Lorenzo Snow affirmed at a special priesthood meeting in the Salt Lake City Temple, *"...there are many here now under the sound of my voice, probably the majority, who will live to go back to Jackson County and assist in the building of that temple."* (Dialogue: A Journal of Mormon Thought, Autumn 1966, p. 74.)

## 102 years after the prophecy

President Joseph Fielding Smith said, *"I firmly believe that there will be some of that generation who were living when this revelation was given who shall be living when this temple is reared, and I do not believe that the Lord has bound himself to accomplish the matter within one hundred years from 1832, but he has the power to accomplish this before 1932, if he wills... I have full confidence in the word of the Lord and that it shall not fail."* (The Way To Perfection, Salt Lake City, 1935, p. 270.)

## 131 years after the prophecy

Finally, Joseph Fielding Smith admitted, *"It may be reasonable to assume that in giving this revelation to the Prophet of the Lord did have in mind the generation of people who would still be living within the one hundred years from the time of the announcement of the revelation, and that they would enjoy the blessings of the temple... It is also reasonable to believe that no soul living in 1832, is still living in mortality on the earth."* (Answers to Gospel Questions, Vol. 4, p. 112.)

Today the temple lot in Jackson County, Missouri sits empty. No temple has ever been built on this spot. **D&C 84** is a false prophecy which proves Joseph Smith and all subsequent LDS Prophets/Apostles who affirmed this prophecy were also false prophets.

👁 **Go to: TriGrace.org**
**Under 'Resources' find and print the free PDF download of the *Biblical Tests of a Prophet*.**

Then watch the TGM Tutorial explaining how this visual is used with LDS people.

## Source Fix/Living Hope Video Resources

*The Bible vs Joseph Smith*—In this unique documentary, produced entirely in Israel, a Christian and a Mormon sit down to dialogue about an important question of the faith: How do we know if a prophet is speaking the truth?

Listen in on their fascinating discussion and follow along as they travel throughout the Holy Land in search of the facts. They will put Biblical prophets and Mormon prophets to the same test in order to find out if their predictions actually took place in history. If even one prediction fails to come true, that prophet fails the test!

*The Bible vs Joseph Smith* can be purchased at www.**sourceflix**.com.

## QUESTIONS FOR REVIEW:

**How many false prophecies does it take to disqualify a prophet?**

After studying the PDF download *The Biblical Tests of a Prophet*, list three reasons Joseph Smith was a false prophet:

1.

2.

3.

# S E C T I O N 52
# The Boasting Prophet

🛑 **Turn to the Glossary of Mormon Terms and examine the LDS quotes under 'Joseph Smith'.**

The leaders of modern day Mormonism would love to erase much of the true history of Joseph Smith because they know the reputation of the

LDS Church hinges upon the character of their founding prophet. For this reason, the Church has attempted to whitewash 'the Prophet'.

This whitewashing is evident in a film produced by the LDS Church, in 2005, in honor of Joseph Smith's 200th birthday entitled, *'Joseph Smith, Prophet of the Restoration'*. The producers basically deify Joseph in this documentary. Our ministry has renamed this film *'The Passion of Joseph'*, which seems more appropriate when considering the content.

We would strongly encourage you to watch this video so you can begin to understand the picture-perfect image most Mormons have in regard to their founding Prophet. *(In 2014 this video was being offered by The LDS Church free on-line at: **www.mormonchannel.org/joseph**)*

Because most Mormons view Joseph Smith as the 2nd most important person who ever walked on this earth, it is vital that we expose the true character of Joseph Smith and help Mormons see the truth. One way to do this is to show them Joseph's boasting statement.

## The Boasting Statement

In a public sermon on Sunday, May 26, 1844, Joseph Smith Jr. proclaimed,

> *"I have more to boast of than ever any man had. I am the only man that has ever been able to keep a whole church together since the days of Adam. A large majority of the whole have stood by me. Neither Paul, John, Peter, nor Jesus ever did it. I boast that no man ever did such a work as I. The followers of Jesus ran away from Him; but the Latter-day Saints never ran away from me yet."* (History of the Church, Vol. 6, by the LDS Church, pg. 408-409.)

As you can imagine, this is NOT information the average Mormon wants to hear; so Tri-Grace Ministries has created the *4 Step Boasting Visual* to assist you. This interactive tract will expose two of Joseph's biggest blunders:

**#1.** It exposes the above boasting statement.

**#2.** It exposes Joseph's immoral polygamist relationships.

We have learned from many former Mormons that these shocking facts about Joseph Smith were the deciding factor that led them away from Joseph and into a personal relationship with Jesus

👁 **Go to: TriGrace.org**
**Under 'Resources' find and print the free PDF download of *4-Step Boasting Visual*. Then watch the TGM Tutorial explaining how to use this Visual Aid with LDS people.**

**NOTE:** Many Mormons will question the facts you are showing them. It is important for them to take *The Boasting Visual* home and check out the details for themselves. If they will do this, the truth will rock their world.

## LDS Resources

Those who would like to go one step further might consider purchasing the LDS resource containing the boasting statement. You can purchase the paperback edition of *History of the Church, Volume 6, 1843-1844*, on Amazon.com for about $6.50 *[color of the cover is bright orange]*.

## QUESTIONS FOR REVIEW:
After watching the TGM Tutorial—The *4 Step Boasting Visual,* why this would ROCK virtually any Mormon?

# CHAPTER 14

# THE CHURCH OF JESUS CHRIST VS JESUS CHRIST

# SECTION 53

## Jesus is Our Living Prophet

The LDS Church takes great pride in their living Prophets. In 1980, Ezra Taft Benson gave the following address at Brigham Young University,

***"14 Fundamentals in Following the Prophet—***

*Let us summarize this grand key, these 'Fourteen Fundamentals in Following the Prophet', for our salvation depends on them.*

*1. The prophet is the only man who speaks for the Lord in everything.*

*2. The living prophet is more vital to us than the Standard Works. [The LDS Scriptures: The Bible, Book of Mormon, Doctrine and Covenants, and The Pearl of Great Price.]*

*3. The living prophet is more important to us than a dead prophet.*

*4. The prophet will never lead the Church astray.*

*5. The prophet is not required to have any particular earthly training or credentials to speak on any subject or act on any matter at any time.*

*6. The prophet does not have to say 'Thus Saith the Lord', to give us scripture.*

*7. The prophet tells us what we need to know, not always what we want to know.*

*8. The Prophet is not limited by men's reasoning.*

*9. The prophet can receive revelation on any matter, temporal or spiritual.*

*10. The prophet may advise on civic matters.*

*11. The two groups who have the greatest difficulty in following the prophet are the proud who are learned and the proud who are rich.*

*12. The prophet will not necessarily be popular with the world or the worldly.*

*13. The prophet and his counselors make up the First Presidency—the highest quorum in the Church.*

*14. The prophet and the presidency—the living prophet and the First Presidency—follow them and be blessed—reject them and suffer.*

*"I testify that these fourteen fundamentals in following the living prophet are true. If we want to know how well we stand with the Lord then let us ask ourselves how well we stand with His mortal captain… the Living Prophet"* (Liahona, June, 1981, Ezra Taft Benson, First Presidency Message, 'Fourteen Fundamentals in Following the Prophet', an Address given Tuesday, February 26, 1980 at Brigham Young University.)

**NOTE:** This talk was strategic for Ezra because President Spencer W. Kimball was 85 years old, and Ezra was next in line for the presidency of the LDS Church.

The LDS Church has exalted the position of 'prophet' to the highest level on earth. He is the authority on both temporal and spiritual issues and is to be absolutely believed and followed. [And, LDS people wonder why we call this church a 'cult'.]

Mormons believe their 'living prophets' give their church special authority from God. LDS people will often ask, "We have a living prophet, do you have a living prophet?"

### Yes, We Have a Living Prophet!

When a Mormon asks this question we would suggest you answer them this way, "Yes, of course we have a living prophet. You do know that ALL Christian churches have a living prophet, don't you?" This response will shock them and might open an opportunity to share the following Bible lesson with them.

**Jesus is Our Living Prophet**—The Following chain of references will prove that Jesus is our living prophet today.

**A Prophet Like Moses**—Moses prophesied that God would send a special prophet.

> **Deuteronomy 18:15, 18-19,** *"The LORD thy God will raise up unto thee a Prophet from the midst of thee, of thy brethren, like unto me; unto him ye shall hearken… I will raise them up a Prophet from among their brethren, like unto thee, and will put my words in his mouth; and he shall speak unto them all that I shall command him. And it shall come to pass, that whosoever will not hearken unto my words which he shall speak in my name, I will require it of him."*

### Jesus claimed to be 'That Prophet'

> Jesus said in **John 5:46,** "For had ye believed Moses, ye would have believed me; for he wrote of me."

### Jesus was recognize as 'That Prophet'

> The people of Jesus' day recognized Jesus as 'that prophet'.
> **John 6:14,** "Then those men, when they had seen the miracle that Jesus did, said, This is of a truth that prophet that should come into the world."

The Apostle Peter later told the 1st Century Church—Jesus was 'that prophet'.
> **Acts 3:22-26,** *"Moses truly said unto the fathers, A prophet shall the Lord your God raise up unto you of your brethren, like unto me; him shall ye hear in all things whatsoever he shall say unto you. And it shall come to pass, that every soul, which will not hear that prophet, shall be destroyed from among the people. Yea, and all the prophets from Samuel and those that follow after, as many as have*

*spoken, have likewise foretold of these days… Unto you first God, having raised up his Son Jesus, sent him to bless you, in turning away every one of you from his iniquities."*

### Jesus Is the Final Prophet

> **Luke 16:16,** *Jesus said, "The law and the prophets were until John: since that time the kingdom of God is preached, and every man presseth into it."*

> **Hebrews 1:1-2,** *"God, who at sundry times and in divers manners spake in time past unto the fathers by the prophets, Hath in these last days spoken unto us by his Son."*

> **Hebrew 13:5,** *"Be content with such things as ye have: for he hath said, I will never leave thee, nor forsake thee."*

### The Spirit of Jesus will Guide Us

> **John 14:16-18,** Jesus said, *"I will pray the Father, and he shall give you another Comforter, that he may abide with you for ever; Even the Spirit of truth; whom the world cannot receive, because it seeth him not, neither knoweth him: but ye know him; for he dwelleth with you, and shall be in you. I will not leave you comfortless: I will come to you."*

> **John 16:13,** *"Howbeit when he, the Spirit of truth, is come, he will guide you into all truth."*

### A Personal Relationship With Jesus

We have the Spirit of Christ living in us.
> **Romans 8:9-10,** *"But ye are not in the flesh, but in the Spirit, if so be that the Spirit of God dwell in you. Now if any man have not the Spirit of Christ, he is none of his. And if Christ be in you, the body is dead because of sin; but the Spirit is life because of righteousness."*

If we have the Spirit of Jesus living in us, why do we need a modern day prophet? We believe Jesus is alive and He personally guides every believer throughout their life. Our living Prophet, Jesus Christ, is the most important person who ever lived, so he trumps all other prophets.

**Colossians 2:6-7,** *"As ye have therefore received Christ Jesus the Lord, so walk ye in him: Rooted and built up in him, and stablished in the faith, as ye have been taught, abounding therein with thanksgiving."*

## QUESTIONS FOR REVIEW

**Read through the LDS *14 Fundamentals in Following the Prophet* and summarize them in one sentence.**

**How do we know for certain that Jesus is 'that prophet' spoken of in Deuteronomy 18:15-19?**

**Explain in your own words why don't we need a modern day prophet?**

# S E C T I O N 54
# The Words of Jesus

The Church of Jesus Christ of Latter-day Saints has a significant problem in regard to Jesus. Although the LDS Church claims to BELIEVE IN Jesus, they really don't BELIEVE Jesus. In other words, the LDS Church only gives lip service to Jesus. They use Jesus like a mascot to call themselves Christians, but in reality Jesus is not all that important in the day-to-day life of a Mormon.

👁 **If you have not already done so, Go to: TriGrace.org. Under 'Resources' find and print the free PDF download of the *4 Step Eternal Marriage* visual. Then watch the TGM Tutorial explaining how this Visual Aid is used with Mormon people.**

Now, imagine you are the 'Mormon' in the tutorial and consider the four topics outlined:
**#1.** *Eternal/Temple Marriage,*
**#2.** *The Pre-Mortal life/Preexistence,*
**#3.** *The Great Apostasy, and*
**#4.** *Priesthood Authority*
*(ALL are **vital** doctrines in the LDS Church.)*

If you were LDS, how would it make you feel to realize that Jesus never taught any of these doctrines; and in fact, He disagreed with these doctrines? This is a powerful witnessing method!

Now, ask yourself: Is it right for Mormons to call The Church of Jesus Christ of Latter-day Saints a 'Christian' church when Jesus disagrees with all four of these foundational LDS doctrines? Shouldn't the Church of Jesus Christ agree with Jesus Christ?

## Challenge LDS People With Jesus!

My point in this exercise should be obvious. In reality, Mormons follow Joseph Smith not Jesus Christ. Mormon people are told the doctrines of their Church were taught by Jesus; but because their church discredits the Bible and discourages them from reading it, most LDS people never study the teachings of Jesus for themselves.

## The '4 STEP WORDS OF JESUS' Visual

TGM has created a simple visual to challenge LDS people in regard to the words of Jesus. Our approach is simple—we just want LDS people to start reading the words of Jesus for themselves and think about what Jesus actually taught. After all, Jesus is the most important person who ever lived on earth and His words are the most important words ever spoken.

👁 **Go to: TriGrace.org**
**Under 'Resources' find and print the *4 Step Words of Jesus Visual*. Then watch the Tutorial showing how this TGM visual is used with LDS people.**

## 4 simple Questions:

**1.** Would you agree with the Christian belief that Jesus is the most important person who ever lived on this earth?

**2.** Would you also agree that the Words of Jesus are the most important words ever spoken?

**3.** Jesus said, *"If you continue in my word, then are you my disciples indeed; And you shall know the truth, and the truth shall make you free." (John 8:31-32.)*

**4.** Are the Words of Jesus the absolute truth?

As Christians, we believe the words of Jesus are vital to our relationship with Him. We believe life on this earth is all about knowing Jesus and following His teachings. Show your LDS friend some of the things Jesus said about the importance of His own words.

## Jesus promised to preserve the truth of His words to all generations when He said:

*"Heaven and earth shall pass away, but my words shall not pass away."* (**Matthew 24:35, Mark 13:31, & Luke 21:33**.)

## Jesus said His words were absolute truth:

*Jesus said, "If ye continue in my word, then are ye my disciples indeed; And ye shall know the truth, and the truth shall make you free... I am the way, the truth, and the life, no man comes to the Father but by Me.'"*(**John 8:31-32; 14:6**.)

## In Luke 6, Jesus asked the people:

*"Why call ye me, Lord, Lord, and do not the things which I say?"*

Jesus then went on to claim the following about the importance of His teachings:

*"Whosoever cometh to me, and heareth my sayings, and doeth them, I will shew you to whom he is like: He is like a man which built an house, and digged deep, and laid the foundation on a rock: and when the flood arose, the stream beat vehemently upon that house, and could not shake it: for it was founded upon a rock. But he that heareth, and doeth not, is like a man that without a foundation built an house upon the earth; against which the stream did beat vehemently,*

*and immediately it fell; and the ruin of that house was great."* (**Luke 6:46-49**.)

## The words of Jesus will judge us in the final judgment:

*"He that rejecteth me, and receiveth not my words, hath one that judgeth him: the word that I have spoken, the same shall judge him in the last day."*(**John 12:48.**)

## Everyone who loves truth listens to Jesus:

*"To this end was I born, and for this cause came I into the world, that I should bear witness unto the truth. Every one that is of the truth heareth my voice."* (**John 18:37.**)

Our point is this—If Jesus truly is the Way, the Truth, and the Life, He is not only the most important person who ever lived, but the truths He taught are the most important words ever spoken to mankind. We should, therefore, devote our lives to studying and following His words.

## The Challenge

The next step in this process is to present your LDS friend with a simple 'Challenge'.

Explain that the Bible contains four eye witness accounts of Jesus Christ's life and teachings – Matthew, Mark, Luke, and John.

Then challenge them to read the Gospel of John—THIS WEEK—with the eyes of a child, because Jesus said,

**Matthew 18:3,** *"Verily I say unto you, Except ye be converted, and become as little children, ye shall not enter into the kingdom of heaven."*

The following points will help LDS people to truly think about what Jesus is saying. Ask them to read the gospel of John and think about these three things:

**1.** Look for truths taught by Jesus which might surprise you.

**2.** Try to find a place where Jesus taught the religious beliefs you hold to be most precious.

**3.** Align your thinking and beliefs with the truths taught by Jesus no matter what it costs!

As they read, we can rest assured that the Holy Spirit will reveal the truth to them because:

*"The word of God, is quick, and powerful, and sharper than any two-edged sword, piercing even to the dividing asunder of soul and spirit, and of the joints and marrow, and is a discerner of the thoughts and intents of the heart."* (**Hebrews 4:12**.)

And God says, *"So shall my word be that goeth forth out of my mouth: it shall not return unto me void, but it shall accomplish that which I please, and it shall prosper in the thing whereto I sent it."* (**Isaiah 55:11**.)

If we can get Mormon people into God's Word, Jesus will draw them to Himself.

## QUESTIONS FOR REVIEW

**What is the basic strategy behind *THE 4 STEP JESUS VISUAL*?**

**Why will this approach work with any Mormon who will take our 'Challenge' and read the Gospel of John with the eyes of a child?**
> ***(See God's promises to us in Hebrews 4:12 and Isaiah 55:11.)***

# S E C T I O N **55**
# The Jesus Survey for Mormons

As was discussed in the previous two sections, Mormonism only gives lip service to Jesus and his teachings. They claim to believe in Jesus, but they really don't really believe Jesus.

The Jesus Survey *(for Mormons)* is six simple questions that can be presented to any Mormon in an easy to use survey format.

**NOTE:** As you study *The Jesus Survey*, you will notice that it also includes the four topics found in the *4 Step Eternal Marriage Visual*. We call these topics the '4 pillars of Mormonism' because, when these four doctrines are dismantled, the LDS world view will collapse.

Before proceeding with this chapter, you should first take *The Jesus Survey* yourself.

👁 **Go to: TriGrace.org**
**Under 'Resources' find and print the free PDF download of *The Jesus Survey*. (Page 2 of the survey gives the correct answers—don't Cheat!)**

So, how did you do?

**NOTE:** If you give this survey to Christians, they will usually get at least 4 out of 6 correct. If you give this same survey to Mormons, they will usually miss at least 4 out of 6.

We will briefly discuss each question so you understand why this survey works so well with LDS people.

**QUESTION #1.** Jesus demonstrated on several occasions that even the most wicked of sinners would be forgiven:
A. Eventually, through repentance process which would lead them to righteous living.
or
B. Immediately, by simply coming to Jesus and exercising a humble faith in Him.

### Mormonism
Forgiveness within Mormonism is a very defined process that must be strictly followed if forgiveness is to be attained.

🛑 **Turn to the Glossary of Mormon Terms and read the LDS definition of 'Forgiveness'.**

### Jesus and Forgiveness
In **Luke 7:36-50**, Jesus immediately forgave a prostitute because she simply worshiped Him.

Jesus said, *"Her sins, which are many, are forgiven."* (Also consider **Matthew 9:2-8**.)

Also consider the Father's immediate forgiveness in the story of the prodigal son found in **Luke 15:11-24.**

## Biblical Forgiveness is Immediate

**1 John 1:9,** *"If we confess our sins, he is faithful and just to forgive us our sins, and to cleanse us from all unrighteousness."*

It is significant to note that according to the Bible, all forgiven sins are totally forgotten, never to be remembered again:

**Psalm 103:12,** *"As far as the east is from the west, so far hath he removed our transgressions from us."*

**Isaiah 38:17,** *"Thou hast cast all my sins behind thy back."*

**Micah 7:19,** *"Thou wilt cast all their sins into the depths of the sea."*

**Hebrews 8:12** and **10:17,** *"I will be merciful to their unrighteousness, and their sins and their iniquities will I remember no more... And their sins and iniquities will I remember no more."*

*(Compare **Doctrine and Covenants 82:7** which totally contradicts this wonderful Bible promise.)*

**QUESTION #2.** In regard to preexistence, Jesus stated that:

A. He was the only person who had pre-existed in the presence of the Father and had come down to the earth.

or

B. We all had pre-existed with our Father in Heaven and should view the entire human race as sons and daughters of God.

## Mormonism

The pre-mortal existence is foundational to the entire worldview of Mormonism—the end goal of Mormonism is exaltation *(to one day become a God just like Heavenly Father.)* Exaltation is founded in the Preexistence and being literal children of God which makes us genetically sons of deity.

**STOP** Turn to the Glossary of Mormon Terms and read the LDS definition of 'Pre-Mortal Life or Preexistence'.

## Jesus on Preexistence

The LDS doctrine of the Preexistence has many theological problems, but we will only focus on the fact that Jesus said He was the only person who preexisted with the Father in Heaven.

**NOTE:** To reduce repetition, refer back to Section 46, 'The Premortal Life/The Preexistence of Spirits', where the following verses are outlined: **John 17:24-25, John 5:37-38, John 6:46, John 7:28-29,** and **John 8:54-55**.

We will look at one verse here to make the point:

**John 8:23,** *"And he said unto them, Ye are from beneath; I am from above: ye are of this world; I am not of this world."*

**QUESTION #3.** (True or False) Jesus taught His followers the sanctity and importance of an eternal marriage relationship which would extend far beyond the future resurrection.

## Mormonism

According to the LDS Prophets, eternal marriage is the 'Crowning Ordinance' of Jesus Christ's gospel. Temple marriage, however, is one topic that has no scriptural support. No one in the Bible or in the Book of Mormon was ever married in a temple or was ever married for time and all eternity.

**STOP** Turn to the Glossary of Mormon Terms and read the LDS definition of 'Celestial Marriage'.

## Jesus on Marriage in the Afterlife

Only once did Jesus discuss the topic of marriage in the afterlife. This narrative is found in **Matthew 22:23-30**. Consider the story and the question posed to Jesus:

*"The same day came to him the Sadducees, which say that there is no resurrection, and asked him, saying, Master, Moses said, If a man die, having no children, his brother shall*

*marry his wife, and raise up seed unto his brother. Now there were with us seven brethren: and the first, when he had married a wife, deceased, and, having no issue, left his wife unto his brother: Likewise the second also, and the third, unto the seventh. And last of all the woman died also. Therefore in the resurrection whose wife shall she be of the seven? for they all had her."*

If eternal marriage was a principle of Jesus Christ's gospel, this was the perfect opportunity to preach a sermon on the wonders of 'celestial marriage'—but, Jesus didn't do that.

Think about the question posed to Jesus, *"In the resurrection whose wife shall she be of the seven? For they all had her."* If celestial marriage was the 'crowning ordinance' of Jesus Christ's gospel, he would have asked these men, *"Was this woman married to any of her husbands in the temple for time and all eternity?"*

Jesus did not ask that question because no one was ever married in a Jewish temple. Instead Matthew records:

*"Jesus answered and said unto them, Ye do err, not knowing the scriptures, nor the power of God. For in the resurrection they neither marry, nor are given in marriage, but are as the angels of God in heaven."*

**QUESTION #4.** In regard to priesthood, Jesus Christ:

A. Spoke often with His disciples about the importance of the priesthood and ordained them with priesthood authority to act in His name.

or

B. Never spoke about the importance of any priesthood nor is it recorded that He ordained his Apostles with priesthood authority.

🛑 **Turn to the Glossary of Mormon Terms and read the LDS Definition for: 'Priesthood'.**

## Mormonism

LDS 'priesthood authority' is probably the most emphasized doctrine in the LDS Church. In the minds of Mormon people, this is the part of the 'restored LDS gospel' of Jesus Christ that means the most to them.

Every worthy male believes he holds both the Aaronic and the Melchizedek priesthoods, and these priesthoods give him special authority to administer the ordinances of the 'restored gospel' of Jesus Christ.

## Jesus on the Priesthood

Jesus must not have considered the topic of priesthood authority to be important at all because he never once discussed priesthood with his disciples. The word 'priesthood' is not found in the gospels, and almost every use of the word 'priest' in the gospels is in reference to the Jewish priests with whom Jesus was in continual conflict.

Jesus consistently taught that all power and authority would come through the gift of the Holy Ghost/Spirit, Jesus said:

***Acts 1:8**, "Ye shall receive power, after that the Holy Ghost is come upon you: and ye shall be witnesses unto me both in Jerusalem, and in all Judaea, and in Samaria, and unto the uttermost part of the earth."*

In Acts Chapter 2, this is exactly what happened—the gifts of the Spirit came through the Holy Ghost. These gifts had nothing to do with any 'priesthood'.

The most important point when considering the 'Aaronic' and/or 'Melchizedek' priesthoods is this: there is absolutely no instruction given by Jesus or by any of His Apostles concerning the need for 'priesthood authority' in the letters to the New Testament churches.

The only New Testament book that addresses the topic of the Aaronic and Melchizedek priesthoods is the book of Hebrews. This book, however, does not support LDS theology. In Hebrews, the Aaronic priesthood is weak, obsolete and passing away. Also, only one person is said to be a 'priest forever after the order of Melchizedek'—JESUS. Check it out, every time this Melchizedek priest is mentioned, it is always in the singular. The only priest who is ever said to be in the likeness of Melchizedek is Jesus.

## Does 'Ordained' = 'Priesthood?'

LDS people directly link the Biblical word 'ordained' with 'priesthood'. Every time Mormons see the word 'ordained'—in their mind—they assume it means ordained to the priesthood. However, Biblically this is not the case.

## In the Bible 'Ordained' is not synonymous with 'Priesthood':

- Burnt offerings were ordained by God (**Numbers 28:6**.)
- Feasts of Israel were ordained to be kept on appointed days (**1 Kings 12:32**.)
- The land of Palestine was ordained to be Israel's dwelling place (**1 Chronicles 17:9**.)
- Ungodly priests were ordained by ungodly kings (**2 Chronicles 11:15**.)
- Praise psalms were ordained to be used in public worship (**2 Chronicles 23:18**.)
- Musical instruments were ordained to be used in public worship (**2 Chronicles 29:27**.)
- Heavenly bodies (sun, moon, and stars) were ordained to shine in the heavens (**Psalm 8:3**.)
- The lineage of David (the line of the Messiah) was ordained by God (**Psalm 132:17**.)
- God ordained peace for Israel (**Isaiah 26:12**.)
- 'Tophet' fiery judgment on the ungodly was ordained by God (**Isaiah 30:33**.)
- Prophets were ordained (**Jeremiah 1:5**.)
- Warriors were ordained to kill (**Daniel 2:24**.)
- The Chaldeans/Babylonians were ordained to destroy Israel (**Habakkuk 1:6-12**.)
- The twelve Apostles were ordained to preach the gospel and perform miracles (**Mark 3:14-15**.)
- All Believers in Jesus are ordained to do good works (**John 15:16; Ephesians 2:10**.)
- The Lord's Apostles were ordained to be witnesses of Jesus Christ's death and resurrection (**Acts 1:22**.)
- Jesus was ordained to be the judge of all mankind (**Acts 10:42; Acts 17:31**.)
- Believers in Jesus are ordained to eternal life (**Acts 13:48**.)

- Elders were ordained to be the spiritual leaders in the early church (**Titus 1:5**.)
- The decrees of the Apostles were ordained to be preached in all the churches (**Acts 16:4**.)
- The Old Testament Law was ordained to condemn sinful mankind (**Romans 7:7-12**.)
- Government leaders are ordained by God (**Romans 13:1**.)
- Preaching the gospel of salvation through the crucifixion of Jesus Christ was ordained by God (**1 Corinthians 2:1-8**.)
- Paying pastors to preach the gospel was ordained by God (**1 Corinthians 9:14**.)
- Paul was ordained as the Apostle to preach the gospel to the Gentiles (**1 Timothy 2:7**.)
- Israel's High Priest was ordained to offer animal sacrifices to atone for the people's sins (**Hebrews 5:1, 8:3, 9:6**.)
- Ungodly men are ordained to condemnation (**Jude 1:4**.)

👁 Go to: TriGrace.org
**Under 'Resources' find and print the free PDF download of *Ordained is NOT Synonymous with Priesthood*.**

**QUESTION #5.** (True or False) Jesus said that after his departure the Church would fall into a state of total apostasy because wicked men would arise who would take away many of the precious truths that He had taught.

## Mormonism

LDS people have the lowest regard for the Christian church because they believe the LDS Heavenly Father told Joseph Smith:

*"They [the Christian denominations] were all wrong; and... all their creeds were an abomination in his sight; that those professors were all corrupt; that: 'they draw near to me with their lips, but their hearts are far from me.'"* (Pearl of Great Price, Joseph Smith History 1:19.)

🛑 **Turn to the Glossary of Mormon Terms and read the LDS definitions of 'Great Apostasy, The', and 'Christianity'.**

## Jesus said this about His Church

**Matthew 16:18**, *"I will build my church; and the gates of hell shall not prevail against it."*

**Matthew 24:35,** Jesus said, *"Heaven and earth shall pass away, but my words shall not pass away."*

**Matthew 28:20,** Jesus made this promise to His Church, *"I am with you alway, even unto the end of the world. Amen."*

**Acts 1:8,** Jesus told his 1st Century disciples, *"Ye shall receive power, after that the Holy Ghost is come upon you: and ye shall be witnesses unto me both in Jerusalem, and in all Judaea, and in Samaria, and unto the uttermost part of the earth."*

NO WAY could the Christian church fall into a state of total apostasy! If the 'Great Apostasy' happened as the LDS Church describes, then Jesus is a false prophet, but Jesus is not a liar, He is *"the way, the truth, and the life."* (**John 14:6**.)

During Jesus Christ's final moments on earth, as he was being questioned by Pilate, He said, *"To this end was I born, and for this cause came I into the world, that I should bear witness unto the truth. Every one that is of the truth heareth my voice."* (**John 18:37**.)

If we truly believe in Jesus, we must also believe that Jesus always spoke the truth.

**QUESTION #6.** (True or False) Jesus taught that after death people will be given a second chance to receive the gospel – those who repent can move from a place of tortured remorse to a place of peace and comfort.

### Mormonism

LDS people hate the Christian view of hell! They don't want to picture hell as a place of fiery judgment. They choose to believe it is a place where people will only suffer the torments of remorse. In LDS theology ALL (except the sons of perdition) will have the opportunity to repent and eventually be saved to one of three LDS kingdoms of glory.

**(STOP)** Go to the Glossary of Mormon Terms and read the LDS definitions for 'Hell', 'Damnation', 'Eternal Damnation', and 'Eternal Punishment'.

### Jesus Defined Hell as Eternal Punishment

In the gospel story of the Rich Man and Lazarus, Jesus eliminates any hope for second chances after death when he explains:

**In Luke 16:19-26,** *"Between us and you there is a great gulf fixed, so that those who want to pass from here [paradise] to you cannot, nor can those from there [hell] pass to us."*

Jesus taught more about eternal destruction in hell than any other prophet, Jesus said:

**Matthew 7:13,** *"wide is the gate, and broad is the way, that leadeth to destruction, and many there be which go in thereat."*

**Mark 9:43-44,** *"It is better for thee to enter into life maimed, than having two hands to go into hell, into the fire that never shall be quenched: Where their worm dieth not, and the fire is not quenched."* (**also vs. 45-48**.)

**Matthew 25:46,** *"These shall go away into everlasting punishment: but the righteous into life eternal."*

And in the book of Revelation He says:

**Revelation 20:10, 14-15,** *"The devil that deceived them was cast into the lake of fire and brimstone, where the beast and the false prophet are, and shall be tormented day and night for ever and ever... And death and hell were cast into the lake of fire. This is the second death. And whosoever was not found written in the book of life was cast into the lake of fire."*

It is ironic that the LDS Church approaches the doctrine of hell in such a light hearted manner because the Book of Mormon warns that the Devil will deceive people into believing there is no such thing as an eternal fiery hell.

**2 Nephi 28:21-22,** *"Others will he [the devil] pacify, and lull them away into carnal security, that they will say: All is well in Zion;*

*yea, Zion prospereth, all is well—and thus the devil cheateth their souls, and leadeth them away carefully down to hell. And behold, others he flattereth away, and telleth them there is no hell; and he saith unto them: I am no devil, for there is none—and thus he whispereth in their ears, until he grasps them with his awful chains, from whence there is no deliverance."*

It is sad that LDS people have been pacified and lulled into a false sense of security by a Church that calls itself Christian yet denies the very teachings of the one they call Savior.

### The Jesus Challenge

Tri-Grace Ministries has also produced a handout version of the Jesus Survey that can be passed out like a tract at an LDS event. One thing to keep in mind is that the answers are given on the back of this handout, so admonish those receiving this handout NOT TO CHEAT. Ask them to do the survey first, then look at the answers.

👁 **Go to: TriGrace.org**
**Under 'Resources' find and print the free PDF download of *The Jesus Challenge* .**

### QUESTIONS FOR REVIEW
**Why do most Mormons miss 4 out of 6 of the questions in the Jesus Survey?**

**Why do you think they get any of them right?**

**Why is the Jesus Survey effective with Mormons, what does the Survey reveal to them?**

**When a Mormon hears the Biblical word 'ordained' what do they immediately think?**

# SECTION 56
# Mormonism and Racism

🛑 **Go to the Glossary of Mormon Terms and read the LDS definition of 'Blacks'.**

This section is written to expose the inherent racist nature of Mormonism. This section is not written to accuse LDS people of being racists.

### I am Not A Racist

As a born again Christian, I would say I am colorblind when it comes to race. Yes, I do notice that human beings have a variety of skin colors; but this observation does not cause me to feel racist in any way. In fact, I actually appreciate the diversity within the human family. I see great diversity in all of creation because we have a Creator God who happens to be very imaginative.

### The God of the Bible is Not a Racist

The God of the Bible is not racist, nor did He create humans with varying degrees of lighter or darker skin to denote their level of righteousness. There are no statements in God's Word, the Bible, which would indicate that light skin is a blessing or a symbol of righteousness. Nor are there any comments in the Bible to indicate that darker skin is a curse which resulted from the rebellious actions of individuals (not in this life or in any 'pre-earth' life.) It is abhorrent for me to even consider the idea that God might be a racist.

### God is 'Colorblind'

I can confidently state that the God of the Bible is colorblind too. He loves all the people of this whole world—red, yellow, black and white—exactly the same. He came to this earth in the person of Jesus Christ to die for the sins of the whole world, for the sins of white and black alike.

My Bible says", *There is none righteous no not one."* **(Romans 3:10.)**

117

This means we are all in the same spiritual condition—black and white alike are all sinners in need of a Savior. Jesus offers the same salvation to all without prejudice:

*"Whosoever will, may come."* (**Romans 10:13**.)

We serve an awesome Savior of love, and His great love has always been extended to the entire human race on an equal basis.

## LDS People Today are NOT Racist

I am also a Christian who loves and has a deep appreciation for LDS people. I have many good things to say about the Mormons. They are a nice, hardworking, friendly, and kind people who would give you the shirt off their back if you had a need. I don't believe most Mormon people today would encourage racism. I have LDS friends who have adopted children of various nationalities with dark skin, and these individuals love their adopted children like their own. This does not mean Mormonism is not racist, and that concerns me.

## Kudos to the LDS Church for Ending Their Racist Restrictions

I want to give credit where credit is due; and in recent years, LDS church leaders have made huge concessions and great strides to eradicate the racist restrictions of their past. Until 1978, people with dark skin were not allowed to be ordained into the LDS priesthood, nor were people with dark skin allowed to enter the Mormon temples. People with white skin were not allowed to 'mix their seed' with those of darker skin. Thankfully, these racist regulations have been rescinded, and today blacks have an equal standing in the LDS Church. However, this does not eliminate the racism embedded within Mormonism.

## Racism Can Never Be Completely Erased From Mormonism For Three Reasons...

### REASON #1 – Prophets, Seers, and Revelators of the LDS Church were Racists

Racism cannot be eliminated from the LDS religion because there is no way to erase the fact that LDS Prophets and Apostles from the past (men who claimed to be spokespersons for God) issued racist revelations in the name of God.

The fact that LDS Prophets were racist can clearly be seen in their writings prior to 1978.

From the very founding of the LDS Church, men who claimed to be living prophets of God made unbelievable racist comments about people groups with dark skin.

**Joseph Smith**—The founding prophet of Mormonism was a racist. Joseph Smith said,
*"Had I anything to do with the negro, I would confine them by strict law to their own species, and put them on a national equalization."* (History of the Church, Vol. 5, pp. 217-218.)

The fact that there happen to be a few examples in early LDS history where Joseph was kind to some African American families does not change the fact that he was racist in his thinking. Some (not many) slave owners were kind to their slaves—I feel certain Joseph Smith would have promoted kindness to slaves.

**Brigham Young**—followed in Joseph's footsteps by making racist comments like:
*"You see some classes of the human family that are black, uncouth, uncomely, disagreeable and low in their habits, wild, and seemingly deprived of nearly all the blessings of the intelligence that is generally bestowed upon mankind. The first man that committed the odious crime of killing one of his brethren will be cursed the longest of any one of the children of Adam. Cain slew his brother. Cain might have been killed, and that would have put a termination to that line of human beings. This was not to be, and the Lord put a mark upon him, which is the flat nose and black skin."* (Journal of Discourses, Vol. 7, p.291, Remarks by President Brigham Young, delivered in the Tabernacle, Great Salt Lake City, October 9, 1859, Reported by G. D. Watt.)

Racist comments like these were abundant in the early days of Mormonism and even into the mid 1900's LDS Prophets were still making outrageous racial comments.

**Joseph Fielding Smith**—The 10th LDS President and Prophet said,

*"Not only was Cain called upon to suffer, but because of his wickedness he became the father of an inferior race. A curse was placed upon him and that curse has been continued through his lineage and must do so while time endures. Millions of souls have come into this world cursed with a black skin and have been denied the privilege of Priesthood and the fullness of the blessings of the Gospel. These are the descendants of Cain. Moreover, they have been made to feel their inferiority and have been separated from the rest of mankind from the beginning." (The Way to Perfection, p. 101, 1931.)*

**The Church and the Negro**, by Elder John Lewis Lund, contains unbelievable LDS quotes about the 'African race',

*"Brigham Young made a very strong statement on this matter when he said, 'I would like the President of the United States and all the world to hear this. Shall I tell you the law of God in regard to the African race? If the white man who belongs to the CHOSEN SEED mixes his blood with the seed of Cain, the penalty under the law of God, is death on the spot. This will always be so'. God has commanded Israel not to intermarry. To go against this commandment of God would be to sin. Those who willfully sin with their eyes open to this wrong will not be surprised to find that they will be separated from the presence of God in the world to come." (The Church and the Negro, by John Lewis Lund, p. 54.)*

These quotes are undeniable, which causes problems for those who would attempt to defend the honor of the LDS Church. Their only recourse is to point out the fact that many 'Christians' have also been racist. Regrettably this is true, and as a Christian, I am shocked that any person who would name the name of Jesus Christ would consider a person in the human family as inferior due to the color of their skin.

There is, however, a big difference between 'professing Christians', who were racist in complete contradiction to God and the Bible, and Mormon Prophets, who were racist in perfect agreement with the scriptures of the LDS Church.

## REASON #2 – The LDS Scriptures Were and Still Are Racist

Racism cannot be separated from Mormonism because it cannot erase the fact that racism is, even today, promoted in the LDS scriptures.

I would challenge anyone to show me from the Bible that racism was promoted according to God's word. The Prophets of the Bible did not promote racism. There are numerous examples from the Bible where God's Prophets associated with, worked side-by-side with, and intermarried with people of all nationalities.

When the Israelites were freed from their slavery in Egypt, a 'mixed multitude' of foreign slaves left with them (the mixed multitude certainly contained African slaves) and Moses married an Ethiopian (dark skinned) woman. Solomon welcomed and honored the Queen of Sheba (an African queen.)The Apostle Paul said there is no distinction between Jew or Gentile, Slave or Free (which would include all people groups), Male or Female—we are all one in Christ.

## The LDS Scriptures Promote Racism

The Mormon Prophets who promoted racism did so because the LDS scriptures promote racism, consider the racist statements found in LDS scriptures today.

**Moses 7:8,** *"For behold, the Lord shall curse the land... and there was a blackness came upon all the children of Canaan, that they were despised among all people." (***Pearl of Great Price, Moses 7:8***.)*

**NOTE:** the book of Moses should NOT be confused with the books written by Moses in the Holy Bible.

**2 Nephi 5:21,** *"And he had caused the cursing to come upon them, yea, even a sore cursing, because of their iniquity. For behold, they had hardened their hearts against him, that they*

*had become like unto a flint; wherefore, as they were white, and exceedingly fair and delightsome, that they might not be enticing unto my people the Lord God did cause a skin of blackness to come upon them"*

**3 Nephi 2:14-15,** *"And it came to pass that those Lamanites who had united with the Nephites were numbered among the Nephites; And their curse was taken from them, and their skin became white like unto the Nephites."*

We can disagree with the Mormon prophets for making racial statements in the name of God, but we really cannot blame them because they were teaching what the LDS scriptures proclaim to be truth. The real question is this: why would any human being, especially anyone with dark skin, ever want to be a part of a religion where racism is promoted in that religion's scriptures?

### REASON #3 – The LDS God Is a Racist

Most importantly, the racism of Mormonism cannot be ignored or erased because the God of Mormonism, who called Joseph Smith to start the Mormon religion, is a racist.

In the Book of Mormon there is a class system set forth. Those who are more righteous are light skinned, those who are less righteous are dark skinned. So in the LDS worldview, where did it all start?

According to LDS theology, prior to the creation of this world there was a great council of the Gods in Heaven, and all of God's spirit children were summoned to this meeting. *(Supposedly, we were all in attendance.)* In this meeting, two of God's spirit sons stepped forth, Jesus and Lucifer. They each proposed a plan of salvation for our earth. The council of Gods chose to accept Jesus Christ's plan of salvation and, as a result, Lucifer rebelled. His rebellion caused a great war in Heaven.

All of God's spirit children chose sides in this conflict, 1/3 fought for Lucifer, and 2/3 fought with Jesus—1/3, however, did not fight valiantly in this war.

The spirit children who teamed with Lucifer were judged to be 'sons of perdition' and were cast out of Heaven, destined to become the demonic spirits who serve the Devil.

The spirit children who fought valiantly with Jesus were blessed to be born into the world with white skin.

The spirit children who did not fight valiantly were judged and destined to be born into this world cursed with a black skin.

**NOTE:** The LDS Church today is trying to distance itself from this early teaching of Mormonism, but it is undeniable that the early prophets of the Mormon Church taught this doctrine.

(STOP) **Turn to the Glossary of Mormon Terms and read the LDS definition for 'Blacks'.**

### The 'Root' of the Racism Problem

Once again, those who would defend the honor of the LDS Church in regard to racism have a problem because the root of the problem is not the racism taught by LDS Prophets, nor is it the racism promoted in LDS scriptures. The root of the problem is the fact that Joseph Smith claimed his new-found religion was ordained by God.

If Joseph Smith was being truthful, and Mormon doctrine was inspired by God, the root of racism is their God. According to LDS theology, it was their God who determined that black skin would be a curse and used the mark of black skin to differentiate the righteous from the unrighteous. It was also their God who inspired Book of Mormon prophets to say white skin is exceedingly fair and delightsome and black skin is loathsome and a curse.

Even LDS Leaders understood this to be the case. Consider this statement by LDS Apostle, Bruce R. McConkie:

*"The negroes are not equal with other races where the receipt of certain spiritual blessings are concerned, particularly the priesthood and the temple blessings that flow therefrom, but this inequality is not of man's origin. **It is the Lord's doing**, is based on his eternal laws of justice, and grows out of the lack of spiritual*

*valiance of those concerned in their first estate [the pre-mortal life]." (Mormon Doctrine, Bruce R. McConkie, 1966, p. 527-528.)*

## Which God do you Choose?

Why would any human being, especially anyone with dark skin, ever want to be a part of a religion where racism is promoted by that religion's prophets, scriptures, and God? I don't know about you, but I choose a God who is not a racist. I choose the God of Christianity. I don't want a God that invented a class system for human beings based upon skin color. I want a God that blesses ALL who place their trust in Him and love their neighbor as themselves. I want a God who will judge those who are evil and wicked—those who do not love Him and do not treat others with equal respect and honor.

### Can the LDS Church Fix This Problem?

Yes, they can! They need to repent and be completely honest with the LDS people.

The outrageous racial statements made by LDS Prophets in the name of God prove they were NOT true prophets of God, they were false prophets. They must admit this and ask the LDS people to forgive them.

The LDS scriptures are not God's word! God would never make racist comments like the ones contained in the Book of Mormon. The leadership must admit the LDS scriptures are frauds and ask the LDS people to forgive them for this deception.

The God of the Bible is not a racist, so the LDS Church needs to admit that the gods of Mormonism are NOT true. They need to apologize to the LDS people for leading them into idolatry and ask the LDS people to forgive them.

Then the LDS Church needs to turn to the one and only true God and follow Him alone. They need to place their trust in the only true Word of God, the Bible. They need to start believing what Jesus Christ taught and place their faith and trust in Him alone for their salvation. The LDS gospel needs to be trashed, and the true gospel of Jesus needs to start being proclaimed. They need to stop promoting their abominable LDS temple works and turn their temples into houses of

prayer for all people as Jesus said, "Is it not written, 'My house shall be called a house of prayer for all nations? But you have made it a 'den of thieves.'"

If, and only if, they will do these things can they totally fix this problem.

👁 **Go to: TriGrace.org**
**Under 'Resources' find and print the *Mormonism and Racism* visual. Then watch the Tutorial showing how this visual is used with LDS people.**

### QUESTIONS FOR REVIEW
**Which LDS racism quote is most offensive to you? Why?**

**Name the three reasons racism can never be totally erased from Mormonism?**
   **1.**

   **2.**

   **3.**

**In what significant way is the LDS Church still racist today even though they allow blacks to fully participate in the LDS religion?**

# APPENDIX 1
# GLOSSARY OF MORMON TERMS

# A

**Adam**—Also known as Michael the Archangel and the Ancient of Days, see Ancient of Days.

"The first man. The father of the human race. Before his earth life, he was known as Michael. He led the righteous in the war in heaven. He helped in the creation of the earth." (*Gospel Principles*, LDS Church, Glossary/Adam, 1979/1990.)

"Our great prince, *Michael*, known in mortality as *Adam*, stands next to Christ in the eternal plan of salvation and progression... In the creation of the earth, Michael played a part second only to that of Christ. When Lucifer rebelled and there was war in heaven, it was Michael who led the hosts of the faithful in casting Satan out. When the time came to people the earth, the spirit Michael came and inhabited the body formed from the dust of the earth, the living soul thus created being known as *Adam.*" (*Mormon Doctrine*, McConkie, 1966, p. 491.)

**Ancient of Days**—See Adam

"When Adam was placed on this earth all his former knowledge was taken away. Yet the Lord has made known to us that Adam lived before and had experiences as Michael, the great prince, who was chosen to stand as the head of the human family on this earth as the Ancient of Days." (*The Way to Perfection*, Joseph Fielding Smith, 1931, p. 18.)

"Daniel in his seventh chapter speaks of the Ancient of Days; he means the oldest man, our Father Adam... He *(Adam)* is the father of the human family, and presides over the spirits of all men... The Son of Man stands before him, and there is given him glory and dominion. Adam delivers up his stewardship to Christ... but retains his standing as head of the human family." (*Teachings of the Prophet Joseph Smith*, Joseph Fielding Smith, p. 157.)

**Adultery**—In the LDS Church, adultery is a sin like unto murder in that it can become an unforgivable sin. Commit adultery once and, through a long repentance process, you can be forgiven; but if you commit adultery again, it cannot be totally forgiven—Two strikes and you're out!

"Next to Murder in Seriousness—The enormity of this sin is underlined by numerous scriptures... The Lord apparently rates adultery close to premeditated murder... The grievousness of the sin enhances the difficulty of repenting. Sometimes offenders reach the point of no return and cannot repent... The penalty in this life is similarly clearly defined: 'Thou shalt not commit adultery; and he that committeth adultery, and repenteth not, shall be cast out'. (D&C 42:24)... The sin is forgivable providing the repentance is sufficiently comprehensive. 'But if he doeth it again, he shall not be forgiven, but shall be cast out.'" (D&C 42:26.) (*The Miracle of Forgiveness*, Kimball, p. 62-63, 72-73.)

**Apostate**—Anyone who was a member of The Church of Jesus Christ of Latter-day Saints and who left the Church is termed an 'apostate'. It is taught by the LDS Church that gross sin is the initial cause of apostasy, followed by the departure of the Holy Ghost—which then allows Satan to take possession of the person's mind and which will cause the person to lose faith in truths that can only be found in the LDS Church. This departure from truth will ultimately result in excommunication from the LDS Church making them 'sons of perdition'—sealed to Satan for all eternity. Apostates are, therefore, treated by the LDS Community with the greatest contempt. Often, apostates will lose their jobs or their businesses will go bankrupt (because the LDS community may totally shun them.) They also lose their social status in the community which means they lose friends and sometimes even family (through divorce.) The fear of being called an 'apostate' often manipulates LDS people into staying in the Church, long after they understand Mormonism to be false.

"…*The apostate*—the man who is bitter in his soul, who has known the truth but has turned away from the light and rejected the gospel." (*Doctrines of Salvation*, Joseph Fielding Smith, Vol. 2, p. 188.)

"*Fate of Apostates*— …Almost without exception when a person leaves the Church, it is due to *transgression.* The Spirit of the Lord will not dwell in unclean tabernacles, and *when the Spirit is withdrawn, darkness supersedes the light, and apostasy will follow… In the Church when a man sins and continues without repentance, the Spirit is withdrawn, and when he is left to himself the adversary takes possession of his mind and he denies the faith…* But *when he turns away, he still knows that he once had the light.* The Lord has said of such: 'All those who know my power, and have been made partakers thereof, and suffered themselves through the power of the devil to be overcome, and to deny the truth and defy my power—They are they who are the sons of perdition, of whom I say that it had been better for them never to have been born'. …*Severity Of Judgment Upon Apostates*— …Let it be remembered, however, that the punishment of the apostate, no matter who he is or what degree of knowledge he may have attained, shall be most severe. 'Hearken and hear, O ye my people, saith the Lord and your God… ye that hear me not will I curse, *that have professed my name, with the heaviest of all cursings*'. …*Excommunicated Persons Lose All Blessings*—What will be the status of a person born under the covenant if excommunicated from the Church? When a person is excommunicated from the Church, every blessing is withdrawn and lost…" (*Doctrines of Salvation,* Joseph Fielding Smith, Vol. 3, p. 308-311.)

**Atonement of Christ**—According to Mormonism, the atonement took place mostly in the Garden of Gethsemane *(and partially on the cross at Calvary.)* Although Mormonism gives lip service to the cross, the greatest suffering and the actual atonement is believed to have taken place in the Garden.

Mormonism also divides the atonement into two parts; the first is unconditional atonement, the second conditional atonement. Unconditional atonement is 'salvation by grace' for all people *(except sons of perdition)* and is resurrection from the grave/immortality—living in one of the three LDS kingdoms of glory. Conditional atonement is complying with the LDS laws, commandments, and ordinances which will then determine which kingdom of glory a person has earned. In its fulness, conditional atonement can earn the most valiant persons eternal life/exaltation or in-other-words godhood.

"It was in Gethsemane that Jesus took on Himself the sins of the world, in Gethsemane that His pain was equivalent to the cumulative burden of all men, in Gethsemane that He descended below all things so that all could repent and come to Him… He suffered the pains of all men in Gethsemane so they would not have to suffer if they would repent. Only then did He voluntarily submit to death." (*Teachings of Ezra Taft Benson*, p.14-15.)

"PASSION OF CHRIST— …The sectarian world falsely suppose that the climax of his torture and suffering was on the cross—a view which they keep ever before them by the constant use of the cross as a religious symbol. The fact is that intense and severe as the suffering was on the cross, yet the great pains were endured in the Garden of Gethsemane. It was there that he trembled because of pain, bled at every pore, and suffered both in body and in spirit… It was there he underwent his greatest suffering for men, taking upon himself, as he did, their sins on conditions of repentance." (*Mormon Doctrine*, McConkie, 1966, p. 555.)

"Twofold Nature of Atonement. The atonement of Jesus Christ is of a twofold nature. Because of it, all men are redeemed from mortal death and the grave, and will rise in the resurrection to immortality of the soul. Then again, by obedience to the laws and ordinances of the gospel, man will receive remission of individual sins, through the blood of Christ, and will inherit exaltation in the kingdom of God, which is eternal life." (*Doctrines of Salvation*, Joseph Fielding Smith, Vol. 1, p. 123.)

"ATONEMENT AND SINS UNTO DEATH. *Joseph Smith taught that there were certain sins so grievous that man may commit, that they will place the transgressors beyond the power of the atonement of Christ. If these offenses are committed, then the blood of Christ will not cleanse them from their sins even though they repent. Therefore their only hope is to have their own blood shed to atone, as far as possible, in their behalf.*" (*Doctrines of Salvation*, Joseph Fielding Smith, Vol. 1, pp. 135-136.)

## Authority—See Priesthood.

# B

**Baptism**—By immersion is synonymous with being 'born again' and receiving the gift of the Holy Ghost.

"Baptism is the first saving ordinance of the gospel… *Being Born Again.* Through the ordinance of baptism and confirmation, you were born again into a new life. The Savior said to Nicodemus, 'Except a man be born of water and of the Spirit, he cannot enter into the kingdom of God' (John 3:5.)" (*True to the Faith*, LDS Church, 2004, p. 21, 25.)

"*Why must we be baptized?* WE MUST BE BAPTIZED FOR THE REMISSION OF OUR SINS… WE MUST BE BAPTIZED BEFORE WE CAN RECEIVE THE GIFT OF THE HOLY GHOST… WE MUST BE BAPTIZED TO ENTER THE CELESTIAL KINGDOM… Baptism by immersion by one having the proper authority is the only true and acceptable way of being baptized." (*Gospel Principles*, LDS Church, 1979/1990, Ch. 20, 'Baptism'.)

**Baptism for the dead**—LDS people go to LDS temples to do works for the dead. Baptism for the dead is just one of the proxy works performed for the dead in LDS temples.

"Ordinances for the Dead—People who have died without essential gospel ordinances may receive those ordinances through the work done in temples. You may do this work in behalf of your ancestors and others who have died. Acting for them, you can be baptized and confirmed, receive the endowment, and participate in the sealings of husband to wife and children to parents." (*True to the Faith*, LDS Church, 2004, p. 171-172.)

"'The greatest responsibility in this world that God has laid upon us, is to seek after our dead'. because we cannot be saved without them. …while it is necessary to preach the gospel in the nations of the earth, and to do all the other good works in the Church, yet the greatest commandment given us, and made obligatory, is the temple work in our own behalf and in behalf of our dead." (*Doctrines of Salvation*, Joseph Fielding Smith, Vol. 2, p. 149.)

**[NOTE: 1 Corinthians 15:29,** *"Else what shall they do which are baptized for the dead, if the dead rise not at all? why are they then baptized for the dead?"* **How should you respond to a Mormon who brings up this Biblical passage in support of 'baptism for the dead?'**

The key to interpreting this passage is the CONTEXT. You will notice in verse 29 the word 'they' is used. Then, in verse 30 'we' is used. These two verses have two different groups of people in mind. In verse 29, 'they' corresponds with the 'false teachers' who were discussed in **1 Cor. 15:12**. In verse 30 'we' are the Christians who are being persecuted for their belief in the resurrection. The Apostle Paul is the master of sarcasm. In his writings, when something is ridiculous, Paul often uses sarcasm to expose the error. In verse 29 Paul is using sarcasm to point out the fact that the false teachers are contradicting themselves—if there is no resurrection from the dead, why then are 'they' having people get baptized for the dead—it would be pointless.

Another idea you can bring up with your LDS friend is the fact that no 'baptisms for the dead' are ever talked about in the Book of Mormon which is supposed to contain the 'fulness of the everlasting gospel'—see the 'Introduction' to the Book of Mormon. The fact that works for the dead are never mentioned in the Book of Mormon supports our interpretation of **1 Cor. 15:29**. Plus, because 1 Cor. 15 is the only place where 'baptism for the dead' is mentioned in either the Bible or the Book of Mormon proves this to be an isolated practice not associated with the Lord's true Church or it would be mentioned in more than just this one place.]

**Bible**—The LDS Church goes to great lengths to discredit the authority of the Bible. The Book of Mormon describes how the early Christian Church fell into apostasy and corrupted the Bible *(see 1 Neph Chapter 13.)* On the one hand, the LDS Church uses the Bible to authenticate its claim to be 'Christian' and on the other hand undermines the Bible by teaching LDS people not to trust it.

"We believe the Bible to be the word of God as far as it is translated correctly." (The Pearl of Great Price, 'Eighth Article of Faith', LDS Church, 1981.)

"The Bible, as it has been transmitted over the centuries, has suffered the loss of many plain and precious parts." ('Letter Reaffirms Use of King James Bible', President Ezra Taft Benson, Gordon B. Hinckley, & Thomas Monson, *Church News*, June 20, 1992, p. 3.)

"What shall we say then, concerning the Bible's being a sufficient guide? Can we rely upon it in its present known corrupted state, as being a faithful record of God's word? We all know that but a few of the inspired writings have descended to our times... Who knows how many important doctrines and ordinances necessary to salvation may be buried in oblivion in some of the lost books? ...But the Bible has been robbed of its plainness; many sacred books having been lost, others rejected by the Romish Church, and what few we have left, were copied and recopied so many times, that it is admitted that almost every verse has been corrupted and mutilated to that degree that scarcely any two of them read alike." (Orson Pratt, *Divine Authenticity of Book of Mormon, No. 3* (December 1, 1850), and *The Seer*, Orson Pratt, 1853-54, p. 213.)

**Blacks**—Although the LDS Church is trying to distance itself from the teachings of LDS Prophets and Apostles in regard to the 'blacks/negroes' or really anyone who has skin that is not 'white and delightsome' *(see 2 Nephi 5:21)*, the fact remains—the official doctrines of Mormonism past cannot be erased! Mormonism was and still is a racist religion.

"NEGROES—In the pre-existent eternity various degrees of valiance and devotion to the truth were exhibited by different groups of our Father's spirit offspring. One-third of the spirit hosts of heaven came out in open rebellion and were cast out without bodies, becoming the devil and his angels. The other two-thirds stood affirmatively for Christ… Of the two-thirds who followed Christ, however, some were more valiant than others… Those who were less valiant in pre-existence and who thereby had certain spiritual restrictions imposed upon them during mortality are known to us as the *negroes*. Such spirits are sent to the earth through the lineage of Cain, the mark put upon him for his rebellion against God and his murder of Abel being a black skin… Negroes in this life are denied the priesthood; under no circumstances can they hold this delegation of authority from the Almighty… The present status of the negro rests purely and simply on the foundation of pre-existence… The negroes are not equal with other races where the receipt of certain spiritual blessings are concerned, particularly the priesthood and the temple blessings that flow therefrom, but this inequality is not of man's origin. It is the Lord's doing, is based upon his eternal laws of justice, and grows out of the lack of spiritual valiance of those concerned in their first estate." (*Mormon Doctrine*, McConkie, 1966, p. 526-528.)

[**NOTE:** Thankfully, in 1978, the restrictions placed upon African Americans or anyone with darker colored skin was rescinded by the LDS Church and they now have equal standing in the LDS Church— BUT, there is really no way for the LDS religion to 'fix' this problem because in order to do so, they need to not only trash the past restrictions that were placed upon the blacks but they also need to trash their scriptures which promote racism and their God who is the original racist! The only way to 'fix' this is to trash the entire religion, turn to the Jesus Christ of the Bible and the gospel of the Bible, and join the ranks of true Christianity.]

## Born Again—See Baptism.

**Book of Abraham**— Since its publication in 1842, the Book of Abraham has been a source of controversy. Non-Mormon Egyptologists have raised a united voice disagreeing with Joseph Smith's explanations of the Egyptian facsimiles. They have also asserted that damaged portions of the papyri have been reconstructed incorrectly. The controversy intensified in 1966 when portions of the Joseph Smith Papyri were found and subsequently returned to the LDS Church. The translation of the Egyptian text by both Mormon and non-Mormon Egyptologists has shown that the rediscovered portions bore no relation to the original 'Book of Abraham' text.

"A translation from some Egyptian papyri that came into the hands of Joseph Smith in 1835, containing writings of the patriarch Abraham… A Translation of some ancient Records, that have fallen into our hands from the catacombs of Egypt.—The writings of Abraham while he was in Egypt, called the Book of Abraham, written by his own hand, upon papyrus." (Pearl of Great Price Introductory Note, and the 'Book of Abraham' Introductory Note.)

"*Book of Abraham*— …Abraham was the original author, and the scriptural account contains priceless information about the gospel, preexistence, the nature of Deity, the creation, and priesthood, information which is not otherwise available in any other revelation now extant." (*Mormon Doctrine*, McConkie, 1966, p. 564.)

**Book of Mormon**—The Book of Mormon is considered to be the most important of the four books recognized as inspired scripture by the LDS Church. It is interesting to note that the Book of Mormon does not support many of the strange and unique doctrines of the LDS Church.

"The Prophet Joseph Smith said: 'I told the brethren that the Book of Mormon was the most correct of any book on earth, and the keystone of our religion, and a man would get nearer to God by abiding by its precepts, than by any other book.'" *(Book of Mormon, INTRODUCTION, paragraph 6.)*

"Of the four great standard works of the Church—the Bible, the Book of Mormon, the Doctrine and Covenants, and the Pearl of Great Price—I would particularly urge you to read again and again the Book of Mormon and ponder and apply its teachings." (*The Teachings of Ezra Taft Benson*, p. 557.)

"It is the Book of Mormon, not the Bible, that prepares men… for the Second Coming of the Son of Man. And when the eternal ledgers are finally balanced, more souls will have been saved in the celestial kingdom—ten thousand times over—because of the Book of Mormon than have so obtained because of the Bible." (*A New Witness for the Articles of Faith*, McConkie, p. 394.)

# C

**Celestial Kingdom**—Heavenly Father's dwelling place, the highest LDS heaven. Only those who earn celestial glory will have the opportunity to one day reach the state of exaltation or godhood in the celestial kingdom.

"*Celestial Glory for Those Who Keep the Whole Law*—To enter the *celestial* and obtain exaltation it is necessary that the *whole law be kept*." (*The Way to Perfection*, Joseph Fielding Smith, p. 206.)

"Highest among the kingdoms of glory hereafter is the *celestial kingdom*. It is the kingdom of God… An inheritance in this glorious kingdom is gained by complete obedience to gospel or celestial law." (*Mormon Doctrine*, McConkie, 1966, p. 116-17.)

"NOT HALF THE LATTER-DAY SAINTS TO BE SAVED. Those who receive the *fullness* will be privileged to view the face of our Father. *There will not be such an overwhelming number of Latter-day Saints who will get there.* President Francis M. Lyman many times has declared… I believe, that *if we save one-half of the Latter-day Saints, that is, with an exaltation in the celestial kingdom of God, we will be doing well.* Not that the Lord is partial, not that he will draw the line as some will say, to keep people out. He would have every one of us go in if we would; but there are laws and ordinances that we must keep; if we do not observe the law we cannot enter." (*Doctrines of Salvation*, Joseph Fielding Smith, Vol. 2, p. 15.)

**Celestial Marriage**—Only LDS people who are 'worthy' may be married in an LDS Temple for time and all eternity. To enter the LDS temple one must certify their worthiness in two interviews—a Bishop's interview and a Stake Presidency interview. Approval is based upon individual worthiness through compliance with LDS law—those who are deemed worthy will then receive a 'Temple Recommend' which grants them entrance into the LDS temples.

"The prophets have uniformly taught that the consummate and culminating element of God's great plan for the blessings of his children is eternal marriage… President Howard W. Hunter described celestial marriage as 'The Crowning Gospel Ordinance.'" ('Eternal Marriage', Elder F. Burton Howard, *Ensign*, May, 2003, p. 92.)

"Celestial marriage is the gate to an exaltation in the highest heaven within the celestial world… *The most important things that any member of the Church of Jesus Christ of Latter-day Saints ever does in this world are: 1. To marry the right person, in the right place, by the right authority; and 2. To keep the covenant made in connection with this holy and perfect order of matrimony—thus assuring the obedient persons of an inheritance of exaltation in the celestial kingdom.*" (*Mormon Doctrine*, McConkie, 1966, p. 118.)

**Christianity**—The multitudes of Gentiles who believe in the Christian Jesus and who were led astray by the great and abominable Church, the Church of the Devil *(see **1 Nephi Chapters 13-14.**)*

"The people called Christians are shrouded in ignorance, and read the Scriptures with darkened understandings." (*Journal of Discourses 7:333*, Brigham Young, October 8, 1859.)

"Every Latter-day Saint knows that following the death of the apostles, Paul's prophecy was fulfilled, for there were many 'grievous wolves' that entered the flock, and men arose 'speaking perverse things', so that the doctrines were changed and the true Church of Jesus Christ ceased to be on the earth." (*Man, His Origin and Destiny*, Joseph Fielding Smith, p. 467.)

One BYU professor explained, "Since whoever does not belong to 'the church of the Lamb of God' belongs to 'the church of the devil', as Nephi announced, then all systems of worship outside of The Church of Jesus Christ of Latter-day Saints would be classified as 'the church of the devil' by Nephi's definition." *(*Kent B. Jackson, "'Watch and Remember': The New Testament and the Great Apostasy"; John M. Lundquist and Stephen D. Ricks, eds., *By Study and Also by Faith: Essays in Honor of Hugh W. Nibley on the Occasion of His Eightieth Birthday, 27 March 1990, 1:87.*)

**Council of the Gods**—In heaven, the LDS religion teaches that there were councils held by the Gods to make the necessary decisions in regard to the creation of our earth.

"COUNCIL IN HEAVEN—There were many meetings, conferences, *councils*, and schooling sessions held among the Gods and their spirit offspring in pre-existence. Among other things, at these various assemblages, plans were made for the creation and peopling of this earth and for the redemption and salvation of the offspring of Deity... Joseph Smith speaks of 'the head of the Gods' calling 'a council of the Gods' to arrange for the creation and peopling of the earth. He also speaks of 'the grand council of heaven' in which those destined 'to minister to the inhabitants of the world' were 'ordained' to their respective callings." (*Mormon Doctrine*, McConkie, 1966, p. 163-164.)

**Creation**—The creation of our earth was directed by the Father and organized by Jesus Christ, many preexistent spirit children of God also participated in the creation of this world. The LDS Church teaches matter and/or the elements are eternal, so our earth and everything on it was created from existing matter—they do not believe in creation 'ex nihilo'—a Latin phrase meaning 'out of nothing'.

"Under the direction of his Father, *Jesus Christ created this earth*. No doubt *others helped him*, but it was Jesus Christ, our Redeemer, who, under the direction of his Father, came down and organized matter and made this planet... We are told by our Father in heaven that *man is eternal*; that he has always existed, and that *all life on this earth came from elsewhere*... ADAM AND OTHERS HELPED IN CREATION. It is true that Adam helped to form this earth. He labored with our Savior Jesus Christ. I have a strong view or conviction that there were others also who assisted them. Perhaps Noah and Enoch; and *why not Joseph Smith,* and those who were appointed to be rulers before the earth was formed?" (Doctrines of Salvation, Joseph Fielding Smith, Vol. 1, p. 74-75.)

Joseph Smith taught, "Now, I ask all who hear me, why the learned men who are preaching salvation, say that God created the heavens and the earth out of nothing? The reason is, that they are unlearned in the things of God, and have not the gift of the Holy Ghost... You ask the learned doctors why they say the world was made out of nothing; and they will answer, 'Doesn't the Bible say He *created* the world?' And they infer, from the word create, that it must have been made out of nothing. Now, the word create came from the word baurau which does not mean to create out of nothing; it means to organize; the same as a man would organize materials and build a ship. Hence, we infer that God had materials to organize the world out of chaos—chaotic matter, which is element… The pure principles of element are principles which can never be destroyed; they may be organized and re-organized, but not destroyed. They had no beginning, and can have no end." (*Teachings of the Prophet Joseph Smith*, Joseph Fielding Smith, p. 350-352.)

**Cross**—LDS people will not wear a cross *(of course there is always the exception to the rule)* nor will the LDS Church display the cross on or in their churches. As with the Bible, they give lip service to the cross but for all practical purposes the importance of the cross is ignored in the theology of Mormonism.

"To bow down before a cross or to look upon it as an emblem to be revered because of the fact that our Savior died upon a cross is repugnant to members of the Church of Jesus Christ of Latter-day Saints… To many, like the writer, such a custom is repugnant and contrary to the true worship of our Redeemer. Why should we bow down before a cross or use it as a symbol? Because our Savior died on the cross, the wearing of crosses is to most Latter-day Saints in very poor taste and inconsistent to our worship. Of all the ways ever invented for taking life and the execution of individuals, among the most cruel is likely the cross." (*Answers to Gospel Questions*, Joseph Fielding Smith, Vol. 4, p. 17.)

"For us, the cross is the symbol of the dying Christ, while our message is a declaration of the Living Christ." ('The Symbol of Our Faith', Gordon B. Hinckley, *Ensign*, April 2005, p. 3.)

"It was in Gethsemane, on the slopes of the Mount of Olives, that Jesus made his perfect atonement by the shedding of his blood—more so than on the cross… (see D&C 19:16-20.)" (*A Bible! A Bible!*, Robert J. Matthews, p. 282.)

# D

**Damnation—*See Eternal Damnation*—**In LDS theology, not keeping the commandments will dam a person in the afterlife (dam as in a water dam that stops the progress of a river.) Those who fail to keep all of the LDS laws will be stopped in their eternal progression or damned—barred from their full potential to one day become a God.

"DAMNATION—What is damnation? *It is being barred, or denied privileges of progression, because of failure to comply with law.* All who fail to enter into the celestial kingdom are damned, or *stopped in their progression*, but they will enter into some other glory which they are entitled to receive." (*Doctrines of Salvation*, Joseph Fielding Smith, Vol. 2, p. 227.)

**Devil—*See Satan***

**Doctrine and Covenants**—The Doctrine and Covenants are the modern day revelations of the Church of Jesus Christ of Latter-day Saints.

"The Doctrine and Covenants is a collection of divine revelations and inspired declarations given for the establishment and regulation of the kingdom of God on the earth in the last days… Most of the revelations in this compilation were received through Joseph Smith, Jun., the first prophet and president of The Church of Jesus Christ of Latter-day Saints. Others were issued through some of his successors in the Presidency *(see headings to Sections 135, 136, and 138, and Official Declarations 1 and 2.)* …The Doctrine and Covenants is unique because it is not a translation of an ancient document, but is of modern origin and was given of God through His chosen prophets for the restoration of His holy work and the establishment of the kingdom of God on the earth in these days." (Doctrine and Covenants, 'Explanatory Introduction', by the LDS Church, 1981.)

# E

**Elohim**—The LDS name of God the Eternal Father, Heavenly Father.

"*Elohim*, as understood and used in the restored Church of Jesus Christ, is the name-title of God the Eternal Father, whose firstborn Son in the spirit is *Jehovah*—the Only Begotten in the flesh, Jesus Christ." (*Jesus the Christ*, Talmage, p. 38.)

"JEHOVAH THE FIRSTBORN. Among the spirit children of Elohim, the first-born was and is Jehovah, or Jesus Christ, to whom all others are juniors.—Improvement Era, Vol. 19, p.940." (*Gospel Doctrine*, Joseph F. Smith, 1977, p. 70.)

"That Child to be born of Mary was begotten of Elohim, the Eternal Father, not in violation of natural law but in accordance with a higher manifestation thereof; and, the offspring from that association of supreme sanctity, celestial Sireship, and pure though mortal maternity, was of right to be called the 'Son of the Highest." (*Jesus the Christ*, Talmage, p. 81.)

**Endowment**—A sacred covenant performed by worthy Mormons in LDS temples.

"Certain special, spiritual blessings given worthy and faithful saints in the temples are called *endowments*, because in and through them the recipients are endowed with power from on high... So sacred and holy are the administrations performed that in every age when they have been revealed, the LORD has withheld them from the knowledge of the world and disclosed them only to the faithful saints in houses and places dedicated and selected for that purpose... All temple ordinances, except baptism for the dead, pertain to exaltation [*becoming gods*] in the celestial kingdom... These sacred ordinances are administered for the living and on a proxy basis for the dead also." (*Mormon Doctrine*, McConkie, 1966, p. 226-227.)

**Eternal Damnation—*See also Eternal Punishment***—Eternal is not associated with the eternal wrath of God upon sinners, or punishment that has no end. Eternal Damnation can be likened to a water 'dam' which prevents the flow of a man's progression upward to godhood.

**Temporary punishment imposed upon those in the LDS Spirit Prison is one form of 'eternal damnation'.**
"This type of eternal damnation ceases when the offender has finally come forth in the resurrection. In this sense, eternal damnation is the type, kind, and quality of torment, punishment, or damnation involved rather than the duration of that damnation. In other words, *eternal* is the name of the kind of punishment involved... Eternal punishment is, thus, the kind of punishment imposed by God who is *Eternal*, and those subject to it may suffer there-from for either a short or a long period. After their buffetings and trials cause them to repent, they are freed from this type of eternal damnation." (*Mormon Doctrine*, McConkie, 1966, p. 236.)

**After the final judgment, all who are assigned to a lesser glory than the celestial glory experience 'damnation', this is the second form of 'eternal damnation'—this is similar to a water dam that stops the progress of a river.**
"WHAT IT MEANS TO BE DAMNED. What is damnation? *It is being barred*, or *denied privileges of progression, because of failure to comply with law.* All who fail to enter into the celestial kingdom are damned, or *stopped in their progression*, but they will enter into some other glory which they are entitled to receive." (*Doctrines of Salvation*, Joseph Fielding Smith, Vol. 2, p. 227.)

"*Eternal damnation* is the opposite of eternal life, and all those who do not gain eternal life, or exaltation in the highest heaven within the celestial kingdom, are partakers of eternal damnation. Their *eternal condemnation* is to have limitations imposed upon them so that they cannot progress to the state of godhood."(*Mormon Doctrine*, McConkie, 1966, p. 234.)

**Eternal Families**—The promise that 'families are forever' for those who are worthy and have had their families sealed to them in an LDS temple.

"*THE FAMILY CAN BE ETERNAL*— ...President Brigham Young explained that our families are not yet ours. The LORD has committed them to us to see how we will treat them. Only if we are faithful will they be given to us forever... *The Eternal Family*—Our family can be together forever. To enjoy this blessing we must be married in the [LDS] temple... When we are married in the temple by the authority of the Melchizedek Priesthood, we are married for time and eternity. Death cannot separate us. If we obey the commandments of the LORD, our families will be together forever as husband, wife, and children."(*Gospel Principles*, LDS Church, 1979/1990, Ch. 36, 'The Family Can Be Eternal'.)

**Eternal Life**—VERY IMPORTANT! Eternal life is works-based and must be earned by obeying all the principles of the LDS gospel. Eternal life is not the same as Immortality. Everyone will be given an immortal/eternal existence in one of the three Mormon heavens. Eternal life is the same thing as LDS Exaltation—Eternal life/Exaltation is progression to godhood in the celestial kingdom.

"IMMORTALITY AND ETERNAL LIFE COMPARED. Immortality and eternal life are two separate things, one distinct from the other. Every man shall receive immortality, whether he be good, bad, or indifferent, for the resurrection from the dead shall come to all. Eternal life is something in addition. None shall receive eternal life save it be those who keep the commandments of the LORD and are entitled thus to enter in his presence... Very gladly would the Lord give to everyone eternal life, but since that blessing can come only on merit—through the faithful performance of duty—only those who are worthy shall receive it." (*Doctrines of Salvation*, Joseph Fielding Smith, Vol. 2, p. 4-5.)

"Eternal life is not a name that has reference only to the unending duration of a future life; immortality is to live forever in the resurrected state, and by the grace of God all men will gain this unending continuance of life. But only those who obey the fullness of the gospel law will inherit eternal life... Thus those who gain eternal life receive exaltation...They are gods." (*Mormon Doctrine*, McConkie, 1966, p. 237.)

**Eternal Marriage**—See Celestial Marriage.

**Eternal Progression**—The eternal world view of Mormonism—all human beings, progress from an eternal 'intelligence', to a pre-mortal spirit child of God, to mortality, to immortality, and if they are worthy to eternal life/exaltation—eventual godhood in the Celestial Kingdom.

"We believe in a God who is Himself progressive, who's majesty is intelligence; whose perfection consists in eternal advancement—a Being who has attained His exalted state by a path which now His children are permitted to follow, whose glory it is their heritage to share. In spite of the opposition of the sects, in the face of direct charges of blasphemy, the Church proclaims the eternal truth: 'As *man is, God once was; as God is, man may be.*" (*The Articles of Faith*, Talmage, p. 430.)

"If Jesus Christ was the Son of God, and John discovered that God the Father of Jesus Christ had a Father, you may suppose that He had a Father also. Where was there ever a son without a father? And where was there ever a father without first being a son? ...Paul says that which is earthly is in the likeness of that which heavenly, hence if Jesus had a Father, can we not believe that *He* had a Father also?" (*Teachings of the Prophet Joseph Smith*, Joseph Fielding Smith, p. 373.)

"ETERNAL PROGRESSION A FUNDAMENTAL PRINCIPLE OF THE GOSPEL— …God himself is still increasing and progressing in knowledge, power, and dominion, and will do so, worlds without end. It is just so with us." (*Doctrines from the Prophets, Alma P. Burton*, Wilford Woodruff, p. 155.)

**Eternal Punishment**—Is not punishment forever, but rather punishment from God whose name is Eternal.

"…For, behold, I am endless, and the punishment which is given from my hand is endless punishment, for Endless is my name. Wherefore—Eternal punishment is God's punishment. Endless punishment is God's punishment." (**D&C 19:10-12**.)

"Eternal punishment is, thus, the kind of punishment imposed by God who is *Eternal*, and those subject to it may suffer there-from for either a short or a long period. After their buffetings and trials cause them to repent, they are freed from this type of eternal damnation." (*Mormon Doctrine*, McConkie, 1966, p. 236.)

**Exaltation**— Exaltation is synonymous with eternal life. Exaltation is becoming a God, just like Heavenly Father, through obedience to all the laws and ordinances of the Mormon gospel.

"WHAT IS EXALTATION? Exaltation is eternal life, the kind of life that God lives… We can become Gods like our Heavenly Father. This is exaltation." (*Gospel Principles*, LDS Church, 1979/1990, Ch. 47, 'Exaltation'.)

"LEARN HOW TO BE GODS—You have got to learn how to be gods yourselves, and to be kings and priests to God, the same as all gods have done before you, namely, by going from one small degree to another, and from a small capacity to a great one; from grace to grace, from exaltation to exaltation." (*Doctrines from the Prophets,* Alma P. Burton, 'Joseph Smith', p. 169.)

"REQUIREMENTS FOR EXALTATION—Latter-day Saints are taught that now is the time to fulfill the requirements for exaltation (see **Alma 34:32-34**.) President Joseph Fielding Smith said, "In order to obtain the exaltation we must accept the gospel and all its covenants; and take upon us the obligations which the LORD has offered; and walk in the light and understanding of the truth; and 'live by every word that proceedeth forth from the mouth of God' …In other words, each person must endure in faithfulness, keeping all the Lord's commandments until the end of his life on earth." (*Gospel Principles*, LDS Church, 1979/1990, Ch. 47, 'Exaltation'.)

**Excommunication—*See Apostate***

# F

**Fall, The**—The fall of Adam and Eve in the Garden of Eden was a fall in the right direction.

President Joseph Fielding Smith said, "'The Transgression of Adam—Many Christian sects mistakenly teach that Adam's transgression and fall were contrary to God's plan for his children… Adam made the wise decision, in fact the only decision that he could make'. …President Wilford Woodruff said: 'Adam and Eve came to this world to perform exactly the part that they acted in the Garden of Eden; and I will say, they were ordained of God to do what they did, and it was therefore expected that they would eat of the forbidden fruit in order that man might know both good and evil…' President Marion G. Romney dispels any doubt as to Adam's understanding of his action: '…I do not look upon Adam's action as a sin. think it was a deliberate act of free agency. He chose to do that which had to be done to further the purposes of God.'" (*Search These Commandments*, LDS Church, 1984, p. 238-239.)

"SIN HAD TO COME INTO THE WORLD—Some may regret that our first parents sinned. This is nonsense. If we had been there, and they had not sinned, we should have sinned. I will not blame Adam or Eve. Why? Because it was necessary that sin should enter into the world… no one could ever receive an exaltation without being acquainted with its opposite… The LORD knew they would do this, and he had designed that they should." (*Doctrines from the Prophets*, Alma Burton, 'Brigham Young', p. 6.)

"GREAT BLESSINGS RESULTED FROM THE TRANSGRESSION—Some people believe that Adam and Eve committed a serious sin when they ate of the tree of knowledge of good and evil. However, latter-day scriptures help us understand that their fall was a necessary step in the plan of life and a great blessing to all mankind." (*Gospel Principles*, LDS Church, 1979/1990, Chapter 6, 'The Fall of Adam and Eve'.)

**Feelings**—In the LDS Church, truth is determined by 'feelings'.

**D&C 9:8-9**, "Behold, I say unto you, that you must study it out in your mind; then you must ask me if it be right, and if it is right I will cause that your bosom shall burn within you; therefore, you shall feel that it is right. But if it be not right you shall have no such feelings, but you shall have a stupor of thought that shall cause you to forget the thing which is wrong."

"In order to know that the Book of Mormon is true, a person must read, ponder, and pray about it. The honest seeker of truth will soon come to feel that the Book of Mormon is the word of God… In answer to our prayers, the Holy Ghost will teach us truth through our feelings and thoughts." (*Preach My Gospel*, LDS Church Manual, 2004, p. 38-39.)

**First Vision**—In 1820 Joseph Smith, as a teenage boy, *[supposedly]* had a spiritual encounter with Heavenly Father and his Son, Jesus Christ.

**The Official LDS Version of the First Vision (1838)—Recorded in the Pearl of Great Price:**
"I was at this time in my fifteenth year… It was on the morning of a beautiful, clear day, early in the spring of eighteen hundred and twenty… I kneeled down and began to offer up the desires of my heart to God. I had scarcely done so, when immediately I was seized upon by some power which entirely overcame me, and had such an astonishing influence over me as to bind my tongue so that I could not speak. Thick darkness gathered around me, and it seemed to me for a time as if I were doomed to sudden destruction.

But, exerting all my powers to call upon God to deliver me out of the power of this enemy which had seized upon me, and at the very moment when I was ready to sink into despair and abandon myself to destruction—not to an imaginary ruin, but to the power of some actual being from the unseen world, who had such marvelous power as I had never before felt in any being—just at this moment of great alarm, I saw a pillar of light exactly over my head, above the brightness of the sun, which descended gradually until it fell upon me.

It no sooner appeared than I found myself delivered from the enemy which held me bound. When the light rested upon me I saw two Personages, whose brightness and glory defy all description, standing above me in the air. One of them spake unto me, calling me by name and said, pointing to the other— *This is My Beloved Son. Hear Him!*

My object in going to inquire of the Lord was to know which of all the sects was right, that I might know which to join. No sooner, therefore, did I get possession of myself, so as to be able to speak, than I asked the Personages who stood above me in the light, which of all the sects was right (for at this time it had never entered into my heart that all were wrong)—and which I should join.

I was answered that I must join none of them, for they were all wrong; and the Personage who addressed me said that all their creeds were an abomination in his sight; that those professors were all corrupt; that: 'they draw near to me with their lips, but their hearts are far from me, they teach for doctrines the commandments of men, having a form of godliness, but they deny the power thereof'.

He again forbade me to join with any of them; and many other things did he say unto me, which I cannot write at this time. When I came to myself again, I found myself lying on my back, looking up into heaven." (Pearl of Great Price, Joseph Smith History 1:7, 14-20.)

"FIRST VISION— ...This transcendent vision *[the 'First Vision']* was the beginning of latter-day revelation; it marked the opening of the heavens after the long night of apostate darkness... Through it the creeds of Christendom were shattered to smithereens, and because of it the truth about those Beings whom it is life eternal to know began again to be taught among men. With this vision came the call of that Prophet who, 'save Jesus only', was destined to do more 'for the salvation of men in this world, than any other man that ever lived in it'. This vision was the most important event that had taken place in all world history from the day of Christ's ministry to the glorious hour when it occurred... When Joseph Smith, then but a youth in his 15$^{th}$ year... returned from that sacred spot, he had the sure knowledge—for his eyes had seen and the Holy Ghost... had born record to his soul—that the Father and the Son were two glorified Personages in the express image of each other." (*Mormon Doctrine*, McConkie, 1966, p. 285-286.)

**Forgiveness**—Total forgiveness is only granted when all the commandments of the LORD are kept.

"Your Heavenly Father has promised forgiveness upon total repentance and meeting all the requirements, but that forgiveness is not granted merely for the asking. There must be works—many works—and an all-out, total surrender, with a great humility and 'a broken heart and a contrite spirit'. It depends upon you whether or not you are forgiven, and when. It could be weeks, it could be years, it could be centuries before that happy day when you have the positive assurance that the LORD has forgiven you." (*Miracle of Forgiveness*, Kimball, pp. 324-325.)

"This progress toward eternal life is a matter of achieving perfection. Living all the commandments guarantees total forgiveness of sins and assures one of exaltation through that perfection which comes by complying with the formula the LORD gave us. In his Sermon on the Mount he made the commandment to all men: 'Be ye therefore perfect, even as your Father which is in heaven is perfect' (Matt. 5:48.) Being perfect means to triumph over sin. This is a mandate from the LORD. He is just and wise and kind. He would never require anything from his children which was not for their benefit and which was not attainable. Perfection therefore is an achievable goal." (*The Miracle of Forgiveness*, Kimball, pp. 208-209.)

**Fulness of the Gospel**—All the required ordinances and laws of the LDS gospel.

"FULNESS OF THE GOSPEL.—*By fullness of the gospel is meant all the ordinances and principles that pertain to the exaltation in the celestial kingdom.*" (*Doctrines of Salvation*, Joseph Fielding Smith, Vol. 1, p. 160.)

# G

**Gethsemane**—*(see Atonement)*

**God**—An exalted man.

"...the *[LDS]* Church proclaims the eternal truth: *'As man is, God once was; as God is man may be.'"* (*Articles of Faith*, Talmage, pg. 430.)

"*God an Exalted Man— ...God himself was once as we are now, and is an exalted man, and sits enthroned in yonder heavens...* I am going to tell you how God came to be God. We have imagined and supposed that God was God from all eternity. I will refute that idea, and take away the veil, so that you may see... *It is the first principle of the Gospel to know for a certainty the Character of God... he was once a man like us*; yea, that God himself, the Father of us all, dwelt on an earth, the same as Jesus Christ himself did." (*Teachings of the Prophet Joseph Smith*, Joseph Fielding Smith, pp. 345-346.)

"EXTENT OF GOD'S POWER. I do not believe in the doctrine held by some that God is only a Spirit and that he is of such a nature that he fills the immensity of space, and is everywhere present in person, or without person, for I can not conceive it possible that God could be a person, if he filled the immensity of space and was everywhere present at the same time. It is unreasonable, a physical, a theological inconsistency, to imagine that even God the eternal Father would be in two places, as an individual, at the same moment. It is impossible." (*Gospel Doctrine*, Joseph F. Smith, 1977, pp. 55-56.)

**Godhead**—Three separate Gods: God the Father, God the Son, and God the Holy Ghost. These three individuals are one in purpose but not literally one God, they are not one being—one substance.

Joseph Smith proclaimed, "I will preach on the plurality of Gods... I have always declared God to be a distinct personage, Jesus Christ a separate and distinct personage from God the Father, and that the Holy Ghost was a distinct personage and a Spirit: and these three constitute three distinct personages and three Gods." (*Teachings of the Prophet Joseph Smith*, Joseph Fielding Smith, p. 370.)

"Three separate personages—Father, Son, and Holy Ghost—comprise the Godhead. As each of these persons is a God, it is evident, from this standpoint alone, that a *plurality of Gods* exists. To us... these three are the only Gods we worship. But in addition there is an infinite number of holy personages, drawn from worlds without number, who have passed on to exaltation and are thus gods." (*Mormon Doctrine*, McConkie, 1966, p. 576-577.)

**Godhood**—Exaltation is another LDS term for godhood.

"Man is a god in embryo and has in him the seeds of godhood, and he can, if he is will, rise to great heights. He can lift himself by his own bootstraps as no other creature can do. He was created not to fail and degenerate but to rise to perfection like his Lord Jesus Christ." (*The Teachings of Spencer W. Kimball*, p. 28.)

"GODHOOD— ...That exaltation which the saints of all ages have so devoutly sought is *godhood* itself. Godhood is to have the character, possess the attributes, and enjoy the perfections which the Father has... They are gods." (*Mormon Doctrine*, McConkie, 1966, p. 321.)

**Gospel, The LDS**—A combination of the atonement of Jesus Christ plus: water baptism, laying on of hands to receive the Holy Ghost, temple endowments, temple marriage, love and worshiping God with all your heart, faith in Jesus, chastity, repentance, tithing, honesty, truthfulness, obeying the Word of Wisdom, baptisms for the dead, keeping the Sabbath day holy, attending church meetings, godly family life, daily family prayers, honoring parents, teaching the LDS gospel to others, studying the scriptures, obeying the Mormon prophets, true charity, and keeping all the Lord's commandments until the end of your life on earth—*(see Gospel Principles, LDS Church, 1979/1990, Ch. 47, 'Exaltation'.)*

"The gospel is a program of action—of *doing* things." (*Miracle of Forgiveness*, Kimball, p. 208.)

"GOSPEL—The *gospel* of Jesus Christ is the plan of salvation. It embraces all the laws, principles, doctrines, rites, ordinances, acts, powers, authorities, and keys necessary to save and exalt men in the highest heaven hereafter... The preparatory gospel 'is the gospel of repentance and of baptism, and the remission of sins, and the law of carnal commandments'. ...The *fulness of the gospel* consists in those laws, doctrines, ordinances, powers, and authorities needed to enable men to gain the fulness of salvation." (*Mormon doctrine*, McConkie, 1966, p. 331-333.)

"THE GOSPEL IS SIMPLE IN ORDER THAT ALL MAY UNDERSTAND." [*WHAT??? How is the LDS gospel simple?*] (*Doctrines from the Prophets*, Alma P. Burton, p. 220.)

**Great Apostasy, The**—The Total Apostasy of the Christian Church happened shortly after the death of the Lord's Apostles and lasted until Joseph Smith brought about the 'restoration of the gospel' through the establishment of the LDS Church.

"The Great Apostasy... occurred after the Savior established His Church. After the deaths of the Savior and His Apostles, men corrupted the principles of the gospel and made unauthorized changes in Church organization and priesthood ordinances. Because of this widespread wickedness, the Lord withdrew the authority of the priesthood from the earth. During the Great Apostasy, people were without divine direction from living prophets... Parts of the holy scriptures were corrupted or lost... This apostasy lasted until Heavenly Father and His Beloved Son appeared to Joseph Smith in 1820 and initiated the restoration of the fulness of the gospel." (*True to the Faith*, LDS Church, 2004, p. 13.)

"A self-suggesting interpretation of history indicates that there has been a great departure from the way of salvation as laid down by the Savior, a universal apostasy from the Church of Christ. Scarcely had the Church been organized by the Savior, whose name it bears, before the powers of darkness arrayed themselves for conflict with the organized body... Ages of darkness came upon the earth; the power of Satan seemed almost supreme." (*The Articles of Faith*, Talmage, p. 200-201.)

In Joseph Smith's 'First Vision', God the Father and Jesus Christ supposedly gave him this message, "When the light rested upon me I saw two Personages, whose brightness and glory defy all description, standing above me in the air. One of them spake unto me, calling me by name and said, pointing to the other—*This is my Beloved Son. Hear Him*! My object in going to inquire of the Lord was to know which of all the sects was right, that I might know which to join... (for at this time it had never entered into my heart that all were wrong)... I was answered that I must join none of them, for they were all wrong; and the Personage who addressed me said that all their creeds were an abomination in his sight; that those professors were all corrupt; that: 'they draw near to me with their lips, but their hearts are far from me, they teach for doctrines the commandments of men, having a form of godliness, but they deny the power thereof'. He again forbade me to join with any of them." (Pearl of Great Price, Joseph Smith History 1:17-20.)

# H

**Heaven**—Three kingdoms of glory or three levels of heaven: the Celestial heaven—for perfected Mormons only; the Terrestrial heaven—for unworthy yet moral Mormons and moral non-Mormons; the Telestial heaven—for bad Mormons (who are not Sons of Perdition) and wicked non-Mormons.

"The Lord has told us of three degrees of glory. There are three 'heavens', as it is often referred to. We call them the telestial, terrestrial, and the celestial. I cannot for a minute conceive the telestial being hell either, because it is considered a heaven, a glory. The Prophet Joseph Smith told us that if we could get one little glimpse into the telestial glory even, the glory is so great that we would be tempted to commit suicide to get there." (Patriarch Eldred G. Smith, BYU Speeches of the Year, March 10, 1964, p. 4.)

"In their final judgment, the children of God will be assigned to a kingdom of glory for which their obedience has qualified them. In his letters to the Corinthians, the Apostle Paul described these places. He told of a vision in which he was 'caught up to the third heaven' and 'heard unspeakable words, which it is not lawful for a man to utter' (2 Cor. 12:2, 4.) Speaking of the resurrection of the dead, he described 'celestial bodies', 'bodies terrestrial' (1 Cor. 15:40), and 'bodies telestial' (JST, 1 Cor. 15:40), each pertaining to a different degree of glory. He likened these different glories to the sun, to the moon, and to different stars (see 1 Cor. 15:41.)" (*Ensign,* Conference Edition, May, 1995, *Apostasy and Restoration,* Dallin H. Oaks, p. 86.)

"KINGDOMS OF GLORY.—Contrary to the views found in the uninspired teachings and creeds of modern Christendom, there are in eternity *kingdoms of glory* to which all resurrected persons (except the sons of perdition) will eventually go. These are named: *celestial, terrestrial,* and *telestial*—the glory of each being beyond mortal comprehension... The glory to be received by individuals in the kingdoms of glory hereafter will be in direct proportion to their obedience and diligence in this life, for all men will be judged in accordance with their particular works." (*Mormon Doctrine,* McConkie, 1966, p. 420-421.)

**Heavenly Parents**—Mormonism teaches that all men and women were born as spirit children to Father God and a Mother Goddess in the pre-mortal existence.

"All men and women are in the similitude of the universal Father and Mother, and are literally the sons and daughters of Deity... –Joseph F. Smith, John R. Winder, Anthon H. Lund, November, 1909." (Messages of the First Presidency, Vol. 4, 'The Origin of Man', The Church of Jesus Christ of Latter-day Saints, James R. Clark, p. 203.)

"MOTHER IN HEAVEN—Implicit in the Christian verity that all men are the spirit children of an *Eternal Father* is the usually unspoken truth that they are also the offspring of an *Eternal Mother.* An exalted and glorified Man of Holiness could not be a Father unless a Woman of like glory, perfection, and holiness was associated with him as a Mother. The begetting of children makes a man a father and a woman a mother whether we are dealing with a man in his mortal or immortal state." (*Mormon Doctrine,* McConkie, 1966, p. 516.)

**Heavenly Father**—The first of three separate Gods in the LDS godhead. His name is 'Elohim' and he produced all the spirits of mankind by having relations with his wife *(or wives)* in the Celestial kingdom.

"The Father of Our Spirits—One of life's great questions is 'Who am I?' A beloved Primary song helps even little children answer this question. We sing, 'I am a child of God, and he has sent me here'. ...You are a literal child of God, spiritually begotten in the Premortal life. As His child, you can be assured that you have divine, eternal potential and that He will help you in your sincere efforts to reach that potential." (True to the Faith, LDS Church, p. 74.)

"'*Father' as Literal Parent*— ...God the Eternal Father, whom we designate by the exalted name-title 'Elohim', is the literal Parent of our Lord and Savior Jesus Christ, and of the spirits of the human race." (Messages of the First Presidency, Vol. 5, The Church of Jesus Christ of Latter-day Saints, p. 26.)

"The Church of Jesus Christ of Latter-day Saints, basing its belief on divine revelation, ancient and modern, proclaims man to be the direct and lineal offspring of Diety... Man is the child of God, formed in the divine image and endowed with divine attributes, and even as the infant son of an earthly father and mother is capable in due time of becoming a man, so the undeveloped offspring of celestial parentage is capable, by experience through ages and aeons, of evolving into a God." (Messages of the First Presidency, Vol. 4, The Church of Jesus Christ of Latter-day Saints, 'The Origin of Man', p. 206.)

**Hell**—Hell is a temporary place of punishment. The vast majority who suffer there will eventually end up in the Telestial kingdom (the lowest heaven.)

"That part of the spirit world inhabited by wicked spirits who are awaiting the eventual day of their resurrection is called *hell*... There they suffer the torments of the damned; there they welter in the vengeance of eternal fire; there is found weeping and wailing and gnashing of teeth; there the fiery indignation of the wrath of God is poured out upon the wicked... Hell will have an end... After their resurrection, the great majority of those who have suffered in hell will pass into the telestial kingdom; the balance, cursed as sons of perdition, will be consigned to partake of endless wo with the devil and his angels." (*Mormon Doctrine*, McConkie, 1966, pp. 349-350.)

**Holy Ghost**—The third member of the godhead is the Holy Ghost. In LDS theology, the Holy Ghost is not the Holy Spirit *(see 'Holy Spirit'.)*

"A PERSONAGE OF SPIRIT. The Holy Ghost is the third member of the Godhead. *He is a Spirit, in the form of a man*... The Holy Ghost is a personage of Spirit, and has a spirit body only... As a Spirit personage *the Holy Ghost has size and dimensions. He does not fill the immensity of space*, and cannot be everywhere present in person at the same time." (*Doctrines of Salvation*, Joseph Fielding Smith, Vol. 1, p. 38.)

"The Holy Ghost as a personage of Spirit can no more be omnipresent in person than can the Father or the Son... The Holy Ghost in person may visit men and will visit those who are worthy... but may not tarry with them." (*Latter-day Prophets Speak*, Daniel H. Ludlow, 'Joseph F. Smith', March, 1909, p. 284.)

"Well, let me tell you, the Holy Ghost is a man; he is one of the sons of our Father and our God; and he is that man that stood next to Jesus Christ, just as I stand by brother Brigham." *(Journal of Discourses, Vol. 5, Heber C. Kimball, August 23, 1857, p.179.)*

"The Holy Ghost, sometimes called the Comforter, is the third member of the Godhead, and is a personage, distinct from the Holy Spirit... It seems not improbable that He uses the Holy Spirit to perform His labors." (*Evidences and Reconciliations*, John Widtsoe, p. 173.)

**Holy Spirit**—The Holy Spirit is not the Holy Ghost. The Holy Spirit is not a person, but is a divine essence, a force, or fluid which permeates all that exists. The Holy Spirit proceeds from the presence of God to fill the immensity of space. [This is a confusing doctrine that even most LDS people do not comprehend.]

"The chief agent employed by God to communicate his will to the universe is the holy spirit, which must not be confused with the Holy Ghost, the personage who is the third member of the Godhead. The holy spirit permeates all the things of the universe, material and spiritual. By the holy spirit the will of God is radio-transmitted, broadcast as it were. It forms what may be called the great system of communication among the intelligent beings of the universe. The holy spirit vibrates with intelligence; it takes up the word and will of God as given by him or by his personal agents, and transmits the message to the remotest parts of space. By the intelligent operation and infinite extent of the holy spirit, the whole universe is held together and made as one unit." (*A Rational Theology*, John Widtsoe, p. 72-73.)

"Jesus Christ, a little babe like all the rest of us have been, grew to be a man, was filled with a divine substance or fluid, called the Holy Spirit, by which he comprehended and spake the truth in power and authority; and by which he controlled the elements, and imparted health and life to those who were prepared to partake of the same." (*The Essential Parley*, P. Pratt, p. 186.)

"The Holy Spirit is the agent, means, or influence by which the will, power, and intelligence of God, and the Godhead… may be transmitted throughout space. The Holy Spirit, vicariously called the Spirit of God, the Light of Christ, the Spirit of Truth, proceeds from the presence of God to fill the immensity of space." (*Evidences and Reconciliations*, John A. Widtsoe p. 172.)

# I

**Immortality**—Immortality is salvation by grace alone, is associated with being resurrected from the grave, and is a free gift bestowed upon all mankind. Immortality is to live forever, but Immortality is not Eternal life *(see 'Eternal Life'.)*

"*Unconditional or general salvation*, that which comes by grace alone without obedience to the gospel law, consists in the mere fact of being resurrected. In this sense, salvation is synonymous with immortality; it is the inseparable connection of body and spirit so that the resurrected personage lives forever… *This kind of salvation eventually will come to all mankind, excepting only the sons of perdition.*" (*Mormon Doctrine*, McConkie, p. 669.)

"Immortality comes to us all as a free gift by the grace of God alone, without works of righteousness. Eternal life, however, is the reward for obedience to the laws and ordinances of his gospel." (*A Light unto the World*, David B. Haight, p. 8.)

## Inspired Version of the Bible or the Joseph Smith Translation (JST)—The Joseph Smith
Inspired Version of the Bible was Joseph Smith's attempt to 'fix' the Bible. Even though the Joseph Smith Translation (JST) is called a 'translation', there were no ancient manuscripts used in the editing process, rather Joseph Smith was supposedly 'inspired' to make the changes he made. Consider John 1:1-2 in the JST…

*(JST)*—**John 1:1-2** "In the beginning was the *gospel preached through the Son. And the gospel was the word, and the word was with the Son, and the Son was with God, and the Son was of God.* The same was in the beginning with God."

This is just one of many significant changes made to the Bible by Joseph Smith to see more examples and how we use the JST with LDS people…

👁 Go to:
http://trigrace.org/Resources.html
to print free PDF download of *We believe the Bible to be the word of God as far as it is translated correctly*. Then watch the TGM Tutorial pertaining to this Visual Aid.

**Intelligences**—LDS theology states that the base essence of each human being is eternal—as eternal as God himself. The eternal, uncreated essence of each person is called 'intelligence' or 'an intelligence." Even amongst LDS scholars the exact understanding of an 'intelligence' is a mystery.

"MAN WAS ALSO IN THE BEGINNING WITH GOD— …Some of our writers have endeavored to explain what an intelligence is, but to do so is futile, for we have never been given any insight into this matter beyond what the Lord has fragmentarily revealed. We know, however, that there is something called intelligence which always existed. It is the real eternal part of man, which was not created nor made. This intelligence combined with the spirit constitutes a spiritual identity or individual." (*Answers to Gospel Questions*, Joseph Fielding Smith, Vol. 4, p. 127.)

"*Man's eternal nature*—Under the uninspired teachings of men and creeds as they apply to man… it was taught that while man's body was created by God, his origin was purely an earthly one. We believe that before the creation of the body, all men existed as intelligences, these intelligences were not created or made, neither indeed can they be; the intelligent entity in man which we call spirit or soul is a self-existing entity, uncreated and eternal. Thus man is crowned with the dignity which belongs to his divine and eternal nature." (*Conference Reports*, Hugh B. Brown, April 1969, p. 51.)

# J

**Jehovah**—In the pre-mortal existence, Jesus Christ's name was Jehovah, He was the firstborn spirit son of Heavenly Father.

"*Elohim*, as understood and used in the restored Church of Jesus Christ, is the name-title of God the Eternal Father, whose firstborn Son in the spirit is *Jehovah*—the Only Begotten in the flesh, Jesus Christ." (*Jesus the Christ*, Talmage, p. 38.)

"JEHOVAH, THE FIRSTBORN. Among the spirit children of Elohim, the first-born was and is Jehovah, or Jesus Christ, to whom all others are juniors.—*Improvement Era*, Vol. 19, p. 940." (Gospel Doctrine, Joseph F. Smith, 1977, p.70.)

"At the great council in heaven, God stood in the midst of His spirit-children and appointed 'the noble and great ones' to future positions of leadership after they should become mortals. In that assembled throng there was 'one like unto God'. This glorious personage volunteered to be the Savior of the world… This individual… was none other than Jehovah of the Old Testament, and when He lived in mortality He was Jesus Christ of the New Testament… The appointment of Jesus to be the Savior of the world was contested by one of the other sons of God. He was called Lucifer, son of the morning… this spirit-brother of Jesus desperately tried to become the Savior of mankind." (The Gospel Through the Ages, Milton R. Hunter, p. 15.)

**Jesus Christ**—The LDS Church asserts its belief in a different Jesus than the Jesus of Christianity.

### A 'Different Jesus'

"In bearing testimony of Jesus Christ, President Hinckley spoke of those outside the Church who say Latter-day Saints 'do not believe in the traditional Christ'. 'No, I don't. The traditional Christ of whom they speak is not the Christ of whom I speak. For the Christ of whom I speak has been revealed in this the Dispensation of the Fulness of Times. He together with His Father, appeared to the boy Joseph Smith in the year 1820, and when Joseph left the grove that day, he knew more of the nature of God than all the learned ministers of the gospel of the ages.'" ('Crown of Gospel is Upon Our Heads', Gordon B. Hinckley, *Church News*, June 20, 1998, p. 7.)

"It is true that many of the Christian churches worship a different Jesus Christ than is worshipped by the Mormons or The Church of Jesus Christ of Latter-day Saints." (*Ensign*, Conference Edition, May, 1977, 'The Living Christ', Bernard P. Brockbank, p. 26.)

### The pre-mortal Jesus was a spirit child born to Heavenly Father and a Heavenly Mother

"Jesus was born of heavenly parents in a premortal world—he was the firstborn of our Heavenly Father." (*Ensign*, Conference Ed., November 1983, 'Your Sorrow Shall Be Turned to Joy', Robert D. Hales, p. 67.)

### Jesus is our oldest spirit brother in the pre-mortal life

"We worship Elohim, the Father of Jesus Christ... Elohim, the God we worship, is the Father of our spirits and Jesus Christ, his first Begotten Son in the spirit creation and his Only Begotten Son in the flesh, is our Eldest Brother." (*Doctrines of Salvation*, Joseph Fielding Smith, Vol. 1, p. 106.)

### Jesus and Lucifer are spirit brothers born to the same Heavenly Father

"Long before you were born a program was developed by your creators... The principal personalities in this great drama were a Father Elohim, perfect in wisdom, judgment, and person, and two sons, Lucifer and Jehovah [Jesus]." (*Teachings of Spencer W. Kimball*, p. 32-33.)

### The LDS Heavenly Father had a physical relationship with the virgin Mary to conceive Jesus

"The Church of Jesus Christ of Latter-day Saints proclaims that Jesus Christ is the Son of God in the most literal sense. The body in which He performed His mission in the flesh was sired by that same Holy Being we worship as God, our Eternal Father. Jesus was not the son of Joseph, nor was He begotten by the Holy Ghost. He is the Son of the Eternal Father." (*The Teachings of Ezra Taft Benson*, p. 7.)

### The LDS Jesus was married to plural wives and fathered children

"I discover that some of the Eastern papers represent me as a great blasphemer, because I said, in my lecture on Marriage, at our last Conference, that Jesus Christ was married at Cana of Galilee, that Mary, Martha, and others were his wives, and that he begat children... for even the Father himself honored that law by coming down to Mary, without a natural body, and begetting a son; and if Jesus begat children, he only 'did that which he had seen his Father do.'" (*Journal of Discourses*, Vol. 2, Orson Hyde, March 18, 1855, p. 210.)

"One thing is certain, that there were several holy women that greatly loved Jesus – such as Mary, and Martha her sister, and Mary Magdalene; and Jesus greatly loved them, and associated with them much... If all the acts of Jesus were written, we no doubt should learn that these beloved women were His wives." (*The Seer*, Orson Pratt, p. 159.)

*Jesus had to earn godhood by keeping the LDS gospel*

"Jesus became a God and reached His great state of understanding through consistent effort and continuous obedience to all the Gospel truths and universal laws." (*The Gospel Through the Ages*, Milton R. Hunter, p. 51.)

**Joseph Smith**—The founding prophet of the Church of Jesus Christ of Latter-day Saints.

"Joseph Smith, the Prophet and Seer of the Lord, has done more, save Jesus only, for the salvation of men in this world, than any other man that ever lived in it." (**Doctrine and Covenants 135:3**.)

"If it had not been for Joseph Smith and the restoration, there would be no salvation. There is no salvation outside The Church of Jesus Christ of Latter-day Saints." (*Mormon Doctrine*, McConkie, 1966, p. 670.)

"Whosoever confesseth that Joseph Smith was sent of God to reveal the holy Gospel to the children of men... that spirit is of God, and every spirit that does not confess that God has sent Joseph Smith, and revealed the everlasting Gospel to and through him, is of Antichrist." (Journal of Discourses Vol. 8, p. 176, *Discourses of Brigham Young*, 1977, p. 435, Discourses of Brigham Young, 1925, p.666.)

"President Brigham Young stated: 'Joseph Smith holds the keys of this last dispensation, and is now engaged behind the vail [sic] in the great work of the last days.... No man or woman in this dispensation will ever enter into the celestial kingdom of God without the consent of Joseph Smith.... He holds the keys of that kingdom for the last dispensation—the keys to rule in the spirit-world; and he rules there triumphantly.... He was foreordained in eternity to preside over this last dispensation.'" (*Search These Commandments*, LDS Church, 1984, p. 133.)

"The day will come—and it is not far distant, either—when the name of the Prophet Joseph Smith will be coupled with the name of Jesus Christ of Nazareth, the Son of God, as his representative, as his agent whom he chose, ordained and set apart to lay anew the foundations of the Church of God in the world, which is indeed the Church of Jesus Christ." (*Gospel Doctrine*, Joseph F. Smith, 1977, p. 134; *Ensign*, December 2003, 'Joseph Smith: Restorer of Truth', Joseph Fielding Smith, p. 17.)

"Church Stands or Falls With Joseph Smith. Mormonism, as it is called, must *stand or fall on the story of Joseph Smith*. He was either a prophet of God, divinely called, properly appointed and commissioned, or he was one of the biggest frauds this world has ever seen. *There is no middle ground.*" (*Doctrines of Salvation*, Joseph Fielding Smith, Vol. 1, p. 188.)

Joseph Smith stated, "I combat the errors of the ages; I meet the violence of mobs; I cope with illegal proceedings from executive authority; I cut the Gordian knot of powers; and I solve mathematical problems of Universities: WITH TRUTH, diamond truth, and God is my 'right hand man.'" (*Joseph Smith, Times and Seasons 4:375.*)

On May 26, 1844, Joseph Smith preached in a Sunday message, "I have more to boast of than ever any man had. I am the only man that has ever been able to keep a whole church together since the days of Adam. A large majority of the whole have stood by me. Neither Paul, John, Peter, nor Jesus ever did it. I boast that no man ever did such a work as I. The followers of Jesus ran away from Him; but the Latter-day Saints never ran away from me yet." (*History of the Church, LDS Church, Vol. 6, pg. 408-409.*)

Joseph Smith said, "God made Aaron to be the mouthpiece for the children of Israel, and He will make me be god to you in His stead... and if you don't like it, you must lump it." (*Teachings of the Prophet Joseph Smith*, Joseph Fielding Smith, p. 363.)

**Justification**—LDS justification is works based—no one is justified who does not earn it!

"What then is the law of justification? It is simply this: 'All covenants, contracts, bonds, obligations, oaths, vows, performances, connections, associations, or expectations', in which men must abide to be saved and exalted, must be entered into and performed in righteousness so that the Holy Spirit can justify the candidate for salvation in what has been done... As with all other doctrines of salvation, justification is available because of the atoning sacrifice of Christ, but it become operative in the life of an individual only on conditions of personal righteousness." (*Mormon Doctrine*, McConkie, 1966, p. 408.

"One of the most pernicious doctrines ever advocated by man, is the doctrine of 'justification by faith alone', which has entered into, the hearts of millions since the days of the so-called 'reformation.'" (*The Restoration of All Things*, Joseph Fielding Smith, 1964, p 192.)

# K

## Kingdom of God—*See Celestial Kingdom*

**Kolob**—Associated with Heavenly Father's planet or dwelling place. Kolob is a notable star or a planet where the governing of our universe is centered.

"The book of Abraham states that God's physical dominion (throne) is located near a star called Kolob (Abr. 3:2-3.) While it might seem reasonable to suppose that this refers to some distinguishing feature of the universe, all efforts to identify it are speculative and not authoritative. Wherever Kolob is located, its purpose is to 'govern' all planets that are of the same 'order' as the Earth (Abr. 3:9.)" (*Encyclopedia of Mormonism*, BYU, 1:82.)

"Joseph taught that there is a great planet named Kolob, nearest the Celestial Throne, and that it revolves once in a thousand years. That is a day with God... It was such a day that Peter had in mind when he wrote: 'A day with the Lord is as a thousand years, and a thousand years as one day.'" (*Conference Reports*, Orson Whitney, April 1920, p. 123.)

# L

**Lamanites**—*Native American Indians*—According to the Book of Mormon, the Lamanites were Hebrew people who migrated from Jerusalem to the Americas in about 600 BC. Mormonism has made bold claims about the Lamanites stating that they "are the principal ancestors of the American Indians." Recent DNA studies of Native Americans, however, have proven conclusively that the American Indians are not related in any direct way to the Semitic people groups associated with the land of Israel. Rather, Native Americans are directly connected genetically with the people groups found in northeast Asia/Mongolia.

Who are the Lamanites? "With pride I tell those who come to my office that a Lamanite is a descendant of one Lehi who left Jerusalem six hundred years before Christ and with his family crossed the mighty deep and landed in America. And Lehi and his family became the ancestors of all of the Indian and Mestizo tribes in North and South and Central America and in the islands of the sea, for in the middle of their history there were those who left America in ships of their making and went to the islands of the sea... The term Lamanite includes all Indians and Indian mixtures, such as the Polynesians, the

Guatemalans, the Peruvians, as well as the Sioux, the Apache, the Mohawk, the Navajo, and others. It is a large group of great people." ('Of Royal Blood', Spencer W. Kimball, *Ensign*, July 1971, p. 7.)

Gordon B. Hinckley said to the native people of Mexico City, "Bless Thy saints in this great land and those from other lands who will use this temple. Most have in their veins the blood of Father Lehi. Thou hast kept Thine ancient promise. Many thousands 'that walked in darkness have seen a great light.'" (Dedicatory prayer of the Mexico City temple, Gordon B. Hinckley, December, 1983; Church News, 11 Dec. 1983: 4.)

## Lucifer—*See Satan*

# M

**Mankind**—Every person on earth is a literal spirit child of the LDS Heavenly Father and a heavenly mother. Therefore, mankind is the literal offspring of Deity, and has the inherent potential to become Gods. The basic essence of man—his intelligence, however, was not created by God, the LDS Church teaches—man is a self-existing being.

"The Church of Jesus Christ of Latter-day Saints, basing its belief on divine revelation, ancient and modern, proclaims man to be the direct and lineal offspring of Deity. God himself is an exalted man, perfected, enthroned, and supreme... *Men Are Gods In Embryo*—'Man is the child of God, formed in the divine image and endowed with divine attributes, and even as the infant son of our earthly father and mother is capable in due time of becoming a man, so the undeveloped offspring of celestial parentage is capable, by experience through ages of aeons, of evolving into a god.'" (*The First Presidency—Joseph F. Smith*, John R. Winder, Anthon H. Lund; *Doctrines from the Prophets*, Alma P. Burton, p. 2; & *Achieving a Celestial Marriage*, by the LDS Church, p. 130.)

"*Man Is a Self-Existing Being*—Perhaps the most significant truth about man in the context of his pre-earth existence is that he was not created nor made, that is, did not begin, at his birth into mortality... He has always existed... Birth is not man's beginning. Existence as conscious identities in a per-earth life... was not man's beginning. Indeed man has no beginning... 'The spirit of man is not a created being; it existed from eternity, and will exist to eternity'. This truth about man profoundly affects our concept of man. His basic identity was not created, even by God. Rather, he exists upon the same self-existent principles as does God. Man is a product of the same system of things as is God. God and man are of the same race." (*God and Man*, Oscar W. McConkie Jr., LDS Church, p. 26-29.)

## Marriage—*See Celestial Marriage.*

## Michael, the Archangel—*See Adam.*

**Millennium, The**—During the Millennium, 'Works for the Dead' will be done by LDS people for every person who has ever lived on this earth—this is the primary purpose for the Millennium.

"SALVATION FOR DEAD IN LATTER-DAYS. The work of saving the dead has practically been reserved for the dispensation of the fulness of times, when the Lord shall restore all things. It is, therefore, the duty of the Latter-day Saints to see that it is accomplished. We cannot do it all at once, but will have the 1,000 years of the millennium to do it in. In that time the work must be done in behalf of the dead of the previous 6,000 years, for all who need it. Temples will be built for this purpose, and the labor in them will occupy most of the time of the saints." (*Doctrines of Salvation*, Joseph Fielding Smith, Vol. 2, p. 166.)

*"WHAT WILL BE DONE DURING THE MILLENNIUM?* There will be two great works for members of the Church during the Millennium—temple work and missionary work. Some ordinances are necessary for exaltation. These include baptism, the laying on of hands for the gift of the Holy Ghost, and such temple ordinances as the endowment, temple marriage, and the sealing together of family units. Many people have died without receiving these ordinances. People on the earth must perform these ordinances for them. This work is now being done in the temples of the Lord. Because there is too much work to finish before the Millennium begins, it will be completed during that time. Resurrected beings will help us correct the mistakes we have made in doing research concerning our dead ancestors. They will also help us find the information we need to complete our records. The other great work during the millennium will be missionary work. The gospel will be taught with great power to all people." (*Gospel Principles*, LDS Church, 1979/1990, ch. 44, 'The Millennium'.)

**Murder**—According to Mormonism, murder or the shedding of innocent blood, is a sin that can never be totally forgiven.

"And now, behold, I speak unto the church. Thou shalt not kill; and he that kills shall not have forgiveness in this world, nor in the world to come." (**Doctrine and Covenants 42:18.**)

"*The Murderer*—John wrote that 'no murderer hath eternal life abiding in him'. The murderer denies himself salvation in the celestial kingdom, and in this sense he cannot be forgiven for his crime… Another scriptural character responsible for murder—and this in conjunction with adultery—was the great King David. For his dreadful crime, all his life afterward he sought forgiveness. Some of the Psalms portray the anguish of his soul, yet David is still paying for his sin." (*The Miracle of Forgiveness*, Kimball, p.127-128.)

"MURDERERS— …Murderers are forgiven eventually but only in the sense that all sins are forgiven except the sin against the Holy Ghost; they are not forgiven in the sense that celestial salvation is made available to them. After they have paid the full penalty for their crime, they shall go on to a telestial inheritance." (*Mormon Doctrine*, McConkie, 1966, p. 520.)

# N

**Negroes—*See Blacks***

**New Jerusalem, The**—The LDS Church believes Jesus Christ will rule the millennial kingdom from Independence, Missouri—which is 'Zion', where the New Jerusalem will be built.

"For the early Saints, establishing Zion… meant building the city of Zion, or New Jerusalem. In July 1831, the Lord revealed to the Prophet Joseph Smith that the city of Zion should be built in Missouri, with Independence as the center place (**D&C 57:1-3**.)" (*Doctrine and Covenants and Church History Gospel Doctrine Teacher's Manual*, 1999, p. 267.)

"It will be in America – at Jackson County Missouri – that the New Jerusalem will be built; and from there will the Lord govern the world during the Millennium." (*Joshua: Man of Faith*, Mark E. Peterson, p. 76)

# O

**Outer Darkness**—Eternal punishment that lasts forever is only for those deemed worthy of outer darkness—only 'sons of perdition' will be sent to outer darkness with Satan and his fallen angels. The only people who can become sons of perdition are Mormons who have left Mormonism—all other sinners, no matter how bad they may have been, will all eventually receive a degree of glory in the telestial kingdom.

"OUTERDARKNESS—These are they who had testimonies of Jesus through the Holy Ghost and had known the power of the Lord, but allowed Satan to overcome them. They denied the truth and defied the power of the Lord. It would have been better for them if they had never been born. There is no forgiveness for them. They denied the Holy Spirit after having received it. They will not have a kingdom of glory. They will live in eternal darkness, torment, and misery with Satan and his angels forever and ever." (*Gospel Principles*, LDS Church, 1979/1990, ch. 46, 'The Last Judgment'.)

"I think I am safe in saying that no man can become a Son of Perdition until he has known the light. Those who have never received the light are not to become Sons of Perdition. They will be punished if they rebel against God. They will have to pay the price of their sinning, but it is only those who have the light through the priesthood and through the power of God and through their membership in the Church who will be banished forever from his influence into outer darkness to dwell with the devil and his angels. That is a punishment that will not come to those who have never known the truth. Bad as they may suffer, and awful as their punishment by be, they are not among that group which is to suffer the eternal death and banishment from all influence concerning the power of God." (*Conference Report*, Joseph Fielding Smith, "Seek Ye Earnestly...", October, 1958, p. 21.)

# P

**Perfection**—The LDS gospel requires the abandonment of sin before forgiveness can be granted. If repentance is genuine, the person will abandon the sin and never commit that sin again. This means that little by little, LDS people are supposed to be 'perfecting' themselves. The LDS Church teaches its people that perfection is an achievable goal.

"Yea, come unto Christ, and be perfected in him, and deny yourselves of all ungodliness; and if ye shall deny yourselves of all ungodliness, and love God with all your might, mind and strength, then is his grace sufficient for you, that by his grace ye may be perfect in Christ; and if by the grace of God ye are perfect in Christ, ye can in nowise deny the power of God." (**Moroni 10:32**.)

*Repentant Life Seeks Perfection*—"One could multiply references almost indefinitely but enough has been said to establish the point that the repentant life, the life which constantly reaches for perfection, must rely on works as well as on faith. The gospel is a program of action—of *doing* things... Immortality has been accomplished by the Savior's sacrifice. Eternal life hangs in the balance awaiting the works of men.

This progress toward eternal life is a matter of achieving perfection. Living all the commandments guarantees total forgiveness of sins and assures one of exaltation through that perfection which comes by complying with the formula the Lord gave us. In his Sermon on the Mount he made the command to all men: *'Be ye therefore perfect, even as your Father which is in heaven is perfect'. (Matt. 5:48)* Being perfect means to triumph over sin. This is a mandate from the Lord. He is just and wise and kind. He would never require anything from his children which was not for their benefit and which was not attainable. Perfection therefore is an achievable goal... Perfection really comes through overcoming... Christ became perfect through overcoming. Only as we overcome shall we become perfect and move toward godhood. As I have indicated previously, the time to do this is now, in mortality." (*The Miracle of Forgiveness*, Kimball, p. 208-210.)

**Plural Marriage/Polygamy**—The early prophets of Mormonism are responsible for starting the practice of polygamy in the Americas. The mainstream Mormon Church does not condone polygamy at this present time. Mormon splinter groups still involved in this practice are condemned by the LDS Church. The LDS Church does, however, still believe in the eternal principle of plural marriage and does believe polygamy will be practiced by all worthy LDS men in the celestial kingdom.

"The only men who become Gods, even the Sons of God, are those who enter into polygamy." (*Journal of Discourses*, Brigham Young, August 19, 1866, 11:269.)

"We have now clearly shown that God the Father had a plurality of wives, one or more being in eternity, by whom He begat our spirits as well as the spirit of Jesus His First Born, and another being upon the earth by whom He begat the tabernacle of Jesus, as His Only Begotten in this world. We have also proved most clearly that the Son followed the example of his Father, and became the great Bride Groom to whom king's daughters and many honorable Wives were to be married. We have also proved that both God the Father and our Lord Jesus Christ inherit their wives in eternity as well as in time; and that God the Father has already begotten many thousand millions of sons and daughters and sent them into this world to take tabernacles; and that God the Son has the promise that 'of the increase of his government there shall be no end;' it being expressly declared that the children of one of His Queens should be made Princes in all the earth." (*The Seer*, Orson Pratt, p. 172.)

"PLURAL MARRIAGE …In the early days of this dispensation, as part of the promised restitution of all things, the Lord revealed the principle of *plural marriage* to the Prophet [*Joseph Smith*]. Later the Prophet and leading brethren were commanded to enter into the practice, which they did in all virtue and purity of heart despite the consequent animosity and prejudices of worldly people. After Brigham Young led the saints to the Salt Lake Valley, plural marriage was openly taught and practiced until the year 1890. At that time conditions were such that the Lord *by revelation* withdrew the command to continue the practice, and President Wilford Woodruff issued the Manifesto directing that it cease. Obviously the holy practice will commence again after the Second Coming of the Son of Man and the ushering in of the millennium. Plural marriage is not essential to salvation or exaltation." (*Mormon Doctrine*, McConkie, 1966, p. 578.)

**Premortal Life or Preexistence**—The doctrine that all mankind, prior to our earthly existence, were spirit children of heavenly parents.

"Premortal Life—Before you were born on the earth, you lived in the presence of your Heavenly Father as one of His spirit children. In this premortal existence, you attended a council with Heavenly Father's other spirit children. At that council, Heavenly Father presented His great plan of happiness. In harmony with the plan of happiness, the premortal Jesus Christ, the Firstborn Son of the Father in the spirit, covenanted to be the Savior. Those who followed Heavenly Father and Jesus Christ were permitted to come to the earth… Lucifer, another spirit son of God, rebelled against the plan and 'sought to destroy the agency of man'. He became Satan." (*True to the Faith*, LDS Church, 2004, pp. 115-116.)

"*WE ARE CHILDREN OF OUR HEAVENLY FATHER*—God is not only our ruler and our creator; he is also our Heavenly Father. 'All men and women are… literally the sons and daughters of Deity… Man, as a spirit, was begotten and born of heavenly parents, and reared to maturity in the eternal mansions of the Father, prior to coming upon the earth in a temporal [physical] body'. Every person who was ever born on earth was our spirit brother or sister in heaven. The first spirit born to our heavenly parents was Jesus Christ. He is thus our elder brother." (*Gospel Principles*, LDS Church, 1979/1990, Ch. 2, 'Our Heavenly Family'.)

**Priesthood**—Of ultimate importance in the LDS Church is the authority of the LDS Priesthoods. The restoration of 'Priesthood Authority' was one of the most important doctrines of the 'Restored LDS Gospel of Jesus Christ'. Mormonism teaches that only worthy men within the LDS Church who hold the Aaronic and/or Melchizedek priesthoods have any authority from God to administrate His Church on earth. Modern day Christendom lost that authority shortly after the death of the Lord's Apostles and has been in a state of 'Total Apostasy' since that time.

"*WHAT IS THE PRIESTHOOD?* Our Heavenly Father has great power. This power is called the priesthood. By this priesthood power the heavens and the earth were created. By this power, the universe is kept in perfect order. Our Heavenly Father shares his priesthood power with his children on the earth. It is the power and authority by which those who are ordained to this power act in his name to do his work... We must have priesthood authority to act in the name of God to perform the sacred ordinances of the gospel... If a man does not have the priesthood, even though he may be sincere, the Lord will not recognize ordinances performed by him... Men need the priesthood to preside in the Church of Jesus Christ of Latter-day Saints." (*Gospel Principles*, LDS Church, 1979/1990, Ch. 13, 'The Priesthood'.)

"THE GREAT APOSTASY AND THE REFORMATION— ...The glorious Gospel truths proclaimed by the Savior were corrupted by pagan teachings and practices... These facts became apparent to a number of good men, such as Martin Luther, John Calvin, William Tyndale the Wesley brothers, and others, who inaugurated what is known as the Reformation. Through sincere and diligent efforts they attempted to restore the Gospel teachings and practices... But none of them held the holy Priesthood of God, which was absolutely essential if they were officially to establish the true Church of Jesus Christ." (The Gospel Through the Ages, Milton R. Hunter, p. 91.)

"*Priesthood*—The priesthood is the eternal power and authority of God... Male members of the Church may begin their priesthood service when they reach the age of 12. They begin by holding the Aaronic Priesthood, and they later may qualify to have the Melchizedek Priesthood conferred on them." (True to the Faith, LDS Church, 2004, p. 124.)

# R

**Redemption**—The LDS doctrine of redemption falls into two categories: unconditional and conditional. Unconditional redemption is forced upon all and is simply resurrection from the grave, the free gift of immortality. Unconditional redemption grants virtually all men a place in one of the three LDS heavens. Conditional redemption is earned by keeping all the requirements of the Mormon Gospel and only the 'righteous' will earn conditional redemption and enter the celestial kingdom.

"REDEMPTION: CONDITIONAL AND UNCONDITIONAL. '*Conditional redemption* is also universal in its nature; it is offered to all but not received by all; it is a universal gift, though not universally accepted; its benefits can be obtained only through faith, repentance, baptism, the laying on of hands, and obedience to all other requirements of the gospel. '*Unconditional redemption* is a gift forced upon mankind which they cannot reject... Not so with conditional redemption; it can be received or rejected according to the will of the creature. 'Redemption from the original sin is without faith or works; redemption from our own sins is given through faith and works. *Both are the gifts of free grace;* but while one is a gift *forced* upon us unconditionally, the other is a gift merely *offered* to us conditionally. The redemption of the one is *compulsory;* the reception of the other is *voluntary.*" (*Doctrines of Salvation*, Joseph Fielding Smith, Vol. 2, p. 10.)

**Repentance**—Forgiveness of sins is only granted when true repentance is accomplished. True repentance is the total abandonment of sin while in this life.

*"Abandonment of Sin—By this ye may know if a man repenteth of his sins—behold, he will confess them and forsake them.* Doctrine & Covenants 58:43—THERE IS ONE CRUCIAL TEST OF REPENTANCE. This is abandonment of the sin." (*Miracle of Forgiveness*, Kimball, p. 163.)

*Forgiveness Cancelled on Reversion to Sin—*Old sins return, says the Lord in his modern revelations. Many people either do not know this or they conveniently forget it. 'Go your ways and sin no more', the Lord warned. And again, '...Unto that soul who sinneth shall the former sins return, saith the Lord your God'. (D&C 82:7.) ...Those who feel that they can sin and be forgiven and then return to sin and be forgiven again and again must straighten out their thinking. Each previously forgiven sin is added to the new one and the whole gets to be heavy load. Thus when a man has made up his mind to change his life there must be no turning back." (*Miracle of Forgiveness*, Kimball, pp. 169-170.)

"Alma 13:11-12 ...indicates an attitude which is basic to the sanctification we should all be seeking, and thus to the repentance which merits forgiveness. It is that the former transgressor must have reached a 'point of no return' to sin wherein there is not merely a renunciation but also a deep abhorrence of the sin—where the sin becomes most distasteful to him and where the desire or urge to sin is cleared out of the life." (*Miracle of Forgiveness*, Kimball, p. 354-355.)

"And until there is real repentance there can never be forgiveness... Discontinuance of sin must be permanent... Incomplete repentance never brought complete forgiveness... Forgiveness is an absolute requirement in attaining eternal life." (*Miracle of Forgiveness*, Kimball, pp. 154, 176, 212, 261.)

**Restoration, The**—The LDS Church teaches the true gospel of Jesus Christ was utterly corrupted and lost during the period of time known as the 'Great Apostasy' (see Great Apostasy, The.) Joseph Smith, is known to LDS people as 'The Prophet of the Restoration' of the true gospel and the true Church of Jesus Christ. LDS theology says it was through Joseph Smith that Priesthood Authority and the LDS Temple Ordinances were restored to the earth.

"After the Savior ascended to heaven, men changed the ordinances and doctrines that he and his apostles had established. Because of apostasy... The true Church of Jesus Christ was no longer on the earth... [and] the gospel Jesus taught was no longer on the earth... The time had arrived for the true Church of Jesus Christ to be restored to the earth... Through the Restoration the priesthood was returned to the earth... OTHER IMPORTANT TRUTHS WERE RESTORED... These include the following: 1. Our Heavenly Father is a real person with a tangible body of flesh and bones. 2. We existed in premortal life as spirit children of God. 3. The priesthood is necessary to administer the ordinances of the gospel... 7. Family relationships can be eternal, through the sealing power of the priesthood. 8. The temple endowment and sealings are available for both the living and the dead." (*Gospel Principles*, by the LDS Church, 1979/1990, chapter 17, 'The Church of Jesus Christ Today – The Lord Promised to Restore His True Church'.)

**Resurrection—*See Immortality***

# S

**Salvation**—LDS Salvation is a two-fold plan. Unconditional or General Salvation is what Jesus Christ earned for all mankind when he atoned for the original sin of Adam—this is a salvation from the grave through the resurrection of the body which grants Immortality to all men. Conditional or Individual Salvation must be earned by perfectly keeping all the laws and ordinances of the Mormon gospel—those who earn this salvation will have eternal life which is termed exaltation. Those who have earned exaltation will become Gods.

"KINDS OF SALVATION—SALVATION: CONDITIONAL AND UNCONDITIONAL. Christ's sacrifice and death did two things for us: it brought unto us *unconditional salvation* and *conditional salvation.* Sometimes we refer to these as *general salvation* and *individual salvation.*" (*Doctrines of Salvation*, Joseph Fielding Smith, Vol. 2, p. 9.)

"SALVATION. *Unconditional or general salvation*, that which comes by grace alone without obedience to gospel law, consists in the mere fact of being resurrected... *This kind of salvation eventually will come to all mankind, excepting only the sons of perdition...* But this is not the salvation of righteousness, the salvation which the saints seek. Those who gain only this general or unconditional salvation will still be judged according to their works and receive their places in a terrestrial or a telestial kingdom. They will, therefore, be damned; their eternal progression will be cut short... *Conditional or individual salvation,* that which comes by grace coupled with gospel obedience, consists in receiving an inheritance in the celestial kingdom of God. This kind of salvation follows faith, repentance, baptism, receipt of the Holy Ghost, and continued righteousness to the end of one's mortal probation... *Salvation* in its true and full meaning is synonymous with *exaltation* or *eternal life...* This full salvation is obtained in and through the continuation of the family unit in eternity, and those who obtain it are gods... If it had not been for Joseph Smith and the restoration, there would be no salvation. There is no salvation outside The Church of Jesus Christ of Latter-day Saints." (*Mormon Doctrine*, McConkie, p. 669-670.)

"Through the atonement of Christ all mankind *may* be saved, by obedience to the laws and ordinances of the gospel. Salvation is twofold: *General*—that which comes to all men irrespective of a belief (in this life) in Christ—and, *Individual*—that which man merits through his own acts through life and by obedience to the laws and ordinances of the gospel." (*Doctrines of Salvation*, Joseph Fielding Smith, Vol. 1, p. 133-134.)

## Salvation by Grace Alone
—All of mankind will partake of salvation by grace alone, or universal salvation, since all will be given the free gift of resurrection. The Biblical concept of salvation by grace alone through faith alone (apart from works) is scorned by the LDS Church.

"*Faith and Works*— ...One of the most fallacious doctrines originated by Satan and propounded by man is that man is saved alone by the grace of God; that belief in Jesus Christ alone is all that is needed for salvation... Of course we need to understand terms. If by the word 'salvation' is meant the mere salvation or redemption from the grave, the 'grace of God' is sufficient. But if the term 'salvation' means returning to the presence of God... for this one certainly must have the 'grace of God', ...plus personal purity, overcoming of evil, and the good 'works' made so important in the exhortations of the Savior and his prophets and apostles." (*Miracle of Forgiveness*, Kimball, p. 206-208.)

"Christians speak often of the blood of Christ and its cleansing power. Much that is believed and taught on this subject, however, is such utter nonsense and so palpably false that to believe it is to lose one's salvation. Many go so far, for instance, as to pretend, at least, to believe that if we confess Christ with our lips and avow that we accept him as our personal Savior, we are thereby saved. His blood, without other act than mere belief, they say, makes us clean." ('What the Mormons Think of Christ', LDS Church Tract, p. 31.)

"SALVATION BY GRACE— ...One of the untrue doctrines found in modern Christendom is the concept that man can gain salvation (meaning in the kingdom of God) by grace alone and without obedience. The soul-destroying doctrine has the obvious effect of lessening the determination of an individual to conform to all the laws and ordinances of the gospel, such conformity being essential..." (*Mormon Doctrine*, McConkie, p. 670-671.)

## Salvation for the Dead—*See Baptism for the Dead, and Endowments.*

**Satan**—Satan or the Devil, known as Lucifer in the pre-mortal existence was a spirit child of God the Father, a spirit brother of Jesus Christ and a spirit brother of all mankind.

"Satan, also called the... devil, is the enemy of righteousness and those who seek to follow God. He is a spirit son of God who was once an angel... But in the premortal Council in Heaven, Lucifer, as Satan was then called, rebelled against Heavenly Father and the plan of salvation. In this rebellion against God, Satan 'sought to destroy the agency of man'. ...Satan persuaded 'a third part of the hosts of heaven' to turn away from the Father." (*True to the Faith*, LDS Church, 2004, p. 154.)

"We needed a Savior to pay for our sins and to teach us how to return to our Heavenly Father. Our Father said, 'Whom shall I send?' Two of our brothers offered to help. Our oldest brother, Jesus Christ, who was then called Jehovah, said, 'Here am I, send me'...Satan, who was called Lucifer, also came, saying: 'Behold, here am I, send me, I will be thy son, and I will redeem all mankind'...After hearing both sons speak, our Heavenly Father said, 'I will send the first'. Jesus Christ was chosen and ordained to be our savior... Because our Heavenly Father chose Jesus Christ to be our Savior, Satan became angry and rebelled. There was war in heaven. Satan and his followers fought against Jesus and his followers. In this great rebellion... One third of the spirits in heaven followed Satan. They were cast down from heaven. Satan and those who followed him were punished. They were denied the right to receive mortal bodies." (*Gospel Principles*, LDS Church, 1979/1990, Ch. 3, 'Jesus Christ our Chosen Leader and Savior'.)

**Scriptures, LDS**—The Bible, Book of Mormon, Doctrine and Covenants, and The Pearl of Great Price.

"The Church of Jesus Christ of Latter-day Saints accepts four books as scripture: the Bible, the Book of Mormon, the Doctrine and Covenants, and The Pearl of Great Price. These books are called the standard works of the Church. The words of our living prophets are also accepted as scripture." (*Gospel Principles*, LDS Church, 1979/1990, Ch. 10, 'Scriptures'.)

**Sons of Perdition**—The only people who are in danger of eternal punishment are former Mormons— LDS people who knew and accepted the fulness of the LDS gospel and then rejected it in this life. These apostate Mormons, unless they repent and come back to the Church, will experience the second death and go to outer darkness with Satan and his fallen angels.

"*What Is the Meaning of Second Death?* ...It is very clear in the Doctrine and Covenants Section 76:30-37, that the only persons who will be completely overcome by this dreadful fate are the sons of perdition who go with the devil and his angels into 'outer darkness.'" (*Answers to Gospel Questions*, Joseph Fielding Smith, Vol. 5, p. 107.)

"Men cannot be sons of perdition until they do receive the Gospel of Jesus Christ, until they themselves hold part of God's authority in the Holy Priesthood, and that having come to the light and to the possession of this power they then do violence to it by becoming traitors to God, and by denying the atonement of the Lord Jesus Christ, and by altogether turning away from the Gospel." (*Collected Discourses*, B.H. Roberts, Vol. 5, p. 139.)

[**NOTE:** In the above quote, 'the Gospel of Jesus Christ' is the LDS gospel, 'the Holy Priesthood' is the LDS Priesthood, and 'the atonement of the Lord Jesus Christ' is the LDS atonement—those who become 'traitors to God' are LDS people who walk away from Mormonism.]

**Spirit World**—The place where all the spirits of this earth go after death. In the spirit world, Mormons preach the gospel to all that never joined the LDS Church while on the earth. Through proxy works for the dead, done in Mormon temples (baptisms and temple works for the dead) and the missionary efforts of deceased Mormons in the afterlife, it is believed that many will accept the teachings of the Mormon Church in the spirit world and eventually work their way to exaltation/godhood.

"Eventually our mortal bodies will die, and our spirits will go to the spirit world. The spirit world is a place of waiting, working, learning, and resting from care and sorrow. Here, our spirits will live until we are ready for our resurrection. Then our mortal bodies will once more unite with our spirits, and we will receive the degree of glory which we have earned... *ARE THERE DIVISIONS IN THE SPIRIT WORLD?* The prophet Alma in the Book of Mormon teaches about two divisions or states in the spirit world... —*(see Alma 40:12-14)*—The spirits are classified according to the purity of their lives and their obedience to the will of the Lord while on earth. The righteous and the wicked are separated, but the spirits may progress from one level to another as they learn gospel principles and live in accordance with them." (*Gospel Principles*, LDS Church, 1979/1990, Ch. 45, 'The Post-Earthly Spirit World'.)

# T

**Three Degrees of Glory—*See Heaven***

**Telestial kingdom—*See Heaven***

**Terrestrial Kingdom—*See Heaven***

**Trinity—*See Godhead*—**Mormonism denies the Christian doctrine of the Trinity, yet believes in a 'Trinity' composed of three separate Gods: God the Father, God the Son; and God the Holy Ghost. Mormons may use the term 'Trinity' according to their own definition.

"*The Godhead: The Trinity*—Three personages composing the great presiding council of the universe have revealed themselves to man: (1) God the Eternal Father; (2) His Son, Jesus Christ; and (3) the Holy Ghost. That these three are separate individuals, physically distinct from each other, is demonstrated by the accepted records of divine dealings with man." (*Articles of Faith*, James E. Talmage, p. 39.)

# V

**Virgin Birth**—Mormonism only gives lip service to the virgin birth. The Mormon doctrine of a Godhead with three separate Gods forces them to reject the Holy Ghost as the agency through which Christ's miraculous conception occurred. If Christ was conceived by the Holy Ghost, he would have to be called the Son of the Holy Ghost, not the Son of the Father. Instead, they teach that God the Father, who has a physical body of flesh and bones, had a relationship with Mary and she conceived in the same natural way that all mothers conceive on this earth. This doctrine destroys the Biblical truth that Christ was virgin born.

"A MODERN PROPHET'S ANSWER—...Now, we are told in scriptures that Jesus Christ is the only begotten Son of God in the flesh. Well, now for the benefit of the older ones, how are children begotten? I answer just as Jesus Christ was begotten of his father... Now, my little friends, I will repeat again in words as simple as I can, and you talk to your parents about it, that God, the Eternal Father, is literally the father of Jesus Christ... Jesus is the only person who had our Heavenly Father as the father of his body." (*Family Home Evening Manual*, Joseph F. Smith, 1972, pp. 125-126.)

"The Church of Jesus Christ of Latter-day Saints proclaims that Jesus Christ is the Son of God in the most literal sense. The body in which He performed His mission in the flesh was sired by that same Holy Being we worship as God, our Eternal Father. Jesus was not the son of Joseph, nor was He begotten by the Holy Ghost. He is the Son of the Eternal Father." (*Teachings of Ezra Taft Benson,* Reed A. Benson, p. 7.)

"Christ was begotten by an Immortal Father in the same way that mortal men are begotten by mortal fathers." (*Mormon Doctrine*, McConkie, 1966, p. 547.)

# W

**Word of Wisdom**—A rather ambiguous list of health laws set forth by the LDS Church. As a part of these dietary laws, LDS people are forbidden to drink any kind of black tea or coffee.

*"The Word of Wisdom is for our physical and spiritual benefit.*—The Word of Wisdom is a law of health revealed by the Lord for the physical and spiritual benefit of His children. On February 27, 1833, as recorded in section 89 of the Doctrine and Covenants, the Lord revealed which foods are good for us to eat and which substances are not good for the human body. He also promised health, protection, knowledge, and wisdom to those who obey the Word of Wisdom" (LDS.org, Topics, 'Word of Wisdom'.)

"Many of our good people have become so weak that, according to the 'Word of Wisdom', they are not worthy to be called Saints... But says one, 'If I am offered a cup of tea or a cup of coffee I cannot refuse it'. Then, according to the word of the Lord, you are too weak to be a Latter-day Saint." (*Official Conference Report*, Elder Joseph F. Smith, April 1880, p. 36.)

"SALVATION AND A CUP OF TEA. You cannot neglect little things. 'Oh, a cup of tea is such a little thing. It is so little; surely it doesn't amount to much; surely the Lord will forgive me if I drink a cup of tea'. Yes, he will forgive you, because he is going to forgive every man who repents; but, my brethren, if you drink coffee or tea, or take tobacco, are you letting a cup of tea or a little tobacco stand in the road and bar you from the celestial kingdom of God, where you might otherwise have received a fulness of glory?" (*Doctrines of Salvation*, Joseph Fielding Smith, Vol. 2, p. 16)?

# Z

**Zion—*See New Jerusalem***

# APPENDIX 2
# BIBLIOGRAPHY

*A Comprehensive History of The Church of Jesus Christ of Latter-day Saints, Century 1, Vol. 1*, by the Church Brigham Young University Press, Provo, Utah, 1965/1976

*Achieving a Celestial Marriage*, Student Manual, Church Educational System, The Corporation of the President of the Church of Jesus Christ of Latter-day Saints, Salt Lake City, 1976/1992

Benson, Ezra Taft, Hinckley, Gordon B., and Monson, Thomas, *"Letter Reaffirms Use of King James Bible"*, *Church News*, June 20, 1992

Benson, Ezra Taft, *The Teachings of Ezra Taft Benson*, Bookcraft, Salt Lake City, 1988

*Book of Mormon, 1830 First Edition*, Herald Heritage Publishing House/Facsimile Reprint, Independence, Missouri, 1973

Burton, Alma P., *Discourses of the Prophet Joseph Smith*, Third Edition, Deseret Book Company, Salt Lake City, 1965

Burton, Alma P., *Doctrines of the Prophets*, Bookcraft Inc., Salt Lake City, 1970

Clark, James R., *Messages of the First Presidency, Vol. 4, 1901-1915*, The Church of Jesus Christ of Latter-day Saints, Bookcraft, Salt Lake City, 1970

Clark, James R., *Messages of the First Presidency, Vol. 5, 1916-1934*, The Church of Jesus Christ of Latter-day Saints, Bookcraft, Salt Lake City, 1971

*Conference Report, April 6, 7, 8, 1880*, The Year of Jubilee, Fiftieth Annual Conference, Official Report, The Church of Jesus Christ of Latter-day Saints, Salt Lake City

*Conference Report, October 10, 11, 12, 1958*, One Hundred Twenty-Eighth Conference, Official Report, The Church of Jesus Christ of Latter-day Saints, Salt Lake City

*Conference Report, April 4, 5, 6, 1969*, One Hundred Thirty-Ninth Conference, Official Report, The Church of Jesus Christ of Latter-day Saints, Salt Lake City

*Doctrine and Covenants, 1835 First Edition*, Herald Heritage Publishing House/Facsimile Reprint, Independence, Missouri, 1971

*Doctrine and Covenants of the Church of Jesus Christ of Latter-day Saints, 1883 edition*, Deseret News Company, Salt Lake City

*Doctrine and Covenants and Church History Gospel Doctrine Teacher's Manual*, LDS Church Manual, Salt Lake City, 1999

*Ensign, The, May, 1977*, The Church of Jesus Christ of Latter-day Saints, Vol. 7, number 5

*Ensign, The, November 1983*, The Church of Jesus Christ of Latter-day Saints, Vol. 13, number 11

*Ensign, The, May, 1995*, The Church of Jesus Christ of Latter-day Saints, Vol. 25, number 5

*Ensign, The, May, 2003*, The Church of Jesus Christ of Latter-day Saints, Vol. 33, number 5

*Ensign, The, April, 2005*, The Church of Jesus Christ of Latter-day Saints, Vol. 35, number 4

*Essential Parley P. Pratt, The*, Signature Books, Salt Lake City, 1990

*Family Home Evening, number 1, 1972*, published by the First Presidency of The Church of Jesus Christ of Latter-day Saints, Salt Lake City

*Gospel Principles*, The Church of Jesus Christ of Latter-day Saints, Salt Lake City, 1979

Haight, David B., *A Light unto the World*, Deseret Book Company, Salt Lake City, 1997

Hinckley, Gordon B., *Dedicatory Prayer at the Mexico City Temple*, Church News, 11 Dec., 1983: 4, Mexico City, Mexico Temple, Dedicated 2-4 December, 1983

Hunter, Milton R., *The Gospel through the Ages*, Stevens and Wallis, Inc., Salt Lake City, Utah, 1945, "To the Quorums of the Melchizedek Priesthood, George F. Richards, President of the Council of the Twelve

Jesse, Dean C., *Personal Writings of Joseph Smith, Revised Edition,* Deseret Book, Salt Lake City, Utah, and Brigham Young University Press, Provo, Utah, 1984/2002

*Joseph Smith's "New Translation" of the Bible*, Herald Publishing House, Independence, Missouri, 1970

Kimball, Edward L., *The Teachings of Spencer W. Kimball*, Bookcraft, Salt Lake City, 1982

Kimball, Spencer W., *The Miracle of Forgiveness*, Bookcraft, Salt Lake City, 1969/1997

Ludlow, Daniel H., *Latter-day Prophets Speak*, Bookcraft, Salt Lake City, 1951

Lund, John Lewis, *The Church and the Negro*, 1967

Matthews, Robert J., *A Bible! A Bible!*, Bookcraft, Salt Lake City, 1990

McConkie, Bruce R., *A New Witness for the Articles of Faith*, Deseret Book Company, Salt Lake City, 1985

McConkie, Bruce R., *Mormon Doctrine, 2nd Edition*, Bookcraft, Salt Lake City, 1966

McConkie, Bruce R., *What the Mormons Think of Christ*, Deseret News Press, Salt Lake City

McConkie Jr., Oscar W., *God & Man*, The Church of Jesus Christ of Latter-day Saints, Salt Lake City, 1963

Pratt, Orson, *Divine Authenticity of Book of Mormon*, No. 3 (December 1, 1850)

Pratt, Orson, *The Seer, 1853-54*, Eborn Books, 1990

*Preach My Gospel*, LDS Church Manual, Salt Lake City, 2004

*Scriptures, LDS Triple Combination: The Book of Mormon; The Doctrine and Covenants; The Pearl of Great Price;* The Church of Jesus Christ of Latter-day Saints, Salt Lake City, 1981

*Search These Commandments, Melchizedek Priesthood Personal Study Guide*, The Church of Jesus Christ of Latter-day Saints, Salt Lake City, 1984

Smith, Joseph, the Prophet, *History of the Church of Jesus Christ of Latter-day Saints, Period I, Vol. III,* Published by the Church, Deseret News, Salt Lake City, 1948

Smith, Joseph, the Prophet, *History of the Church of Jesus Christ of Latter-day Saints, Period I, Vol. V,* Published by the Church, Deseret News, Salt Lake City, 1949

Smith, Joseph, the Prophet, *History of the Church of Jesus Christ of Latter-day Saints, Period I, Vol. VI,* Published by the Church, Deseret Book Company, Salt Lake City, 1950

Smith, Joseph F., *Gospel Doctrine,* Deseret Book Company, Salt Lake City, 1977

Smith, Joseph Fielding, *Answers to Gospel Questions, Vol. IV,* Deseret Book, Salt Lake City, 1963

Smith, Joseph Fielding, *Answers to Gospel Questions, Vol. V,* Deseret Book, Salt Lake City, 1972

Smith, Joseph Fielding, *Doctrines of Salvation, Vol. 1,* Bruce R. McConkie, Bookcraft, Salt Lake City, 1954

Smith, Joseph Fielding, *Doctrines of Salvation, Vol. 2,* Bruce R. McConkie, Bookcraft, Salt Lake City, 1955

Smith, Joseph Fielding, *Doctrines of Salvation, Vol. 3,* Bruce R. McConkie, Bookcraft, Salt Lake City, 1956

Smith, Joseph Fielding, *Man... His Origin and Destiny,* Deseret Book, Salt Lake City, 1954

Smith, Joseph Fielding, *Teachings of the Prophet Joseph Smith,* Deseret Book, Salt Lake City, 1976

Smith, Joseph Fielding, *The Restoration of All Things,* The Deseret News Press, 1964

Smith, Joseph Fielding, *The Way to Perfection,* published by the Genealogical Society of Utah, printed by The Deseret News Press, 1931

Talmage, James E., *Jesus The Christ,* published by the Church, Deseret Book, Salt Lake City, 1947

Talmage, James E., *The Articles of Faith,* The Church of Jesus Christ of Latter-day Saints, Salt Lake City, 1952

*True to the Faith-A Gospel Reference,* The Church of Jesus Christ of Latter-day Saints, Salt Lake City, 2004

Widtsoe, John A., *A Rational Theology as taught by the Church of Jesus Christ of Latter-day Saints,* Deseret Book Company, Salt Lake City, 1952

Widtsoe, John A., *Discourses of Brigham Young,* Heber J. Grant for the Church of Jesus Christ of Latter-day Saints, Deseret Book Company, Salt Lake City, 1925

Widtsoe, John A., *Discourses of Brigham Young,* David O. McKay for the Church of Jesus Christ of Latter-day Saints, Deseret Book Company, Salt Lake City, 1977

Widtsoe, John A., *Evidences and Reconciliations,* Bookcraft, Salt Lake City, 1943

Young, President Brigham, *Journal of Discourses, Vol. 2,* published by F. D. Richards, England, 1855

Young, President Brigham, *Journal of Discourses, Vol. 5,* Asa Calkin, Printed by R. James, England, 1858

Young, President Brigham, *Journal of Discourses, Vol. 7,* Amasa Lyman, James and Son, England, 1860

Young, President Brigham, *Journal of Discourses, Vol. 8,* George Q. Cannnon, England, 1861

Young, President Brigham, *Journal of Discourses, Vol. 11,* B. Young, Jun., England, 1867

Young, President Brigham, *Journal of Discourses, Vol. 13,* Horace S. Eldredge, England, 1871

Made in the USA
Columbia, SC
26 July 2021